Robert Manning Strozier Library

APR 9 1992

Tallahassee, Florida

LABOUR MARKET POLICY AND
UNEMPLOYMENT INSURANCE

The Trade Union Institute for Economic Research, FIEF, is a foundation established in 1985 by Landsorganisationen, the Swedish trade union confederation. FIEF's objective, as defined in its constitution, is to 'deepen the academic economic debate through the promotion of enduring research'.

FIEF Studies in Labour Markets and Economic Policy will be published regularly. The series will provide a forum for outstanding scholars to publish applied, policy-oriented research, with background surveys of theory and reviews of empirical research.

FIEF Studies editorial board

Villy Bergström	Director of the Trade Union Institute for Economic Research, FIEF (Managing Editor)
Lars Calmfors	Professor, Institute for International Economic Studies (IIES), University of Stockholm
Michael Hoel	Professor, Oslo University
Bertil Holmlund	Professor, Uppsala University
Karl-Gustaf Löfgren	Professor, University of Umeå
Andrew Oswald	The London School of Economics
Hans T. Söderström	Managing Director of the Business and Social Research Institute, SNS

FIEF panel for this volume

Jonas Agell	Docent, Trade Union Institute for Economic Research (FIEF) and Uppsala University
Dan Andersson	Economist, Swedish Trade Union Confederation
Lars Calmfors	Professor, Institute for International Economic Studies (IIES), University of Stockholm
Bertil Holmlund	Professor, Uppsala University and Trade Union Institute for Economic Research
Per-Olov Johansson	Trade Union Institute for Economic Research (FIEF)
Lars Lundberg	Docent, Trade Union Institute for Economic Research (FIEF)

Per Lundborg	Docent, Trade Union Institute for Economic Research (FIEF)
Karl-Gustaf Löfgren	Professor, University of Umeå
Lars Söderström	Professor, University of Lund
Hans T. Söderström	Managing Director, the Business and Social Research Institute, SNS
Anders Vredin	Trade Union Institute for Economic Research (FIEF)

Invited guests for conferences on papers in this volume

Gary Burtless	The Brookings Institution, Washington DC
Paul Chen	Professor, Department of Economics, Michigan State University
Eskil Wadensjö	Professor, The Swedish Institute for Social Research, University of Stockholm

Labour Market Policy and Unemployment Insurance

Anders Björklund
Robert Haveman
Robinson Hollister
and
Bertil Holmlund

CLARENDON PRESS · OXFORD
1991

HD
5713
L33
1990

Oxford University Press, Walton Street, Oxford OX2 6OR

Oxford   New York   Toronto
Delhi   Bombay   Calcutta   Madras   Karachi
Petaling Jaya   Singapore   Hong Kong   Tokyo
Nairobi   Dar es Salaam   Cape Town
Melbourne   Auckland
and associated companies in
Berlin   Ibadan

Oxford is a trade mark of Oxford University Press

Published in the United States
by Oxford University Press, New York

© *FIEF 1991*

All rights reserved. No part of this publication may be reproduced,
stored in a retrieval system, or transmitted, in any form or by any means,
electronic, mechanical, photocopying, recording, or otherwise, without
the prior permission of Oxford University Press

British Library Cataloguing in Publication Data
Labour market policy and unemployment insurance. — (FIEF
studies in labour markets and economic policy; no. 2).
1. Sweden. Unemployment. Policies of government
I. Björklund, Anders   II. Series
331.1379485
ISBN 0-19-828323-7

Library of Congress Cataloging in Publication Data
Labour market policy and unemployment insurance / [edited by]
Anders Björklund . . . [et al.].
p.   cm.—(FIEF studies in labour markets and economic policy)
Includes bibliographical references and index.
1. Manpower policy. 2. Insurance, Unemployment—Sweden.
I. Björklund, Anders. II. Series.
HD5713.L33   1990   331.12'042—dc20   90-7661
ISBN 0-19-828323-7

Typeset by Colset Private Limited, Singapore
Printed and bound in
Great Britain by Biddles Ltd,
Guildford & King's Lynn

Contents

Introduction
   VILLY BERGSTRÖM   1

**Part I. Direct Job Creation: Economic Evaluation and
Lessons for the United States and Western
Europe**   5
   ROBERT HAVEMAN and ROBINSON HOLLISTER
   with comments by Per-Olov Johansson and
   Anders Björklund

1. Introduction   7
2. Employment and Training Policy: Some Theoretical
Considerations   9
3. Employment and Training Policy: Macro-Economic
and Exchange Rate Implications   16
4. Evaluation of Job Creation Programmes   23
5. What Do We Know about What Works and for
Whom?   34
6. Conclusions and Appendix   59
7. Cost–Benefit Rules for Job-Training Programmes
   PER-OLOV JOHANSSON   66
8. Labour Market Training: The Lesson from Swedish
Evaluations
   ANDERS BJÖRKLUND   86
References for Part I   92

**Part II. The Economics of Unemployment Insurance:
The Case of Sweden**   101
   ANDERS BJÖRKLUND and BERTIL HOLMLUND
   with comments by Gary Burtless and Eskil
   Wadensjö

9. Introduction   103
10. Problems in Insurance Markets   105

11. The Swedish System 110
12. Incentive Effects 138
13. Unemployment Insurance and Income Distribution 159
14. Aspects of Optimal Unemployment Insurance 164
15. Summary and Conclusions 173
16. Comment
    GARY BURTLESS 179
17. Comment
    ESKIL WADENSJÖ 186
References for Part II 191

Index 197

Introduction

In the last fifteen years, macro-economic theory has undergone considerable change. In particular it has become better footed in micro-theory than it was before. The revision of macro-theory has brought about a reformulation of theories of economic policy, including labour market policies.

The research on labour markets has been pursued between two extremes. On the one hand, there is the old Keynesian view of benevolent governments, capable of smoothing cycles and enhancing the efficiency of particular economies by labour market policies such as retraining programmes and job-creating schemes; on the other, there is the belief that unrestricted and unhampered markets will result in full employment and efficient use of resources.

Part I focuses on a paper by Robert Haveman and Robinson Hollister, 'Direct Job Creation: Economies, Evaluation, and Lessons from the US and Western Europe', which reviews the literature and evidence about the role of labour market policies within the two extremes mentioned above.

To what extent can government intervention in the labour market be given theoretical and empirical support? Haveman and Hollister stress the need to see labour market programmes of different kinds (retraining, job creation, subsidies) in the context of the macro-economic situation. Their general conclusion is that recent theoretical developments, such as the efficient wage theories, have re-established a rationale for government labour market policies.

The measurement of effects of labour market programmes has generally become more sophisticated over the years. Unfortunately, European programmes have been investigated for less than the US experiences. Some evaluations have used control groups to stimulate experimental situations. By using benefit–cost analyses, measurements of effects are in principal brought into a general equilibrium framework, as opposed to the partial effects captured by less ambitious studies.

After discussing methods of analysis and measurement of the

effects of labour market programmes, Hollister and Haveman raise the question of what we know about how different programmes work and who are affected. Their review indicates that the broadest counter-cyclical labour market programmes are not well timed in relation to the business cycle, and that the timing is difficult because of long and variable lags. Furthermore, targeted programmes, such as wage subsidies and tax reductions, can have strong employment effects. On the other hand, an interesting programme set up with one control group and two other groups, one with a tax credit voucher and another with a voucher carrying cash reimbursement indicated stigmatization from targeted measures. Chances of employment may even decrease for members of the target groups.

The authors review a great number of job creation policies and labour market programmes, both in Europe and the United States. Generally, studies indicate that these programmes have better results for women than for men, for the less educated and the poor than for the better educated and people with higher income. Skill training programmes for young people may be very effective. However, the authors decline to place great weight on this evidence because proper measurement and analysis has been neglected, especially in Europe.

In an accompanying paper (Chapter 7), Per Olov Johansson derives cost-benefit rules for job-training programmes. Johansson's model contains two production sectors, producing traded and non-traded goods. The firm uses two types of labour, skilled and unskilled, and it invests part of its output. The model is formulated for three periods. Cost–benefit rules for government investment in the retraining of unskilled workers are calculated for three different situations: (*a*) general equilibrium, when prices and wages are flexible, (*b*) classical unemployment, when real wages are stuck at too high a level for full employment, and (*c*) Keynesian unemployment, generated by deficient demand. Johansson's analysis shows that the criteria for government involvement in retraining of the unskilled differ quite a lot between the three situations.

Anders Björklund, commenting on the Hollister–Haveman paper in Chapter 8, points out that Sweden has a history of comparatively low unemployment compared to many OECD economies, but that there has been a considerable extension of the duration of unemployment spells. This increase in duration has occurred concomitantly with various extensions of the benefits of the Swedish unemployment insurance (UI) system.

Part II focuses on a paper by Anders Björklund and Bertil Holmlund that analyses the links between extensions of U I benefits and the duration of and inflow to unemployment in Sweden. Their paper contains a detailed account of the institutional aspects of the Swedish U I system. This is given against the background of general insurance theory, and a rich body of data is presented and analysed. Their analysis stresses the interaction between 'active' labour market policy and 'passive' unemployment compensation.

In Chapter 12, Björklund and Holmlund discuss general issues concerning unemployment insurance and incentives. They survey theoretical and empirical literature mainly from the United Kingdom, the United States, and Sweden. The evidence is broadly that the extension of U I benefits tends to contribute to an extension of unemployment spells. However, despite substantial extensions of the U I system in Sweden, it is not easy to find evidence of strong adverse effects on unemployment. This may be due to the interaction between Sweden's unemployment insurance and its labour market policy, which may have offset increases of unemployment caused by extensions of unemployment insurance.

The Björklund–Holmlund paper ends with a consideration of distributional and normative aspects on unemployment insurance. In Sweden, low experience rating and increasing government subsidies of the financing on unemployment insurance have led to both inter-industry and inter-income class redistributions. Unemployment-prone industries—for instance, the fishing industry and building industry, with high seasonal unemployment—are subsidized at the expense of industries with stable unemployment. The authors also find redistribution between income classes, from high to low.

Discussants on the Holmlund–Björklund paper are Gary Burtless and Eskil Wadensjö.

Villy Bergström
Director, FIEF

PART I

*Direct Job Creation: Economic
Evaluation and Lessons for the United
States and Western Europe*

PART I

1

Introduction

For two decades there has been considerable employment and training activity by the governments of most of the countries in Europe and North America. This seems an appropriate time to review some of this experience in order to assess what we have learned regarding the potential of employment and training efforts and how they might be applied in the current economic and social context.

Most European countries are suffering from extremely high unemployment rates as judged by their own historical standards, and projections by many experts show little hope for improvement for the next five to ten years. Many have increased the magnitude and variety of employment and training efforts in response to this problem.

While the unemployment situation is not as severe in the United States as in most of Europe, unemployment has only recently (1988) achieved levels approximating the 1960s, despite the fact that the recovery following the 1981-2 recession has continued for a record length of time; and even now, certain groups—minorities and youth in particular—have not regained the employment position they had before the recession. There has been a significant shift in labour market policies of the central government following a period of very high job creation activities in the 1970s.

Government employment and training efforts have been significant in magnitude at various times in both Europe and North America; for example, in Sweden it has been estimated that enrolment in public work and training programmes has accounted for as much as 3.5 per cent of the total labour force. In the United States, job creation programmes have been extremely important to particular groups. For example, in 1979 about 40 per cent of employed black teenagers held jobs in the government's Youth Employment Demonstration Projects Act (YEDPA) programmes.

There is thus a set of critical issues for which knowledge about the character and effects of such employment and training programmes could be important. In what follows, we shall assess quite a wide range of such efforts, from direct job creation through education programmes. The focus is on breadth rather than depth of detail in order to highlight what we consider to be major issues.[1]

Our discussion will encompass a wide range of employment and training efforts, extending from complete government production through regional development and anti-discrimination regulations. The major categories that we have in mind, described in the Appendix to this paper, are the following:

— Complete government production
— Shared public private production
— Subsidized activities
— Mixed work and training
— Training
— Enterprise promotion
— Regional and structural support
— Regulations

[1] Readers are advised to consult *Industrial Relations*, 24/1 (Winter 1985), which includes a symposium on active labour market policies and provides a multinational perspective on many of the issues discussed in this study. While the high, sustained rates of unemployment in Europe and the somewhat different experience in the United States provide the backdrop to this review, we shall not attempt to enter into, or evaluate, the debate over the character and causes of these phenomena. Where appropriate, however, we shall emphasize the necessary co-ordination of employment and training efforts with macro-economic and exchange rate policies.

2

Employment and Training Policy: Some Theoretical Considerations

Public employment and training efforts are not always conceded to have economic justification. And even where they are justified as an appropriate public sector activity, the nature of the economic impacts expected from them are often ill defined and poorly understood. Here we try to clarify some of these theoretical issues.

Neoclassical economists tend to regard public employment and training efforts with scepticism. In the absence of any explicit market failure, the burden of proof that such interventions can increase economic well-being, they suggest, lies with those who advocate them. The advocates respond by indicating that where the social benefits of such activities are in excess of social costs, market failure is implicitly present and the intervention is economically justified. The benefits are thought to take several forms: (*a*) increased total output; (*b*) increased total employment; and (*c*) a more equitable distribution of social product or employment.

2.1. Theories of Unemployment: Macro-Economic Theory and Government Labour Market Intervention

Explaining unemployment and how government policies might affect it has been the central problem of economics for over fifty years. It remains perhaps the major area of contending views and unsatisfactory resolution in the profession. It should not be surprising that we cannot present here an adequate, concise summary of theories of unemployment nor attempt an assessment of their merits. What follows is our cursory, personal views of recent developments in this domain as they might apply to government employment and training programmes.

Since the 1930s, government employment measures have been touted as fiscal instruments which can generate increased output at a social cost less than the financial cost owing to the use of underutilized labour and capital resources.[1] One of the earliest refinements of this Keynesian rationale is the 'Swedish' model.[2] Two features of this early formulation stand out because they anticipate many current concerns: (*a*) the necessity to formulate a complementary mix of fiscal, monetary, and labour market policies to increase employment without fuelling inflationary pressures; (*b*) the design of policies appropriate for small, open economies.

Consider, for example, the Rehn–Meidner plan. Excessive inflationary pressure was to be avoided by relatively restrictive monetary and fiscal policy. Simultaneously, active labour market policies —vacancy information, local job creation, mobility allowance, retraining—were to be used to secure resource reallocation consistent with maintaining an internationally competitive economy. In addition, a 'solidaristic wage policy', in which wage differences were to be related only to job content—thus eliminating inter-firm and inter-regional differentials—would help to put pressure on inefficient firms and reward efficient firms. This wage policy would also contribute to social equality and assist in centralized bargaining to constrain inflationary wage demand.[3]

In the late 1970s, responding to stagflation and the problems of disadvantaged workers in the United States, economists began modelling the interaction of public employment programmes and the unemployment–inflation trade-off (see Baily and Tobin 1977). These models investigated, among other things, the conditions under which government employment and training programmes yield more employment gains for any given degree of inflationary pressure than general fiscal expansion does. The concept of the 'non-accelerating-inflation rate of unemployment', or NAIRU, was a central analytical concept in these formulations and stood as a bench-mark against which alternative government policies, including training, direct job creation, and wage subsidies, could be

[1] In ch. 7, Per-Olov Johansson discusses cost–benefit rules for job-training programmes derived under alternative forms of unemployment. Haveman and Krutilla (1967) provide an analytic framework for evaluating public projects in these macro-economic circumstances. See Kesselman (1978).

[2] We hasten to note that our knowledge of the model is quite limited and largely based on the Swedish model as described in Lundberg (1985), Rehn (1985), and Bosworth and Rivlin (1987).

[3] Some of the wage-price aspects of the Swedish model were incorporated in the US Council of Economic Advisers' wage and price guidelines in 1962.

evaluated.[4] The basic idea was that by shifting labour demand towards high unemployment and disadvantaged workers through targeted programmes, the aggregate rate of unemployment consistent with NAIRU could be lowered. The analysis turned on the conditions under which employment and training programmes would have this desired outcome of 'cheating the Phillips curve', both in the short and the long run.

At the same time, interest of theorists in the micro-foundations of macro-economics had been developing. The rational-expectations group argued that involuntary unemployment was unlikely to exist: 'involuntary unemployment is not a fact or phenomenon which it is the task of theorists to explain' (Lucas 1978). Most unemployment was argued to be 'search unemployment'. This view seemed to lead to a subsequent line of theory which reasserted 'classical unemployment' theories, stressing that to the extent that non-search unemployment existed, it was due to rigidities in labour markets introduced by government policies such as the minimum wage or unemployment benefits, or by union power, both of which constrained the natural equilibrating processes of the labour market.

Alternative theories of micro-foundations emerged that were largely based on characterizations of 'the employment relationship'—how labour markets operate. Asymmetric information, implicit contrasts (see Azariadis 1979), overlapping contracts, and 'reputational' considerations were introduced and formally modelled in a general equilibrium framework that could be related to the macro-economic features of unemployment and inflation. Most recently, 'efficiency wage' theories (see Stiglitz 1986; Bulow and Summers 1986) have received a great deal of attention. In 'efficiency wage' models, employers are concerned with costs of turnover, with workers' 'shirking' or morale, with loss of investment in training in firm-specific skills, with paying higher wages than required for simple labour market clearing, and with the related pool of unemployed workers that serves to 'discipline' the employed work force.

Johnson and Layard (1986) draw the threads of these various

---

[4] Other NAIRU-based analyses include Phan-Thuy (1979); Balkenhol (1979); Layard and Nickell (1980); papers by K. Burdett and Bryce Hool, Jeffrey Perloff, and Donald Nichols in Haveman and Palmer, OECD, eds. (1982); (1983); Whitely and Wilson (1983); and Johnson (1983).

theories together. They try to show how supply and demand models that incorporate various elements of these theories can affect the 'natural rate of unemployment', and how some general types of government labour market interventions would affect unemployment (or fail to do so) under the various theoretical regimes. Their results are most relevant to our purposes here, so we briefly review a few of them.

In the simplest, classical supply and demand general equilibrium situation with no distortions in the market, no involuntary employment arises. When distortions are introduced in the form of government benefits and taxes, unemployment and inefficiency may result. A broad employment subsidy financed by a tax in the same market is shown to have no effect on distortion-induced unemployment. Note that the subsidy and the tax to finance it must be jointly considered in the general equilibrium framework.

The form of labour market intervention which does work to offset these distortions in the short run is a 'marginal employment subsidy', i.e. a subsidy paid only for workers added above a given number, and in the long run this does not offset the distortions.

When there are different degrees of distortion in different labour markets, a subsidy in one market financed by a tax in the other may reduce unemployment. This depends on the relative elasticities of supply of labour in the two markets as well as the relative degrees of distortion. As pointed out by one commentator (Bosworth 1986: 134), this is akin to the standard public finance result: taxing inelastically supplied goods to subsidize elastically supplied goods can increase efficiency in many situations. More to the point here, however, Johnson and Layard argue that under this regime, in which unemployment arises due to rigidities in the unskilled labour market, targeted public employment and government training can be effective in reducing unemployment.

Distortions can arise due to monopolistic power of firms or monopsonistic power of unions. The former case, where firms are wage setters, includes efficiency wage considerations which give rise to unemployment. Here it is found that lump-sum subsidies (that is, a fixed amount per worker rather than a proportion of the wage) financed by a proportional tax will increase employment, primarily because the tax makes raising the efficiency wage more expensive and the opportunity costs of the worker in the skilled sector are raised by the subsidy in the unskilled sector. The union models also yield a result in which the lump-sum subsidy with proportional tax-financing increases employment because it increases demand elasticity, which reduces the scope for upward pressure on wages from unions.

It should be pointed out that these theories of unemployment have been continuously revised and elaborated on and, indeed, Stiglitz (1986: 144) warns us that results are often quite sensitive to slight differences in parameterization or specifications of the model. Further, empirical testing of the theories generally lags well behind their initial formulation. None the less, we can venture some lessons to be drawn from these theories.

First, it is important to attempt to trace the effects of labour market programmes which may not be directly interventionist by considering their effects in a general equilibrium context. This gives rise, for example, to sensitivity to displacement concerns in employment and training projects, a topic we review at length below. As Per-Olov Johansson shows in Chapter 7, the cost–benefit rules appropriate for assessing programme impacts will vary under different types of unemployment owing to these general equilibrium considerations.

Second, under certain conditions, wage subsidies, targeted public employment, and government training can work to reduce involuntary unemployment. Under other conditions, apparently sensible policies, e.g. a proportional subsidy and tax, may be unproductive.

Third, our major problem in using the results from these theories of unemployment comes from trying to establish which sets of conditions prevail in any given place and time. If there are certain types of distortions, then particular policies are likely to be effective, but is there, for example, wage rigidity in a given market, and if so, what is the source of that rigidity? The ongoing debates over the causes of the sustained high levels of unemployment in Europe (see e.g. Lawrence and Schultze 1987; Helliwell 1988) illustrate how difficult it is to choose among the theories of unemployment. Are US labour markets significantly less 'rigid' than European markets? Some analysts strongly question this supposition (see Freeman 1988). Recently, US analysts have been focusing on the persistence of inter-industry and inter-regional wage differentials for workers with similar measured characteristics. As Krueger and Summers (1987) have put it, 'since involuntary unemployment can be regarded as confinement to the low wage home production sector of the economy, a finding of significant non-competitive inter-industry wage variations renders plausible claims that economies are subject to chronic involuntary unemployment and casts doubt on the equilibrating properties of the free market'.

Fourth, more empirical testing of the predictions from the various theories of unemployment may help us to recognize when particular forms of government labour market intervention, if any, are appropriate. Present debate over the theories is heated and, in our view, inconclusive.

2.2. Segmented Markets

In the 1960s and early 1970s, institutional and radical economists, especially in the United States, stressed the potential importance of segmentation in labour markets. Labour, they argued, was barred from freely competing across labour markets because of institutional arrangements which effectively created different competitive conditions in various segments of the market. While this perspective has been disputed,[5] the recent growth in interest in efficiency wage models, discussed above, has brought this perspective back into the literature (see Bulow and Summers 1986), and the emphasis on persistent market disequilibrium suggested by the evidence on long-term inter-industry wage differentials has given it a new life among mainstream economists.

In a sense, market segmentation is one characterization of market rigidity of the type modelled by Johnson and Layard. Such segmentation might create a rationale for public labour market activities. If the government programme can move workers from those sectors with an excess supply to markets in which there is a shortage of workers, total production, total employment, or the more equitable distribution of the burdens of unemployment could be achieved. This market-switching gain could occur even if the underlying productivity of workers was unaffected. We shall refer to this below as the market-switching rationale for labour market policies.

---

[5] See Cain (1976) and Wachter (1974). For recent reformulations, see Lang and Dickens (1987).

2.3. Human Capital Formation

The major theoretical justification for government training programmes over the last twenty years has been the economists' human capital model. The embodiment of skills through training raises workers' productivity, and thereby the total social product. Because firms fear loss through attrition of their investment in worker training and upgrading and job changes, they invest less than would be socially optimal (see Johnson 1980). Moreover, because liquidity constraints may make it difficult or expensive for workers to finance training (either directly or through acceptance of lower wages during the training period), the workers may underinvest.

We shall refer to this below as the human capital rationale for labour market policies.

3

Employment and Training Policy: Macro-Economic and Exchange Rate Implications

As recent theorizing on the economics of employment policy suggests, the interactions between these measures and macro-economic (both fiscal and monetary) and exchange rate policies are complex and numerous. Indeed, in a very real sense, all three policy instruments have the same objectives, and measures undertaken in any one area affect the success of interventions in the others. Because these interactions appear to have been so often neglected by policy-makers in the recent past, we raise them here explicitly.

The general goals for all three policy measures are similar: securing and maintaining low unemployment, reducing inflation, and promoting economic growth. A fourth goal, often unstated, is to achieve balance in the trade sector (an objective which often seems disguised as efforts to maintain a historic but arbitrary exchange rate).

3.1. Macro-Economic Considerations Relevant to Employment Policy

Consider, first, the effect of contractionary macro-policy on the success of job creation measures. In such an environment, the burden placed on job creation programmes increases substantially. With labour demand soft, markets slack, and job competition increasing, the placement of trainees or other targeted groups into jobs becomes more difficult. Similarly, the probability that any trainee who finds employment will displace some other workers, either directly or indirectly, increases with the extent of labour market slack. Those groups who judge their jobs to be threatened by such effects increase their opposition to public sector efforts.

At the same time that contractionary policies erode labour

demand (and simultaneously the potential social benefits of job creation programmes), they also have an effect on the supply of potential programme participants. With poorer labour market prospects, the opportunity cost of participating in training programmes decreases for numerous potential participants—their demand for participating, in effect, rises as the programmes are seen as vehicles for mobility from weaker to stronger labour market sectors. Simultaneously, the costs of other inputs to programmes —e.g. space and supervision, materials, and equipment—also fall.

Finally, some job creation programmes produce long-lived public infrastructure outputs—roads, bridges, parks—whose relative value is independent of the business cycle. The decrease in the social cost of the inputs to these activities during a contractionary period should increase the relative attractiveness of these measures at these times. This, of course, is a restatement of the case for counter-cyclical fiscal policy, or the 'shelf of public works'.

During an expansionary (or full employment) period, the reverse of these effects is likely. Placement of trainees will be easier, displacement effects reduced, and the expected social benefits of public programmes increased. Simultaneously, the social costs of job training and job creation will rise as the opportunities of potential trainees improve and the prices of other inputs to the programmes rise. While public works projects appear relatively less economic in such a period, skill-training measures may carry a premium if they are capable of easing private sector bottle-necks or avoiding the onset of price increases.

The lesson of this discussion is clear: job creation measures need to be aligned with macro-economic policy. Skill training has little to commend it when there is a stock of skilled unemployed workers. Similarly, when labour markets are tight, it is uneconomic to pursue social infrastructure projects with workers who must be bid away from private sector activities—especially when such activities can be executed in periods of slack demand. A lesson for the evaluation of labour market programmes is also relevant—placement rates, earnings increases, or other performance indicators observed when employment is high or rising will be inappropriate guides to programme efficiency during other macro-economic circumstances.

3.2. Employment Policy Considerations Relevant to Macro-Economic Measures

For purposes of this more complex interaction, we consider three categories of job creation measures: counter-cyclical, human capital, and market switching. Often, public expenditures for job creation measures are viewed as effective counter-cyclical instruments—with recession in the private sector, unemployed resources which come at low social cost can be used to create outputs whose value persists in the long run and is relatively invariant to the business cycle. Multiplier effects on the output side complement the low social cost of the inputs. The human capital rationale has a similar basis—the creation of skills in the labour force has a long-run investment character, and hence it is the increase in the lifetime productivity of participants, properly discounted, that is relevant in evaluating the social worth of training activities. While these productivity benefits do depend on short-term employment possibilities, longer-term impacts are also relevant. The market-switching rationale views public labour market policies as vehicles for facilitating the movement of labour from declining, excess-supply sectors to those with potential bottle-necks.

Consider, first, job creation programmes in the context of traditional Keynesian considerations. To the extent that such programmes are able to target their impacts on resources that would be unemployed in a recessionary period, net output would be increased, worker skills maintained, enterprise administrative structures kept intact, and depreciating capital used while still of recent vintage. These gains come in addition to the standard expansionary (multiplier) effects associated with expenditure increases.

However, not all the effects of counter-cyclical job creation measures are viewed as gains. For example, recessions have been seen by some as beneficial—as disciplining the market, purging the economy of inefficient practices which develop during an expansion, and constraining excessive wage demands. If this view is accepted, counter-cyclical job creation measures can be viewed as diluting these cleansing effects, and thereby eliminating the long-run efficiency gains that they bring. In a similar perspective, such measures can be viewed as retarding labour mobility and, if output is produced, yielding a less valuable product than the market would yield.

Researchers have also attempted to assess the short- and long-term employment and output growth effects of direct job creation measures relative to general fiscal measures with equivalent revenue effects. While most analysts have found a greater 'bang for the buck' in these resource-targeted measures, there is no general agreement on this issue.[1]

Two additional issues are relevant. First, can direct job creation measures be timed to counter the business cycle rather than reinforce it? Analysts have again compared these measures with general fiscal and monetary counter-cyclical measures, finding that the lag between policy action and labour market impact is shorter for these programmes than for more general measures.[2] Direct experience on the extent to which such programmes can be rapidly mounted, or promptly phased out is mixed.[3]

Second is the question of the effects of the measures on the NAIRU. Again, the relevant comparison is between these direct measures and more general fiscal and monetary policies. Because direct job creation programmes directly reduce employer wage costs (e.g. wage subsidies) or increase the supply of trained labour, they are generally appraised as placing downward pressure on the NAIRU; greater expansion of employment without the generation of inflationary pressure would be possible through such measures than through more general fiscal stimulus (see Bishop and Haveman 1979).

In their roles of creating human capital or facilitating market switching, direct job creation measures also have the potential of cheating the Phillips curve. To the extent that such programmes are

---

[1] Disputes over this issue are found in Haveman and Palmer, eds. (1982), Layard and Nickel (1980), and Whitely and Wilson (1983). Most analysts have based their estimates of the response to wage subsidies on estimates of the elasticity of labour demand in Hamermesh (1976). Two subsequent works, one theoretical and one empirical, suggest that Hamermesh's estimates are too low: see Killingsworth (1985), and Clark and Freeman (1980).

[2] For a theoretical discussion of this issue, see Burdett and Hool (1982).

[3] The employment and training system in the United States was able to build jobs very rapidly under the Youth Employment and Demonstration Projects Act from 1978 to 1981; see Betsey, Hollister, and Papageorgiou (1985: 21) and ch. 3. On the other hand, a number of US studies of purposefully counter-cyclic programmes have concluded that expenditures are allocated too slowly for proper phasing with the cycle; see e.g. Vernez and Vaughan (1978) and US General Accounting Office (1986).

able to target the human capital effects on occupations with the potential for becoming bottle-necks in an expansion, or on the most disadvantaged workers (those operating in labour markets with little upward wage pressure) aggregate unemployment could be driven down further without encountering inflationary effects than would be possible with other policies. Similarly, the selective use of these measures in encouraging worker movement from low- to high-demand sectors or regions can have much the same effect. This is especially true where minimum wages, collective-bargaining arrangements, or social impediments to absolute wage adjustments make market clearing difficult, or where fundamental structural adjustments in industry composition are required because of exogenous changes in technology or demand patterns. To the extent that direct employment measures can facilitate the job switches or employment reallocations associated with a flexible labour market, the NAIRU can be reduced.

In sum, then, on the question of the impact of direct job creation programmes on the NAIRU—the 'bang' associated with the expenditure 'buck'—the weight of the analysis provides a qualified 'yes'. While there are numerous avenues by which economic stimulus can be pushed further without encountering inflationary pressures through direct job creation than through other, less targeted options, the direct empirical evidence on the potential is scanty.[4] This notwithstanding, we judge that the bulk of informed judgement on this issue finds direct job creation measures to be a high potential instrument for securing employment gains at reduced inflation costs. This same opinion, however, would find it essential that these measures be co-ordinated with general macro-economic measures, rather than providing selective expansion in the face of general contraction.

3.3. Exchange Rate Policy and Job Creation Policy

In open economies with a large foreign trade sector, policy-makers are often as much concerned with exchange rates and the balance of payments position as with unemployment and growth; therefore, the

---

[4] Baily and Tobin (1977) and Nichols (1982) provide the earliest and latest estimates of this impact.

interrelationships between exchange rate and foreign trade policy and job creation policy are also relevant. That close ties between macro-economic and exchange rate measures are necessary for effective and co-ordinated policy is well known. Without such co-ordination, for example, expansionary fiscal measures may run into foreign exchange constraints as import demand is stimulated, the balance of payments position is eroded, and/or the exchange rate deteriorates beyond 'acceptable' limits. (What is acceptable, of course, may be simply a matter of national pride, in which case the options available for macro-economic measures are artificially constrained in the interests of perceived standing.)

Consider the example of devaluation as an instrument to raise domestic demand in both export and import substitution sectors. Assume that the conditions necessary for devaluation to be an effective employment stimulus are present—sufficiently high elasticities of export and import demand.[5] Assume as well that the wages and prices in the devaluing economy are not sufficiently tied to import prices to undercut the stimulative effects of devaluation. In this case, devaluation will have the effect of reducing the real wage, leading to an increase in the demand for labour. (Such reductions may well be more acceptable politically than direct cuts in domestic wages.)

In such a situation, a distinct role exists for direct job creation policy. Because the expansion of employment from devaluation will be concentrated in the export and import substitution sectors, skill-training programmes could be oriented towards these sectors if employment bottle-necks or substantial skill-specific demand increases are anticipated. Because the lag between devaluation and demand increases is substantial (the J-curve), time is required to organize and to set training activities in place.

A second example of the foreign trade–job creation nexus concerns long-term strategies to develop internationally competitive industries—the 'infant industry' argument. With such strategies, new activities judged to have high potential for establishing comparative advantage are promoted by government and protected during their formative stages. Although most such assistance is in the form of capital subsidization (e.g. loan subsidies for investment,

---

[5] For a discussion of this and many of the related issues of employment effects of macro- and trade policies applied to an open economy, see Drèze and Modigliani (1981).

special import licensing), job creation programmes in the form of wage subsidies or training programmes could provide equally valuable start-up assistance. They would, at the same time, contribute to long-term employment creation by retarding excessively capital-intensive production methods.

The inverse of this problem is that of easing the adjustment of established industries to changing patterns of international competition—the structural adjustment problem. Given an exchange rate position which is in reasonable equilibrium, the problem here is forecasting, and then accommodating, major long-term shifts in sectoral comparative advantage. Such adjustments often require substantial (and painful) movements of labour resources out of particular activities and regions—recent examples of the collapse of shipbuilding come immediately to mind. In this case, there is a clear need for market-switching forms of job creation programmes to ease the transition. On the other hand, should the industry be in only temporary difficulty, transitional employment policy measures may be in order—wage subsidies to enable the sector to sustain employment and hence to be in a position to take advantage of the next upswing. A difficult question is that of deciding whether a particular industry really is in long-term trouble owing to loss of international position or is, rather, simply at a short-term disadvantage. As one Danish expert recently pointed out:

In Denmark, the textiles industry has been doomed several times due to competition from other countries with much cheaper labor. But impressive efforts on the part of the manufacturers have made this sector one of the strongest growth poles in Danish industry. The production has been automated to a degree which means that Danish clothing and textiles firms can compete with countries with low labor costs in terms of both price and quality. This has also led to increasing employment in this field. (Denmark 1985)

Determining which of these is the appropriate strategy in any particular case is clearly not a simple matter.

These illustrations suffice to indicate the need to co-ordinate labour market policies with exchange rate and foreign trade policy, in much the same manner as with macro-economic policy.

4

Evaluation of Job Creation Programmes

The basic purpose of systematic evaluations of the performance of job creation programmes is to secure information on which to base future decisions regarding the reorientation of programmes or the initiation of new activities.[1] Relevant information can be of various kinds. The most simple and straightforward is the documentation of programme processes—Who entered the programme? What kind of activities were engaged in? What was the administrative structure? What resources were utilized? How many participants completed the programme? A more helpful evaluation would try to assess what difference the activity caused—what events occurred because the programme was undertaken that would not have occurred in its absence? This form of evaluation requires a much higher standard of evidence, since some means of establishing conditions in the absence of the programme—the 'counterfactual'—must be found. The most complete form of evaluation, a benefit–cost analysis, follows directly from the evaluation of programme effects—i.e. if the differences caused by a programme are known, the natural question is to ask whether these effects are worth the resources that were required to create them. A quantitative answer to this question requires both a proper accounting of all of the costs of the programme and a comprehensive estimate of the social benefit that these changes represent.

In this section we discuss several of the most important issues involved in obtaining a consistent and reliable evaluation of direct

---

[1] For a general discussion of the methods for evaluating employment and training programmes, see Cain and Hollister (1983). In this section, we discuss the methods and problems involved in evaluation, not actual evaluations of programmes. In ch. 5 we briefly summarize major findings. Fuller summaries of evaluations of the effects of programmes are provided in *Industrial Relations*, 24/1 (Winter 1985); Betsey, Hollister, and Papegeorgiou (1985); Schwanse (1982). Most of the references to programme evaluation methods and results are from the US literature, as that is where the bulk of efforts on this issue have been located. Western European analysts have shown less interest in these matters.

job creation programmes, moving from the most simple and straightforward evaluation approaches to a variety of the most recently developed methods for generating reliable and useful information.

4.1. Measuring Immediate Impacts

Prior to about 1965, most evaluations of social programmes were simply descriptions of what occurred, sometimes accompanied by the subjective assessments of 'experts' as to the effects. Since that time, however, evaluations have moved beyond the descriptive to take on the more difficult task of trying to establish what happened when the programme was in effect relative to what would have happened otherwise. A basic requirement for assessing the effect of programmes is to secure reliable information on the participants. In the last decade, significant advances in such record-keeping activities have been made; these are often called 'management information systems'. Such systems involve detailed records, maintained in computerized form, on the individuals who participate in a programme. They provide ongoing data to programme administrators in a form designed to aid in management decisions.[2]

Such individualized information is, however, just one building block. The central issue for a reliable evaluation is to determine how these participants would have fared had they not had the benefit of the programme. The primary method for obtaining the counterfactual is the creation of a 'comparison group' of persons who did not participate in the programme.

The most refined method of creating a comparison group is derived from the classical paradigm for a scientific experiment. Subjects are randomly assigned either to receive 'the treatment' or to a 'control group' that receives no treatment. Given a sufficient sample size, the random assignment of individuals effectively reduces the probability that receipt of the treatment will be correlated with particular individual characteristics. The objective is to avoid a case in which, for example, more highly skilled persons are predominantly in the treatment group and unskilled persons are

---

[2] For an unusual attempt to use such records in combination with follow-up data, see Hollister, Kemper, and Wooldridge (1979).

predominantly in the comparison group. This could lead to a mistaken inference that the programme was effective, whereas the superior performance of the treatment group would in fact be due more to the inherent skills of those assigned to it than to the treatment itself.

Until recently, random assignment has rarely been used for programme evaluation purposes. Instead, the usual approach has been to create 'comparison groups' which serve as proxies for the randomly assigned control group.[3] Often, comparison groups are created after the fact, by finding a group of individuals who have similar characteristics to those who participate in the programme. The more similar are the measured characteristics of the two groups, the less likely it is that being in the treatment group will be correlated with some particular trait and the more likely that the evaluation will not be seriously biased. Alternative means of establishing a comparison group involve selecting people who applied for the programme but who were not accepted, or who failed to show up after they were accepted (see e.g. Cain 1968), or selecting people from areas where the programme was not operated (see Mallar *et al.* 1982). Yet another approach has been to construct groups from records which provide information on the characteristics, employment, and earnings of non-participants (see Keifer 1979).

Although constructed comparison groups and randomly assigned control groups are both techniques for securing unbiased estimates of programme impacts, they are not equally effective in achieving this goal. While a constructed comparison group is able to introduce some statistical control into an analysis, and is hence superior to no comparison group at all, recent evidence indicates that analyses based on this technique are not free of bias. The problem is one of the selection bias, whereby some unmeasured characteristic of people—say, motivation—both influences the probability that a person will participate in the programme and affects the person's employment capability even in the absence of the programme. If highly motivated persons are overrepresented in the participant group, they will make the programme effects appear stronger than

---

[3] An important early example in which comparison groups were created from Social Security records on earnings is reported in Ashenfelter (1978). Subsequent studies using comparison groups created from other types of data sources are Bloom and McLaughlin (1982) and Bassi (1984).

they are. Because constructed comparison groups are chosen on the basis of people's observed characteristics, they are not able to control for these unmeasured effects. Only random assignment to treatment and control groups can provide the statistical control required for unbiased evaluation. The evidence amassed from several major evaluations relying on the creation and use of randomly assigned control groups has established that such methods are likely to yield a high level of reliability. On the other hand, a number of important recent studies provide a strong empirical basis for the conclusion that evaluations based on even the most carefully constructed comparison groups may yield erroneous conclusions. We review these studies in Chapter 6 below.

4.2. Dimensions for Assessment

The major objective of job creation programmes is employment, and hence it is the dimensions of employment—rates of employment, hours of work, and earnings—that are assessed. Furthermore, in so far as direct job creation programmes have a long-lived effect on participants, a full evaluation of their worth must consider the work and earnings performance of the worker after he or she has completed the programme. Since participants leave the programme upon completion, special post-programme follow-up data are required for both the participants and the control group.

To ensure that this information is comparable across groups, personal interviews—taken before the programme starts, during its course, and after participation has been completed—form the most common data collection method. These data permit estimation of the changes which are related to participation in the programme by comparing the employment and earnings over time of those participating in the programme and members of the comparison group.[4]

In addition to data on employment-related phenomena, evalua-

---

[4] In some cases, it has been possible to use records regularly collected for other purposes in order to obtain information on some of the topics of concern. Where there is a social security system that requires regular reports of earnings by individual workers, it has been possible to obtain information on the subsequent earning histories of both participants and comparison or control group members (see Ashenfelter 1978). Records collected through the payment of unemployment insurance taxes have also been used (see Gueron, 1986).

tion studies often seek to obtain data on other aspects of participant performance which the programme might affect. Examples include skill achievement; formal educational attainment; health status; criminal activity; utilization of drugs and alcohol; extent of receipt of transfer payments; changes in family structure or circumstances; and attitudes toward work, the community, and self.[5]

Two additional issues in securing reliable post-programme information are important and should be mentioned. The first is the problem of tracing sample members after they have left the programme or reinterviewing control or comparison group members. This is known as 'sample attrition', and its presence has much the same effect in undermining the reliability of evaluations as the selection bias problem mentioned above. When there is substantial attrition, it is not known whether differences that appear between the comparison group and the participants are due to actual differences in behaviour and experience or are due to differences in the characteristics of the individuals that were lost disproportionately from one group as opposed to the other. The statistical techniques that have been used to eliminate the effects of attrition are similar to those developed to deal with the selection bias problem (see Brown 1979; Mallar *et al.* 1982; Skidmore 1984; and Betsey, Hollister, and Papageourgiou 1985; ch. 8).

A second issue is the length of time over which participants and control group members are followed after the programme has been terminated. Because programme effects have been observed in some cases to erode quickly and in other cases to emerge only after a lag (Kemper and Long 1981), it is important to adopt a reasonably long period of post-programme follow-up. In addition to the effects of the programme on participants, others may also feel its impact, either positively or negatively. The most recognized of these effects has already been alluded to—the displacement or substitution impact. Displacement, as we have pointed out, can come either by way of the direct substitution of programme workers for others, or indirectly through the products which might be produced as part of the programme. Evaluation of these displacement effects is difficult.

---

[5] Crime and drug and alcohol abuse were measured for the Supported Work programme (see Hollister, Kemper, and Maynard 1984), and crime was measured for the Job Corps. (See Mallar *et al.* 1982); Betsey, Hollister, and Papageorgiou (1985: app. A) for a discussion of such attitudinal measures and some of their problems.

Also relevant is a related phenomenon involving resources which may be complementary to the outputs or effects of a programme. Training to avoid bottle-necks in the labour market was one rationale of these programmes. When a key skill is provided by the programme, not only are the workers with that skill employed, but so also are other workers who have complementary skills; this employment is also a gain which is properly attributed to the programme. These other-person effects, it should be noted, can arise either during the programme itself or in the post-programme period.

The final effect of the programme which must be evaluated is its own output. Only a few efforts have been made to value the social worth of the product of a programme (see e.g. Mallar *et al*. 1982; Skidmore 1984; and Betsey, Hollister, and Papageorgiou 1985: ch. 8). This estimation is difficult, as programmes are often constrained to produce outputs that will not compete with those produced in the private sector. Such outputs will typically not have a market-established value or will not be highly valued in the social–political process. In addition, a large number of direct job creation efforts have involved environmental improvement outputs or other public goods for which again no market price is observed. To the extent that the output has a social value, however, it must be included in the evaluation.

4.3. Benefit–Cost Analysis[6]

Benefit–cost analysis builds on the measurement of the effects of a programme and attempts to determine if the effort yields an increase in the social value of resources, goods, and services which exceeds the value of the resources used.

Although benefit–cost analysis can be done from several points of view or 'accounting frameworks', the most comprehensive is that of the society as a whole.[7] This framework accounts for all social

---

[6] This section draws heavily upon Kemper, Long, and Thornton (1984). A shorter, slightly different report on this analysis can be found in Haveman and Margolis (1983). This benefit–cost study is generally regarded as the most thorough and complete analysis of a job creation or training programme.

[7] An alternative perspective is from the point of view of the participant. Analysis based on this perspective will indicate if the programme yields gains which are sufficient to induce potential participants to join.

benefits and costs associated with the project or programme and ignores transfers among citizens that may be part of the programme—for example, stipends to participants during a training programme (a transfer from taxpayers to participants). Whereas the social benefits and costs represent real outputs produced (goods and services contributing to consumption or further production) or real inputs used up, transfers shift resources from some citizens to others with no net increase in social output.

Specifying an accounting stance for the benefit–cost analysis is the easy part; the difficult part is developing accurate estimates of the component benefits and costs. In the case of direct job creation programmes, three special problems of analysis exist in addition to the standard issues in benefit–cost studies.[8]

The first of these is the valuation of the outputs that are produced as part of the programme. These in-programme outputs are more often associated with direct job creation programmes than with training or education programmes, and in those few programmes that have been subjected to a comprehensive analysis they have been significant enough to offset a large proportion to the total cost. Those components of in-programme production which either pass through a market and are priced or are similar to other products that are marketed are the easiest to value. Others are not marketed or, if sold, are priced at below market value. Programmes in environmental improvement or public infrastructure are of this sort. In these cases, shadow-valuing techniques must be applied, but heretofore there has been little experience with them and few principles on which to base a generally accepted method (see Kemper and Long 1981).

The second analytic problem peculiar to direct job creation programmes involves the displacement issue touched on earlier. Such displacement could be direct, i.e. worker-for-worker, or indirect, through the competition of goods produced in the public programme with those privately produced. One form of 'direct displacement' is when government-trained or sponsored workers are displacing workers who would have got those jobs in the absence of the government programme. Another term, 'substitution' refers to a similar phenomenon: the government-sponsored worker (through

---

[8] See Mishan (1978) and Haveman and Margolis (1983) for a discussion of the main issues in benefit–cost analysis and the main techniques used in such studies.

training, public service employment, or wage subsidy) is substituted for a worker without such sponsorship. 'Windfall' is the term applied to gains that employers enjoy when the government subsidizes the cost of training or employment which the firm would have undertaken even in the absence of the programme. This issue is complex, and a substantial literature has now been developed on it (see e.g. Johnson 1979; Kemper 1980; Bassi and Ashenfelter 1986). We shall mention a few major aspects.

The possibility that displacement effects will offset the increased earnings and employment of participants exists in all direct job creation programmes. The issue is how significant these effects are likely to be—what proportion of the increased earnings and employment of participants will be cancelled out by displacement? The primary circumstances that affect the degree of displacement are as follows:

1. *The effect of the programme on participant productivity and skills.* If the programme in fact increases participant productivity, there is a presumption of a pre-existing market failure. Without such market impediment, workers would have undertaken the investment on their own. In this case, human capital theory suggests that the benefits of the programme in the form of employment and earnings increases, exist without displacement.

2. *The effect of the programme in moving workers from labour surplus regions to shortage regions.* Even in the absence of a programme-induced increase in productivity, there will be a social gain if underutilized workers are shifted to locations where they will be more fully utilized. This effect, as in the previous case, requires a market impediment to have restrained this mobility in the absence of the programme. Note that the worker who is moved need not have been unemployed him- or herself if the area from which he or she is drawn is a labour surplus area. In this case, 'replacement' would have occurred. This issue of replacement is central to the benefit–cost analysis framework. An important calculated cost of the programme can be the earnings of the proportion of the participants who would have been employed in the absence of the programme. Since they are in the programme rather than employed, the appropriate procedure is to subtract the value of their employment as a cost of the programme; it is an opportunity cost. However, if a worker who is drawn into the programme is quickly replaced by

an unemployed worker in a labour surplus market, this opportunity cost is in fact zero.

3. *Macro-economic circumstances of markets in which participants operate.* The key issue is labour surplus or shortage conditions in the labour markets from which participants are drawn and those in which they are placed. With surplus in the drawing markets, *replacement* is likely, and the departure of the worker implies little or no opportunity cost. Conversely, with surplus in the placement market, *displacement* is likely, and the entry of the worker implies little or no social benefit. In this context, then, macro-economic policy takes on direct relevance to job creation efforts: macro-policy should be such as to accommodate the additional labour supply the productivity generated by the programme if its benefits are to be realized.

Measuring the extent of replacement or displacement is, of course, more difficult than conceptually identifying their effects on the evaluation of programme worth. In the presence of programmes which are small relative to the markets in which they operate, labour market conditions must be assessed in both drawing and placing markets—often small geographical areas with poor data availability—making the identification of programme effects difficult.

There have been a few attempts to measure displacement specifically. Some have proceeded by interviewing the administrators of job creation programmes, asking whether the particular economic activity would have been undertaken without that programme, and then using these subjective estimates to make some assessment of the degree to which there has been, in fact, a net addition of jobs. Such estimates are only as good as the subjective judgement of the administrators (see e.g. Zimmerman 1980; Nathan *et al.* 1981).

A second method has been to estimate an econometric model of employment in a given area in the absence of the programme, based on data series that extend from before it began and continue after its conclusion. The estimates of displacement derived in this way are, obviously, only good if the econometric model is effective at predicting employment in the given labour market area or among a given set of firms in the absence of the programmes (see Crane and Ellwood 1984; Gould, Ward, and Welch 1982).

A very specific method used to estimate displacement involved a special job creation programme which covered all persons of particular ages in a limited set of areas in a few cities. These areas could be matched with other areas with similar characteristics used as comparison groups. The quality of the estimate of displacement achieved by this method depends critically, however, on the exact matching of the comparison areas (discussed further below; see also Farkas *et al*. 1982).

The central lesson regarding displacement estimates is clear, however. When surplus labour exists in markets from which participants are drawn, straightforward control–treatment comparisons of employment differences will understate the net benefits of the programme; when labour surplus exists in markets where participants seek employment, such comparisons will yield an overstatement of net benefits. The task of the analyst is to identify and reflect these considerations in evaluation, even though their precise measurement is difficult. How much labour surplus is there in markets where participants are drawn or placed? Is macro-policy accommodating the changes engendered by the programme, or is it working at cross-purposes?

4.4. Sensitivity Analysis

The final evaluation issue we mention concerns the role of sensitivity analysis. By its very nature, benefit–cost analysis is a comprehensive analytic tool, attempting, when applied to employment programmes, to bring together in one uniform dimension all the social and economic impacts of the programme. Although this is hard to accomplish in practice—because it is difficult to measure impacts, and then difficult to value those which are measurable—the effort to do so is an integral component of a rational public decision process. Because numerous assumptions are necessary in any such analysis, the decision-maker needs to be informed regarding the dependence of the analysis on them. The best that can be done is to make the assumptions as explicit as possible and then to test whether slight variations in those assumptions will have a big effect on the overall estimates of benefits and costs—that is, to do a sensitivity analysis.

In the case of direct job creation programmes, sensitivity analysis is especially important in assessing the long-term effects of the programme on participants. Because these effects may extend through the remaining life-time of the worker, it is necessary to extrapolate the behaviour of those variables that are important to the analysis beyond the period of observation, and extrapolation requires assumptions. These extrapolations of persistence or decay should be made explicit, and their effect on the analysis evaluated.[9]

9 The most comprehensive and effective use of sensitivity analysis is the Supported Work benefit–cost study. See Hollister, Kemper, and Maynard (1984).

5

What Do We Know about What Works and for Whom?

Many analysts have noted the large disparity between Western Europe and the United States in the extent of efforts to evaluate the effectiveness of employment and training programmes.[1] As Schwanse (1982) concluded: 'Most of the European evaluations are confined to relatively simple questions and methodologies. Impact evaluations are almost non-existent'. To our knowledge, this situation persists. In what follows, therefore, we focus on impact evaluations of programmes in the United States, realizing that conclusions regarding this experience may not apply fully to the European situation.

5.1. Broad-Scale Programmes

We define broad-scale programmes to be those that are so open and widely spread in their administration that their impact cannot be evaluated by direct measurements concerning programme participants and a comparison group. This distinction, then, involves both evaluation methodology and programme scope.

5.1.1. Counter-cyclical Programmes

A primary rationale for public employment and training programmes is to counter-balance the effects of the private sector business cycle on employment. The effectiveness of broad counter-cyclical employment-based programmes is difficult to assess; there is no 'counter-factual' indicating what employers would have done had the government programmes not been in place. Short-time compensation programmes have been the primary form of counter-cyclical programme in Europe, but there have been few attempts to

[1] See e.g. Schwanse (1982), and Wilensky (1985).

measure their effectiveness. Two examples characterize this situation. The 1975 short-time compensation programme in Germany was estimated to have reduced the unemployment rate from 5.4 to 4.7 per cent (Schmid 1982), but this estimate was questioned on the grounds that employers would have retained workers even without the subsidy. And while Sweden's heavy subsidization of production in the 1970s is generally viewed as an ineffective attempt to bridge a short-term gap in private sector employment, there is no thorough evaluation of its effectiveness.

A simple way to judge counter-cyclical efforts is in terms of their timing. Bassi and Ashenfelter (1986) point out that for the United States, the timing of explicitly counter-cyclical (as opposed to structural) employment and training expenditures has been poor; from 1973 to 1982, every 1 per cent increase in the unemployment rate was associated with a -0.08 change in real per capita funding for counter-cyclical programmes. Most analysts feel that, because of long lead times, counter-cyclical expenditures such as public works projects often exacerbate the cycle, injecting their stimulus just when recovery is in process. (See US General Accounting Office 1984, a study which used county data in an econometric model to estimate the impact of grants and loans from the Economic Development Administration and which demonstrates the methodological difficulties in evaluating the impact of this type of programme). Improvements in the timing of funding and implementation are needed if such programmes are to be effective.

5.1.2. Wage Subsidies

Economists tend to prefer to promote employment by wage subsidies than by direct government hiring on the grounds that private employers have better established production processes, standards of worker productivity, and marketing networks than new public programmes would.

While these arguments are strong, concerns about windfalls to employers subsidized for workers they would have retained or hired anyway and/or 'displacement' of the output of unsubsidized firms by that of subsidized firms have been expressed as reasons to oppose wage subsidies. While the existence of windfalls to employers would seem to undercut the employment impact of wage subsidies, to determine their effects properly requires the full general equilibrium impact of the subsidies to be evaluated, including the use of windfalls by employers. (As noted above, concerns with displacement effects on both the production and employment studies of the market have been expressed regarding direct public employment as well.) Empirical assessment of the extent of windfalls or displacement of either public or private interventions is very limited.

The most prominent and perhaps the largest wage subsidy programmes are the New Jobs Tax Credit (hereafter NJTC) and the Targeted Jobs Tax Credit (hereafter TJTC) programmes in the United States.

The NJTC programme, which operated in 1977 and 1978, offered tax credits to any firm that increased its employment above 102 per cent of its previous year's employment. The tax credit was 50 per cent of the first $6,000 of the wages paid to workers hired above the 102 per cent level. It is estimated that 1 per cent of the labour force received the subsidy, and the value of the revenue lost was nearly $2 billion.

Evaluation of such a broad-scale programme requires estimation of employment levels in its absence. The most careful estimates for NJTC focused on its effects on employment in the construction and retailing industries, and concluded that in the twelve-month period from mid-1977 to mid-1978, 20 to 30 per cent of the observed employment increase in these industries could be attributed to the subsidy (Bishop and Haveman 1979). The time-series models underlying these estimates may fail to isolate the pure NJTC effect from other macro-changes; nevertheless, these results indicate a substantial positive programme impact on employment. They do not, however, indicate that the social benefits of the intervention exceeded the social costs.

The NJTC was replaced by the TJTC in 1979. Under this programme, private employers receive a two-year subsidy of wages paid for any hired worker from designated target groups. Fifty per cent of the first $6,000 of wage cost for any new hiree is paid for the first year of employment, falling to 25 per cent for the second year. While the NJTC was designed to increase employment generally, the TJTC was targeted on certain disadvantaged groups.

Although the TJTC has been in place since 1979, few attempts have been made to assess its impact overall. Few eligible firms actually utilized the subsidy, but there has been little evidence gathered as to the reasons for this.

Some insight on TJTC has been given by a small experimental study in which able-bodied welfare recipients were randomly assigned to three groups: in the first group, members received a tax credit voucher telling prospective employers that the person was eligible for a TJTC and informing of the terms of the payment; a second group was given a similar voucher, but reimbursement was to be made through a cash payment rather than a tax credit; the third group had no vouchers. While 21 per cent of those without vouchers obtained employment within eight weeks, only 13 per cent of the vouchered groups obtained employment. Among those of the latter who obtained jobs, only a quarter of their employers claimed the subsidy. These results have been interpreted as indicating that a targeted programme can actually stigmatize members of the target group and make their employment chances worse rather than better (see Burtless 1985).

This finding has been widely viewed as providing the first conclusive evidence that targeted government programmes may have a seriously stigmatizing effect. However, some of the analysts involved suggest that other factors may have driven the results. In particular, because local operators were concerned that the control group would resent not receiving the subsidy, all control group members were referred to the Employment Service, where they received the regular services provided; none of the experimental group was given special access to those services. It is true that the US Employment Service is generally regarded as ineffective, particularly in assisting the disadvantaged groups to whom this subsidy was targeted. However, knowing of the experiment, the Employment Service may have made extraordinary efforts on behalf of the controls. Some analysts also felt that the printed description of the subsidy programme given to employers was written in a way that called attention to the limitations of the group's members. Still other analysts have taken the evidence as another example of the peculiar and little-understood response of American employers to wage subsidies. In virtually every small demonstration involving wage subsidies, US employers have been very slow to take advantage of the subsidy offer. Their reluctance seems to be related to the fear that acceptance will lead to greater governmental scrutiny of their books and operations.

Reviewing a number of European evaluations of wage subsidy programmes, Casey and Bruche (1985) describe their overall evaluation as follows:

Despite the very different mechanisms employed (tax refund, exemption from employer social insurance contributions, direct subsidies), levels of support, targeting, and other restrictions, analyses of the multiplicity of European programs come to surprisingly similar conclusions. . . . In general the 'net employment effect' is about 10 per cent, with a maximum of some 25 per cent being reached in the case of the German scheme of 1974–75. This last figure is to be compared to the approximately 45 per cent 'net employment effect' estimated to have been necessary for that particular programme to have been fiscally neutral. (ibid. 42–3)

Because of the need to account for the full general equilibrium implications of the programmes, including 'windfalls' and 'displacements', and the difficulty of doing so, this generalization seems questionable.

A large number of important questions remain regarding the impact of broad-scale wage subsidy programmes on employment. In theory, such subsidies seem an attractive alternative to other forms of public job creation efforts. However, if this expectation is to be tested, improved methodologies for evaluating the effects of such programmes are required, as well as additional wage subsidy interventions designed with impact evaluation as part of the mission.

5.1.3. Direct Job Creation

'Direct job creation' refers to employment programmes in which hiring decisions are made by government (or government-supported entities), and employment is paid for by public revenues. In fact, the boundaries differentiating 'direct job creation' from other government employment and training efforts are fuzzy.[2] In most countries, however, programmes exist which are generally agreed to be 'direct job creation'. To cite just a few: the ABM programme in West Germany, Relief Work in Sweden, the Job Offer Scheme in Denmark, Travaux d'Utilité Collective in France, the Community Programme in the United Kingdom, and the Public Employment Program and Public Service Employment in the United States.

---

[2] Consider for example the case in which the central government provides funds to local governments that cover most but not all costs of a job project which is partially implemented by private organizations that help train workers in the skills necessary to execute the project. Is this 'direct job creation' or 'wage subsidies' or 'skill training'?

A major concern in evaluating direct job creation programmes is the issue of displacement or fiscal substitution. The question here is whether funds provided by the central government to, say, a local government for the purpose of hiring otherwise unemployed workers ultimately pay for positions that would have been supported by the local government in the absence of the subsidy. Initial evaluations of the Public Employment Program in the United States suggested that the extent of such substitution would grow from low levels early in the life of the programme to nearly total substitution over several years (see Johnson and Tomola 1977). These results created doubts as to whether or not such non-targeted direct job creation programmes would have any sustained effect on employment levels. Evaluations of the more targeted public employment programmes that followed the early interventions yielded a more optimistic appraisal. In the first years of a later programme (Public Service Employment), between 40 and 60 per cent of the positions funded were estimated to be net new employment (see Nathan *et al.* 1981; Adams, Cook, and Maurice 1983).

Estimation of the extent of fiscal substitution in direct job creation programmes is difficult, requiring estimates of the level of public employment in the relevant government units in the absence of the programme. Although all of the estimates are clouded with uncertainty because of the inevitable unreliability of this estimated counter-factual, analysts have come to agree on a number of propositions regarding the potential of these programmes:

— Some fiscal substitution inevitably will occur, the degree varying with programme design and the prevailing economic circumstance
— The degree of fiscal substitution is likely to increase over time as government units have time to adjust
— Public employment programmes which explicitly seek to constrain activities that would have been undertaken in their absence yield higher net-to-gross employment ratios
-- Programmes targeted on the disadvantaged will be less vulnerable to fiscal substitution because the skill mix of target-group workers hired does not conform closely to the mix of regular public employees

Three additional observations should be made regarding fiscal substitution. First, even reliable estimates of substitution capture its effects only within the public sector. Private sector responses, including the spending that would have occurred had the funds not been raised through taxation, are not captured. Second, even when fiscal substitution occurs, redistribution of employment towards disadvantaged workers may result if such a target group is designated. Third, tightly constraining a public employment programme to avoid activities in which government units normally engage may force participants into activities which have little skill carryover outside the programme.

One might argue that, to the extent that a direct job creation programme's objectives are largely counter-cyclical, these should not be evaluated by comparing the post-programme earning of participants to those of a comparison group; long-term earnings gains are not the primary objective. However, in assessing the benefits of counter-cyclical programmes one should not ignore the possibility that maintaining workers in employment may prevent the decay of their human capital (skills and work habits)—i.e. that after the end of the cycle, workers maintained in employment through the programme may prove more productive than workers who suffered an extended period of unemployment. Designing and executing a study to actually estimate the extent of such effects is, as far as we know, a challenge not yet taken up.

A primary argument for counter-cyclical programmes is that they utilize resources that would otherwise remain idle. Therefore, a major aspect of their evaluation should be an assessment of the value of output produced. As we have already noted above, only recently have efforts been made to evaluate output produced in employment and training programmes, but the methodology for doing so is becoming established and efforts to do so more common. The closest thing to a direct job creation programme in which the value of output was estimated as part of the evaluation is the National Supported Work Demonstration in the United States. For that programme, the value of output produced by the participants was estimated to be an important component of the benefits, offsetting about 43 per cent of the total costs.

5.1.4. Enterprise Creation

Government efforts to foster the development of private sector enterprises, often as part of regional development plans, have a long history. In the 1980s there has been a renewed emphasis on promotion of enterprises, primarily because of the expected positive impact on aggregate employment. (See Appendix n. 14 for references on enterprise promotion and employment.) The rapid growth in jobs in the US economy in the 1980s was viewed by some as generated by the strong performance of new, often small, enterprises. Enterprise creation fostered by public support, it was felt, could create the same growth. Several countries have undertaken small-scale programmes to enable unemployed persons to remain covered by benefits if starting up a new enterprise, or using unemployment benefits in lump-sum form for enterprise capitalization. As with direct job creation, the performance of enterprise creation efforts is difficult to assess. Again, the establishment of a reliable counter-factual is required. To what extent would the enterprises subsidized by government have been created without the subsidy? Would the activities undertaken in the absence of the programme be more or less labour intensive? One study of an unemployment diversion programme indicates that about 70 per cent of enterprises assisted in this way were in existence after one year (Bloch-Michel *et al.* 1983, cited in Casey and Bruche 1985). Whether this performance is superior to other new enterprises is not known. Moreover, the assisted enterprises are clearly not a representative sample of all new enterprises, and may be either more or less risky. The evaluation problems confronted in assessing these efforts are difficult ones, and the methodology for accurately measuring their effectiveness has not yet been developed.

5.2. Traditional Training and Placement Programmes

Traditional training and placement programmes seek to improve the employability of individuals by providing workers with new skills and placing them in regular private or public employment. Such programmes are aimed at individuals rather than at broad alteration in labour market circumstances, and hence can be evaluated by comparing participants' labour market experience, both during and after the programme, with that of similar individuals who are not participants.

5.2.1. Adults

Consider, first, programmes that have been targeted on the adult population. While there have been substantial training and placement programmes for adults in Europe, there are few evaluations of the net employment gains of participants based on control group comparisons. Hence we again focus on the US experience.

The first substantial employment and training effort in the United States since the Great Depression was that initiated by the Manpower Development and Training Act of 1962, a programme motivated by a perception of increasing structural unemployment. After the War on Poverty began, in 1964, the programme became targeted on disadvantaged workers. By the early 1970s these early efforts had been complemented by a wide range of other training and job creation efforts that were federally sponsored but locally run. The Comprehensive Employment and Training Act of 1973 (CETA) pulled the many such training programmes of different types together under a single administrative structure. This co-ordinated structure remained in place until 1981, when it was replaced by a far smaller programme oriented to the private sector, designed by the Reagan administration under the Job Training Partnership Act (JTPA).

While there were many evaluations of small, particular components of CETA over the years,[3] at the end of the 1970s and into the 1980s major evaluations of the programme centred on the use of the Continuous Longitudinal Manpower Survey (CLMS). A brief sketch of the features of that system will facilitate understanding of the results and the critique of them.

Building on Ashenfelter's earlier work, the US Department of Labor supported the development of data files on large, representative samples of persons participating in the CETA programme in the period 1975–9. The data contained in the files indicated not only the type of programme in which the person was involved but also his or her basic demographic characteristics and labour force status during the year before enrolment. In addition, data on the earnings of these individuals were taken from Social Security Administration (SSA) records and merged with the CLMS records. These data for CETA participants were supplemented with sets of data for other individuals taken from the Current Population Survey (CPS), the monthly representative sample of US households which is the basis

---

[3] Ashenfelter (1978) is generally regarded to have established the paradigm for the evaluation of federal training programs in the United States, although, as the author himself has indicated, it has been superseded by subsequent works cited below.

of national labour force statistics. These CPS data were also merged with SSA data for the individuals in the sample. The CPS sample enabled construction of comparison groups made up of persons who had not participated in the CETA programmes (or at least reported that they had not), with basic demographic information on them as well as their earnings history from the SSA files. The important feature of this combined data source was that because it provided a longitudinal data file on earnings, the impact of CETA programmes could be traced for a period following exit from the programme and compared with the earnings experience of those from the CPS–SSA file who had not participated. To many, this appeared to provide a potentially powerful means to do impact evaluations of CETA programmes.

A large number of evaluations of CETA have been performed utilizing the CLMS (the most recent review, Barnow 1987, examines eleven major studies in detail), as well as several summary assessments of these evaluations (see also Bassi and Ashenfelter 1986: 140–5; Betsey, Hollister, and Papageorgiou 1985: 175–81; Burtless 1984; and Barnow 1987). A few of the studies sought to evaluate CETA overall. They concluded that, at best, CETA had small, positive effects on participants' earnings, and primarily through higher hours of work rather than higher wage rates.

The evaluations of CETA presented not only overall assessments but results further disaggregated by broad types of programmes and by subgroups of the participants according to race (usually defined broadly as minority or non-minority) and sex. The general conclusions seem to be that the programmes were more effective for those with the least previous labour market experience. This showed up more strongly for women than for men, but there were also positive results for the disadvantaged in general.

With respect to programme types, public service employment and on-the-job training were more effective than work experience or classroom training. However, estimates of the effects on earnings for any given programme and population subgroup varied widely, even though roughly the same basic data were being used. For example, among work experience programmes for women, one set of analysts estimated the impact on earnings to be an increase of $800 to $1,300 (Bloom and McLaughlin 1982), while another estimated the impact at $500 (Dickinson, Johnson, and West 1986). Both estimates were statistically significant. There are extended examinations of the possible reasons for the difference in the findings among these studies, but rather than try to summarize them, it is more useful to turn to much more disturbing findings that indicate that the methodology upon which they were based may be fundamentally flawed.

The studies that have shown grave problems with the CETA evaluations depend critically on information drawn from the National Supported Work Demonstration. These findings can be discussed more efficiently if readers are acquainted with the basic features of the Supported Work project, so we digress to sketch them. In any case, the findings from the research on Supported Work are in themselves relevant to our discussion of programme evaluation.

(1) Supported Work. Supported Work was a national demonstration programme which ran from 1975 to 1979. It had four target groups: women who had been on welfare (Aid to Families with Dependent Children) for at least three years; ex-drug addicts; ex-criminal offenders; and youth (17–20 years old) who were high school drop-outs. These groups were felt to need employment assistance because they had not recently, and in some cases never, had a regular connection with the labour market. The objective was to help them establish or re-establish regular employment. Participants were provided subsidized work experience in which work standards were gradually made more demanding, and they were guided by supervisors knowledgeable about the problems of the target groups. Participants could continue in the programme for up to 12 months (18 months in a few sites), after which they had to move on to regular employment (or back to unemployment if they were unsuccessful, even with the programme's assistance, in finding work). Note that this was explicitly not a programme providing skills training; such skills as were obtained were to be the result only of direct work experience. The demonstration was run in fifteen sites across the country, different sites having different combination of the three target groups.

An extensive evaluation of the programme's effects was carried out (fully reported in Hollister, Kemper, and Maynard 1984). The most important feature of this evaluation is that 6,600 applicants to the programme were randomly assigned to be participants or members of a control group. Both participants and controls were interviewed at the point of random assignment and every 9 months thereafter, up to a maximum of about 36 months. A special resurvey done at the end of the evaluation study provided data on youth for 38 to 67 months after initial enrolment. Another important feature of the evaluation is that it provided a very careful and extensive benefit–cost analysis.

The evaluation showed that for all target groups, participants' hours of work and earnings increased relative to the control group during the period they were in the programme (hardly surprising, since both groups were unemployed at the point of random assignment and the participants were given immediate access to the subsidized job). However, in the post-programme period, the evaluation found different impacts for each of the target groups.

The programme had the strongest impact among women on welfare: two years after enrolment they had a 20 per cent higher employment rate, 35 per cent more hours worked, and 48 per cent higher earnings than did the control group. All these differences were statistically significant at conventional levels. The benefit–cost analysis showed that, from the perspective of society as a whole, the net present value of benefits per participant exceeded those of costs by $8,150 (a benefit–cost ratio of about 1 : 3). (Note, however, that the average rate of employment of the participants, while higher than that of the controls, was still a relatively low 42 per cent.)

The evaluation indicated positive but more equivocal results for the ex-addict group. The strongest effects showed up in lower crime rates for the participants, as indicated by statistically significant differences in arrests and incarcerations. The employment effects, while positive in the post-programme period, were statistically significant only for that portion of the group for whom data were available in months 30–36 after enrolment, leaving considerable uncertainty about the strength and reliability of such effects. There were no statistically significant effects on measures (self-reported) of drug and alcohol use. The benefit–cost analysis indicated that the net present value of benefits exceeded costs (by $4,345), but most of the estimated benefits arose from the valuation of the gains from the reduced criminal activity of the ex-addicts who had participated in the programme. (When sensitivity of the results to variations in the underlying assumptions was tested, the conclusion of substantial benefits in excess of costs was robust.)

For the ex-offender group there were no statistically significant impacts on employment or earnings in the post-programme period, nor were there any significant measured effects on the level of criminal activity. There were scattered suggestions that the programme may have reduced drug use, but the patterns over time were not consistent enough to draw any strong conclusions about impacts in this domain. The benefit–cost analysis indicated that the net present value of costs exceeded benefits by $3,180 per participant. There is no evidence here to indicate that Supported Work was likely to be an effective programme for ex-offenders.

Impacts for the youth group were essentially nil in the post-programme period. There were no statistically significant differences in employment or earnings, and no statistically significant long-term impacts on education or training decisions, drug use, or criminal behaviour. The benefit–cost analysis showed that from the point of view of society as a whole, costs exceeded benefits by $1,465 per youth participant.

There were many interesting features of the Supported Work programme and its evaluation. We select a few that are most salient to our review.

Supported Work can be looked upon as a form of direct public job creation (even though specific sites used private sector agencies to some degree). The evidence indicates that, assessed in terms of post-programme effects, this type of intervention works best for women, does not work at all for ex-offenders and low-income youth, and has some positive effects for ex-addicts. Of course, it should be remembered that an objective of direct public job creation can be considered the immediate provision of income for the unemployed in the form of a work opportunity, regardless of its long-term effects. In these terms the programme worked for all four groups, since it raised their incomes above those of the control group during the programme period.[4]

Supported Work is often regarded as a 'work experience' programme, in contrast to e.g. classroom training or job search

---

[4] When evaluated without regard to any gains in post-programme earnings but taking into account reduced transfer payments, the net present value of benefits just about equalled the costs. See Hollister, Kemper, and Maynard (1984: table 8.4, p. 254), which gives costs and benefits from the non-participant perspective. If society prefers to provide income support in forms that involve work rather than cash transfers alone (as they seem to do, at least in the United States and Sweden), then when benefits equal costs in monetary terms, they would exceed costs if account were taken of this social valuation of work.

assistance. As a form of work experience, the effectiveness of this programme varies across the four groups in the same fashion: 'yes', for women on welfare; 'no' for ex-offenders and youth; and 'maybe' for ex-addicts.

Beyond the findings regarding programme effectiveness, the Supported Work evaluation has proved particularly useful for purposes of improving the methodology of evaluating job creation programmes, because the evaluation was carried out in the framework of a random assignment design. The evaluation showed that random assignment to the programme and to a 'no-treatment' control group could indeed be effectively carried out for an employment and training programme involving a very large number of subjects in many sites spread across a nation, and, furthermore, that random assignment design considerably enhanced the power of the subsequent evaluation.

The value of this experience with random assignment has been compounded by the further use of Supported Work data to assess the validity of the comparison group methods used to evaluate CETA, as described above. Two sets of investigators, Fraker and Maynard (1987) and LaLonde (1986), working independently, decided to use the data from Supported Work and from the CLMS–CPS–SSA data base to generate two sets of estimates of the impact of the Supported Work programme, one based on the comparative earnings of participants and the control group created by random assignment, the second based on participant earnings and those of comparison groups created from the CPS data in exactly the same way as for the CETA evaluations. The objective was to determine the extent to which the use of constructed comparison groups, combined with various econometric methods for dealing with selection bias, could yield estimates of the impacts of employment and training programmes that were generally reliable, i.e. unbiased and reasonably precise. The data from Supported Work provided an unusual opportunity for such a test, since the random assignment impact estimates could be taken as a bench-mark of the 'true' programme impacts.

The two sets of investigators tested a wide range of methods for constructing the comparison groups (including all those used by the CETA studies cited above) and a wide range of econometric methods in modelling and estimating programme impacts. The results showed that the comparison group procedures generally provided unreliable estimates of the impact of the programme. They were sensitive to both the method used to select the group and the econometric method used to estimate the impact, but in neither case did one method appear consistently superior to another. They did find that the bias was smaller and the precision greater in estimating the impacts on women on welfare than they were for youth and other male groups, but even for the women, the comparison group estimates ranged from 27 per cent to 159 per cent more than the estimates from the random assignment control group.

These results cast serious doubt on the reliability of the estimates of the impacts of CETA cited above, both according to type of programme and to type of participant. It is probably safe to conclude that CETA had a greater positive impact on women than on men, since the Supported Work programme and several other experimental studies reviewed below support this conclusion. Beyond this, it must be concluded that not much can be said about the impacts of CETA.

(2) Job Training Partnership Act. The most significant change introduced by the Reagan administration's Job Training Partnership Act (JTPA) concerned the structure of control over funds. Funds flow first to states, then to 'service delivery areas', and then to local bodies called Private Industry Councils (PIC). One-half of the members of the PICs (plus the chair) must be from private industry, the view being that since private sector employers will largely be the source of jobs for those completing the programme, they should have a large role in shaping it. PICs control the allocation of resources at the local level.

A strong emphasis on quantitative performance standards—involving post-programme employment and earnings, as well as costs—has developed under JTPA. The local PICs have tended to translate these standards into performance contracts under which the agencies provide the training and other services to participants.

There are some early process evaluations of the implementation of JTPA (e.g. Walker *et al.* 1986), but we know of no impact evaluation studies. An important development can be reported, however. Largely as a result of the problems reviewed above in the use of the CLMS–CPS–SSA data and non-experimental comparison group methodology for the evaluation, an advisory committee to the US

Department of Labor recommended that the evaluation of JTPA be carried out through a limited number of experiments in which subjects would be randomly assigned to programme participation or to a control group. The department accepted and implemented that recommendation, and work has begun this year on the development of sixteen experimental JTPA sites.

(3) Dislocated Workers. Under JTPA, special emphasis was given for the first time to providing training for displaced (or dislocated) workers. As mentioned, federal funds provided to states are passed to local organizations for implementation. Assistance is provided for training, job placement, worker relocation, and child care and transportation while in training.

Identifying dislocated-worker status in a dynamic economy is problematic. Indeed, some analysts have argued that dislocated workers cannot be sufficiently distinguished from the unemployed more generally for the purposes of targeting resources on them (Bendick and Devine 1982). There is a continual flow of workers out of one economic activity and into another, often with a period of unemployment. For example, between January 1979 and January 1984, 11.5 million workers in the United States lost jobs owing to plant closure, plant relocation, or slack work. By the end of 1984, 0.5 million of those who had held their jobs for at least three years prior to lay-off had been unemployed for more than 27 weeks. By some standards, these are dislocated workers.

Evidence on the impact of programmes for dislocated workers is quite limited. A mid-1970s evaluation of a programme for workers dislocated by trade impacts was inconclusive, as most workers simply waited to be recalled to their prior jobs, and most had in fact been recalled in six months (see Corson and Nicholson 1981). Several major dislocated worker training programme demonstrations were implemented and extensively evaluated in the early 1980s.[5] These evaluations provided mixed results. A reasonable conclusion is that a well-structured job search and assistance programme can shorten the period of unemployment and reduce the associated loss of earnings. However, the magnitude of the effects and the conditions

---

[5] These projects were in Detroit, Buffalo, El Paso, and Houston. The evaluations involved both matched comparison groups and random assignment to treatment and control groups. See Kulik, Smith, and Stromsdorfer (1984); Maynard *et al.* (1985).

under which they are likely to obtain remain unclear. Furthermore, major issues remain about how best to target and to implement such programmes. (A comprehensive review of issues and experiences to date is provided in US Congress, Office of Technology Assessment 1986).

(4) Workfare.   In the late 1970s and 1980s, attempts to bring those receiving welfare into the work force have been referred to as 'workfare'. Workfare programmes, which are generally targeted at women as they derive from Aid to Families with Dependent Children, seek to reduce welfare dependency over the long term by providing mandatory training and employment to recipients.

Results have been reported from a number of these projects, primarily those involving a compulsory work requirement. Generally, women taken into the programme were first given job search assistance. If they failed to obtain a job after a period of search, they entered mandatory service. In some cases, this included training; in others, it involved unpaid (i.e. no payment beyond their welfare grant) public sector or private non-profit work, entitled the Community Work Experience Program (CWEP). These demonstration projects were all carried out with random assignment to programme participation or to a control group.

In almost all cases, the studies showed that the programmes had small, positive impacts on employment rates and earnings and, concomitantly, small reductions in welfare benefits received.[6] Because the costs of these programmes are small, ranging from about $150 to $900 per participant, even the relatively small positive impacts were sufficient for benefit–cost analyses to show net social benefits. The results also showed that those with the least labour market experience appeared to gain most. The importance of the random assignment design of the evaluations should be emphasized, as the small estimated effects might well not have been detected in a non-random assignment design, and certainly would have been more strongly questioned. Further, the control group data highlighted the degree to which simply looking at results for programme parti-

[6] Reported in Gueron (1986). The estimated impacts on employment rates were usually statistically significant, whereas the differences in earnings and welfare payments were less often so, probably (given the large variance in these measures) because sample sizes were too small.

cipants could be misleading: in one site, 78 per cent of participants were on welfare at the outset and only 35 per cent were on welfare a year and a half later. But the data from the control group show that most of this decline would have happened anyway: the net programme impact was not a 43 per cent reduction, but a 1 per cent reduction (Gueron 1986: 23). This highlights the subtle findings that can result from careful evaluations: there are indeed statistically significant impacts from programmes of this type, and they appear to more than justify their costs, but they will by no means lead to dramatic changes in the employment of this population nor to huge declines in welfare costs. The rhetoric of the 'workfare' debate in the United States has tended to ignore both parts of this subtle message and to characterize mandatory work and training for welfare recipients either as harsh and ineffective or as a powerful instrument for putting welfare recipients to work and reducing public welfare costs.

A set of studies related to workfare deserves mention, as much for their example of style of analysis as for their findings: Grossman, Maynard, and Roberts (1985); Ellwood (1986); Maynard and Maxfield (1986) (all prepared for the US Department of Health and Human Services by Mathematica Policy Research). These studies focused on questions of targeting training. They sought to determine (*a*) which types of programmes were most effective for which subgroups of the welfare population, and (*b*) which subgroups were most important in determining total welfare costs. The cost-effectiveness of 'workfare' programme resources could be increased by combining findings on these two issues.

The studies were stimulated by previous research on the dynamics of the welfare recipient population, showing that the majority of welfare recipients are on the welfare rolls for short periods, but the majority of welfare resources go for benefits paid to the small group of recipients who are on welfare for long periods. By reanalysing longitudinal data on welfare recipiency and using the total correlation of individual characteristics and the length of time on welfare, it was found that women who have never married and who have a child under 3 years of age are those most likely to become long-term welfare dependants. In order to estimate which types of programme work best for various subgroups of the welfare population, data from five different demonstration programmes were reanalysed. These studies indicated that programmes were more effective for those women with less education, less recent work experience, and a very young child, and that more extensive training programmes were more cost-effective in increasing earnings and reducing welfare payments than short-term job search assistance programmes.

The findings of the two sets of studies were combined in a simulation model designed to test the effects of different combinations of programmes targeted on different subgroups of the welfare population. The results of this work did suggest a revision of previous views. Contrary to the conventional wisdom that targeting on long-term recipients with older children was the superior strategy, the new analysis indicated that intervention at the point of first application to receive benefits, targeted on relatively young women with little education and with young children, would be the most cost-effective. On the basis of this work, a new demonstration design was developed which targets mandatory employment and training resources primarily on teenage mothers who are school drop-outs at the point of their entrance to welfare. It is currently being implemented in two states and involves a full evaluation using random assignment.

These studies are especially interesting because they carefully combined the results of past experimental and non-experimental studies into explicit designs for future programmes, which themselves will be further tested and evaluated.

5.2.2. Youths

Programmes for youth have been a major component of national employment and training efforts in most countries since the mid-1960s; in the late 1970s and early 1980s their share of total resources became even larger. In England, the Youth Training Scheme has been extended to make all 16- and 17-year-old school leavers eligible to participate. In France, the scope of Travaux d'Utilité Collective for those aged 16 to 21 has been greatly expanded. In Ireland the Work Experience Programme, in Sweden the Youth Teams, and in Denmark the Job Creation Law have all become substantial programmes for youth.

In the United States, the most important youth employment and training programmes were supported under the Youth Employment and Demonstration Projects Act of 1978 (YEDPA). The YEDPA umbrella covered a large number of diverse programmes. Moreover, the legislation contained an explicit injunction 'to test the relative efficacy of different ways of dealing with [youth employment problems] in different local contexts' and allocated substantial sums to demonstration and research activities. Although YEDPA was terminated in 1981, a panel was appointed by the National Academy of Sciences in 1983 to review what had been learned from the YEDPA evaluations (see Betsey, Hollister, and Papageorgiou 1985). We draw heavily on the findings of this review.

In addition to the youth component of the Supported Work programme (already discussed), two youth programmes stand out because of their size, the quality of their evaluations, and the concepts they embodied. They are the Job Corps and the Youth Incentive Entitlement Pilot Projects:

(1) Job Corps. This federal programme began in the late 1960s. It is targeted on out-of-school, economically disadvantaged youth aged 14 to 21. The programme is residential: participants live in quarters at the site where the programme services are provided. It provides a complex mix of services, including remedial (basic) education, vocational skills training, work experience, health services, and job search assistance, at sites scattered throughout the United States. In FY 1985 the programme served 120,000 participants.

The major evaluation of the Job Corps was of high quality. Data were gathered for three to four years on a large sample of participants (2,800) and a non-participant comparison group (1,000). The comparison group was carefully drawn from youth eligible for Job Corps but residing in geographic areas where Job Corps enrolment was low. The best econometric methods available were used to try to control for selection bias. A careful cost–benefit analysis was part of the evaluation.

The evaluation found that after participants left the Job Corps, their earnings were 28 per cent higher then those of the comparison group. Educational attainment of the participants increased more than for the comparison group: within the first six months after leaving the Job Corps, the probability of attaining a high school degree or equivalent was .24 for participants versus .05 for those in the comparison group. Similarly, there were positive impacts on the level of criminal acitivity (i.e., participants in the Job Corps committed fewer and less serious crimes).

The study estimated that the net present value of social benefits per enrollee was $2,300 (in 1977 dollars). This positive conclusion was robust under reasonable variations in assumptions.

While this evaluation strongly indicates that the Job Corps is an effective intervention targeted on the disadvantaged youth population, two problems should be noted. First, random assignment was not used to create participant and control groups. Hence even though the comparison group was carefully selected, and state-of-the-art econometric methods were used in the analysis, some doubts regarding potential selection bias remain. Second, while we may conclude that the Job Corps as a whole is effective, there is little evidence regarding which of its several components are the primary contributors to its effectiveness. For example, the contribution of the unique (and expensive) residential character of the programme remains unknown.

(2) Youth Incentive Entitlement Pilot Projects (YIEPP). The Youth Incentive Entitlement Pilot Projects was a demonstration mandated by the US Congress under YEDPA. It ran from March 1978 until August 1981, when it was terminated by the new (Reagan) administration as part of its reorganization of federal employment and training activities under JTPA (described above). The demonstration programme guaranteed disadvantaged youths minimum-wage jobs, part time during the school year and full time during the summer months. No skill training was provided. The programme was a saturation (or 'entitlement') intervention, in that all low-income youths in the target area of a project were guaranteed a job provided that they remained enrolled in school and were making reasonable progress toward a high school diploma. The short-term objectives were to reduce school drop-out rates, provide work experience, and raise participants' incomes during the programme phase. The long-term objectives were to improve employment and earnings after the programme period. There were seventeen demonstration projects across the country, and about 70,000 youths participated.

Evaluation of YIEPP posed a serious problem because of its saturation nature, which made it impossible to draw a comparison group from the same area. The evaluation design called for the comparison of four large-scale programme sites with four non-programme sites. An attempt was made to match the programme sites with comparison sites in terms of important characteristics of the population, industry, and employment.

The evaluation of YIEPP reported statistically significant effects on weekly earnings both for the programme period and beyond. In-programme earnings during the school year were estimated to be 46 to 161 per cent above those in the absence of the programme. Summer earnings increases were estimated to range from 48 to 65 per cent. However, there are reasons to question the accuracy of these estimates, as will be discussed below.

During its operation, YIEPP significantly lowered unemployment rates and raised employment and labour force participation rates of both black and white youths. Importantly, about two-thirds of all youths eligible for the programme in the target sites did participate at some time. This suggests that youths are willing to work at the minimum wage but that, in the absence of a programme like YIEPP, employers are unwilling to hire as many youths at that wage as want to work.

A stated objective of YIEPP was to increase school continuation rates (reduce drop-out rates) of the low-income youth eligible for the programme. Indeed, continued enrolment in education was a condition for continuation in YIEPP. However, the evaluation concluded that the programme had no sustained effects on school continuation rates.

Estimates of the effect of the programme on post-programme employment and earnings were severely limited because of the premature termination of the evaluation study in the fall of 1981. The final analysis focused on the sample of black youth and found that the programme substantially increased the weekly earnings of those eligible. If this is correct, the programme would appear very cost-effective, since it provided both immediate employment and earnings during the programme and favourable post-programme employment and earning experience.

Unfortunately, the studies of YIEPP have serious methodological problems, particularly with respect to post-programme earnings, which highlight the difficulties which any attempt to evaluate 'saturation'-type programmes will face. At the heart of the issue is the feasibility of accurately matching geographic areas so as to create reliable comparison sites. This site-matching procedure is necessary because of the local 'saturation' nature of the programme. The belief that the matching of geographic sites can be accomplished so that the residents of matched sites can be used as comparison subjects requires a belief that all the factors which determine the evolution of the local labour markets have been captured and adequately matched at the outset, and that any changes in the context external to the local area are also measured and controlled for in the analytic model used to estimate programme effects. It seems unlikely that the knowledge of the factors that affect the evolution of local labour markets, and the ability to accurately model and predict that evolution, is sufficiently advanced to rely upon the estimates of impact yielded by evaluations based on this model.

The problems of using matched sites for comparison can be seen in some of the results of the YIEPP study. The final analysis sample was limited in two ways: first, the major analysis excluded whites and Hispanics, even though data had been gathered on them; second, the Denver–Phoenix pair of programme and comparison sites was excluded from the analysis because the Denver programme had 'implementation difficulties'. The exclusion of the Hispanics from the analysis was tied to the exclusion of the Denver–Phoenix pair because the Hispanic sample was highly concentrated in this pair of sites. The rationale for the exclusion of whites was that a large portion of the comparison sample of whites was concentrated in the Louisville site, which experienced very sharp drops in white school enrolments, perhaps because of a controversy over school busing. A third example of site comparison problems can be seen in the individual site results, which show no significant effect on post-programme earnings in the Baltimore site, which had a programme generally regarded as the one best designed and implemented. The evaluators suggest this may be due to an unexpectedly healthy economy in the comparison site, Cleveland. These examples provide concrete evidence that evaluation based on the use of matched comparison sites is quite vulnerable to unpredictable developments.

In sum, YIEPP was an important and sizeable programme designed to investigate the importance of direct job experience during school-attending years for low-income youth, and most specifically the extent to which it might lower school drop-out rates and lead to larger-term increases in income and employment. Many important things were learned from the demonstration about the feasibility of placing large numbers of youth in jobs. It was also learned that a sizeable proportion of youth would take such jobs.

However, in spite of indications that the programme may have had long-term effects on employment and earnings, the method of evaluation is sufficiently weak as to preclude any overall conclusion regarding the effectiveness of this strategy for helping youth.

(3) Overall Findings on Youth Programmes. In 1985 a study conducted by the National Academy of Sciences, Committee on Youth Employment Programmes surveyed over four hundred reports on training programmes focused on youth. Applying criteria for judging the soundness of the evaluation,[7] only twenty-eight evaluations were found to contain reasonably reliable information on impacts. The conclusions from these reliable studies are summarized below.

Following the schema used by the National Academy of Sciences committee, programmes are grouped according to type, and within each type a distinction is made between those aimed primarily at out-of-school youth and those aimed primarily at in-school youth.[8] Only the estimates of post-programme effects are summarized here.

1. *Occupational skills training.* For in-school youth, virtually, no skills training programmes had been adequately evaluated, so no conclusions could be drawn. For out-of-school youth, the Job Corps was the major occupational skills training programme and, as indicated above, an evaluation of very high quality indicated that it was quite effective. The programme had many different components and the evaluation was not designed to assess the components separately, so we do not know, for example, how important was the residential aspect of the programme or its remedial basic education. The benefit–cost analysis showed that, although costs per participant were quite high, the net present value of estimated benefits exceeded that of costs.

2. *Labour market preparation.* This category contains a mix of programme types: career exploration (information on opportunities

---

[7] The criteria were (*a*) pre- and post-programme measurement of relevant aspects of performance, (*b*) the presentation of adequate comparison group data, and (*c*) sample sizes sufficient to enable statistical analysis and minimize attrition biases.

[8] While discrete programme categories are reviewed, many programmes have a variety of components and cannot be considered as falling in only one category. For example, a skills-training programme will have a job placement component at its conclusion.

and requirements); basic education training, often leading to a General Equivalence Degree (GED) certificate (equivalent to US high school completion); orientation to 'the world of work' with some direct job experience. For in-school youth, once again, there was no reliable evidence available. For out-of-school youth these programmes appeared to generate some positive effects on employment in earnings in a 3–8 month post-programme period, but there was no reliable evidence about whether these effects would be sustained for a longer post-programme period.

3. *Temporary jobs*. These programmes provide temporary, often subsidized, employment for youth. The major programme for in-school youth was YIEPP, reviewed above. It must be concluded that we do not know whether it had post-programme effects. This is especially regrettable, because non-experimental work had found a strong relationship between work during the school years and better employment and earnings in the labour market after school (see Meyer and Wise 1982).

The Supported Work demonstration, described above, was the major example for temporary work programmes for out of school work. A careful evaluation based on a random assignment design showed that this programme had no long-term effects on youth, and its costs far outweighed its benefits. However, the programme did serve a particularly disadvantaged segment of the youth population, so it may be that its negative conclusions cannot be generalized to the out-of-school youth population in general.

4. *Job placement*. Programmes in this category devote most of their effort to finding job opportunities for youth and referring youth to an employer which has a reasonable match with the youth's interests and abilities. They usually also include some training in job search techniques, how to prepare résumés, conduct job interviews, and sometimes follow-up support once the youth is placed on a job. For in-school youth they appear to have increased employment and earnings in the year following the programme, but by the second year the effects have disappeared. The conclusions are the same for out-of-school youth in such programmes: short-term positive effects, with comparison group members catching up by the second year.

6

Conclusions and Appendix

In this wide-ranging review of issues and evidence regarding job creation policies and programmes in Europe and the United States, we have been able, at best, to skim over many topics, and have had to omit many details, qualifications, and in-depth analyses. For these reasons, general conclusions are especially risky, but we attempt some here:

1. *Both good institutions and good evaluations are necessary elements for the best employment and training policies* (Europe seems to typify the first, the United States the second), but they seem rarely to occur together.

2. *In general, employment and training programmes have had their greatest impacts and largest social returns for those who have had the least previous labour market experience and are most disadvantaged.* Most evaluations found that programmes work better for women than for men, for those less educated and poorer than for those better educated and with higher income. Even where programmes have had statistically significant effects, the effects have been small relative to the size of the problem, but though small they are often still socially significant.

3. *Intensive, residential skills-training programmes for youth may be very effective.*

4. *Job search and placement efforts produce at least short-term effects in a wide variety of circumstances and are generally of low cost.*

5. *For seriously disadvantaged males, there is little evidence pointing to any particular employment and training policy as effective,* primarily because of the lack of quality evaluation.

6. *Marginal employment subsidies with simple structures, outreach efforts, and minimal interference appear to be a cost-effective labour maket policy to reduce cyclical unemployment.* They deserve more extensive utilization and careful evaluation than they have received in most countries to date.

7. *Employment and training policies cannot be substitutes for*

effective fiscal, monetary, and foreign trade policies. In general, employment and training policies will prove more effective when aggregate demand is increased.

8. *More effort needs to be put into fitting employment and training policies to changes in the general economic context.* This is a problem both of understanding which types of programmes are likely to be most effective in which circumstance and of implementing policies in light of that understanding in a timely fashion. It is important that programmes are started in time to yield effects at the right phase; but also that they are shut down when the changed context makes them less appropriate.

9. *All countries need to devote more resources to systematic learning from their experiences with employment and training programmes.*

The strongest indictment of the past is not that countries have failed to try employment and training policies, but that they have learned so little from their experience. Examples exist which show that carefully designed evaluations, following a few simple rules, can be implemented so as to yield powerful insights. The information they provide is often not good news, but it is important news if the resources used in employment and training programmes are to yield substantial social benefits. Good intentions are not enough.

Appendix: Forms of Employment and Training Efforts

This appendix reviews, in general terms, the wide range of employment and training efforts that have been undertaken.

A. Complete Government Production

This is the purest form of job creation programme by a government, in which the government organizations themselves direct all or nearly all of the factors of production; that is, not only the workers but the supervisors, the provision of materials, the working space, in some cases even the marketing of the product.[1] These programmes can either be directed from the central government organization or, as is more typically the case, they may be

---

[1] Reviews of direct job creation programmes and issues can be found in OECD (1980) and Balkenhol (1980).

directed and controlled on a decentralized governmental basis through regional state, or local government authorities.[2]

B. *Shared Public–Private Production*

In this type of job creation effort, some non-governmental organizational entities are involved in the direction of production, but the public still plays a major control function. The sharing agency is in many cases a non-profit organization.[3] Thus, the government might provide the materials and pay the wage bill, but a non-profit organization such as, say, a charitable organization, a church organization, or a private social welfare agency, would actually organize and supervise the work. Typically, however, the government would maintain control over project selection. In a few cases the sharing agency may be a private for-profit organization.[4] But again, the government would maintain a major control function.

C. *Subsidized Activities*

It is difficult to draw a precise line between shared public–private production and subsidized activities, but the most common form of subsidized activities occurs where the government underwrites the wages, or a portion of the wages, of particular individuals,[5] or for particular types of jobs.[6] The private sector organization, either non-profit or profit, has, largely, the control of the work activity as part of its normal production processes.

In some cases, the subsidization extends beyond wages to other costs that can be related to the particular subsidized job or the particular subsidized person. Sometimes, for example, the subsidy would also extend to supervision costs or even, in a few cases, to costs of materials and tools.[7]

[2] There are many examples of programmes run by state, provincial or local governments, e.g. Relief Work in Sweden, the Youth Conservation Corps in the United States, Job Offer projects in Denmark, but we know of no examples of programmes run completely by officers of the central government.

[3] The projects in the West German A B M and the Community Programme in the United Kingdom are of this form.

[4] In Sweden a small percentage of Youth Teams and in the United Kingdom some of the Community Programme projects involve private profit groups.

[5] There are many examples of these, perhaps the most explicit being the US Targeted Jobs Tax Credit, which has a clearly defined set of individual characteristics that qualify a person for the subsidy.

[6] The US Employment Tax Credit was an example of a broad subsidy attached to the creation of new jobs. Denmark had, until recently, a Job Creation scheme which subsidized particular types of job positions. Several countries have had subsidies which are paid if a job is converted to a job-sharing position or if a worker is encouraged to take early retirement and is replaced by a younger person.

[7] The Community Programme in the United Kingdom provides overhead support in addition to wages.

Subsidization for the purposes of creating or preserving jobs can also take the form of total cost subsidization. That is, instead of attempting to separate out wage costs from other costs of production, the support goes in some form or other to the enterprise as a whole.[8]

It should also be noted that subsidization can come in several forms. It can be a direct flow of funds from the government agency to the private organization, or it can be in the form of vouchers given to individuals[9] which are then reimbursed by the government agency. Other forms which it can take are tax credits, tax deductions, or tax rebates.

D. *Mixed Work and Training*

The most traditional form of mixed work and training is, of course, the apprenticeship system, and some job creation efforts have taken the form of subsidization to apprenticeship programmes for part or all of the wage costs of the individuals involved.[10] In some cases, the government has managed to encourage apprenticeship efforts without subsidization *per se* through threats to intervene in the system if sufficient places are not provided 'voluntarily' by the private sector.

In many cases, governments have tied the subsidization of apprenticeships to a requirement for more formal schooling for some portion of the time that the individual is in the scheme.[11]

Mixed work and training are sometimes referred to as 'alternance training', i.e. a period of pure work is alternated with a period of pure training.[12]

E. *Training*

The usual categories for training are on-the-job training or institutional training.

It is fairly difficult to separate out on-the-job training from the category

[8] Swedish structural support for industries in the mid-1970s is an example, as in the US loan support to Chrysler.

[9] A small experiment to compare the effectiveness of vouchers to individuals *vs.* subsidies to employers was carried out in the United States, but the results were anomalous. See Rivera-Casale, Friedman, and Lerman (1982).

[10] For example, Denmark has recently been providing substantial subsidies for increasing the number of apprenticeships and training places.

[11] The Youth Training Scheme in the United Kingdom, for example, requires 13 weeks out of the year in more basic educational activities, off the job.

[12] The Contract Emploi-Formation in France is an example of this sort of programme.

of apprenticeship just discussed above. Apprenticeship normally involves a more clearly defined curriculum and some testing and certification that a given skill is obtained, whereas on-the-job training normally implies that the organization agrees to put individuals into a specialized work situation for a given period of time so as to allow them to learn skills required for the firm's normal production activities.

Institutional training is, of course, training that takes place outside of the normal work place in formal educational institutions or in specially set up training units.

F. *Enterprise Promotion*

Currently there is a great deal of government interest in programmes to promote new, mostly small-scale, enterprises as a form of job creation.[13] Enterprise promotion in general has, in most countries, been an older government effort, not necessarily directly linked to its job creation potential.[14]

Enterprise promotion can take many forms, most of which provide some assistance to the enterprise through special financial arrangements. In some cases, special assistance in developing management procedures and management skills is also provided.

More recently, governments and private agencies have been setting up enterprise agencies as intermediaries to work at stimulating and co-ordinating efforts among the government sources, large private enterprises, and the smaller new enterprises which are trying to get under way.

G. *Regional and Structural Support*

It can be reasonably argued that many government efforts to reduce regional imbalances in economic activity are, in effect, job creation efforts. Similarly, government support for particular industrial sectors is often motivated by a concern to preserve the employment they provide—or at least to minimize the losses—so structural support can also be, classified in some sense as a job creation effort.

---

[13] See e.g. OECD (1984) and Center for Employment Initiatives (1985).

[14] In the United States in the 1970s the Department of Commerce ran many programmes for assistance to small businesses. In some cases special emphasis was given to providing capital and management assistance to businesses owned by members of minority groups, e.g. Minority Enterprise Small Business Investment Company, and in these cases the objective was primarily to increase the numbers of minority owners of enterprises rather than to increase employment *per se*.

H. Regulations[15]

Many government efforts and actions can be viewed as job creation efforts in that they can affect the level and character of employment provided by the private sector.

1. *Job security*. Legislation had been passed in a number of countries and over several decades defining the conditions of employment contracts which may be made in the private sector with respect to hiring and tenure, and firing or redundancy, (see e.g. ILO 1981: 9–11). In the 1980s, there have been major attempts in some countries to attenuate the more restrictive (for the employer) of these types of legislation, on the grounds that they have created rigidities in the labour market which are detrimental to the dynamic resource reallocations which are critical for job creation.[16]

2. *Hours of work*. In addition to defining circumstances for employment contracts regarding hiring and firing, government regulations also either directly specify, or affect indirectly, the hours of work of a private sector employee.

There are, of course, many dimensions to hours of work—for example, the number of hours that are considered full time and the number of hours that are considered overtime. In addition, the ability of firms to hire part-time workers is sometimes directly legislated or indirectly affected by government regulations.

Annual hours of work are also sometimes affected by legislation bearing on the amount of annual vacation. In recent years there has also been increasing legislation dealing with special leaves from work with maintained job security under special circumstances, such as maternity leaves or parental leaves for early child-rearing, and a number of other special leaves.[17]

One can also think of government regulations regarding hours of work in terms of work over the life-cycle. There are often government regulations dealing with child labour, with the employment of young workers, and, of course, the conditions under which involuntary retirement may be enforced.

3. *Compensation*. Government regulations affect the level of compensation most typically by setting minimum wage levels (see Starr 1981) and the extent of their coverage. More important, the compensation is affected by

[15] For an up-to-date review of evidence regarding effects of regulations on labour market flexibility and job security, see OECD, *Employment Outlook 1985*.

[16] For an example of relatively mild revisions in this direction, see the changes embodied on the West German Employment Promotion Act, effective Jan. 1985.

[17] A number of pieces of legislation bearing on such issues were passed in France in 1984.

the general framework for collective bargaining. In most countries legislation sets the framework for collective bargaining, and the nature of the framework for collective bargaining will usually greatly condition the effects in many of the other dimensions we have already mentioned.

4. *Access and discrimination.* Government regulations affect access to employment, in some cases by requiring positive discrimination in favour of a given type of worker (such as physically handicapped workers), and in other cases by constraining the extent of choice (in terms of hiring, promotion, wages) on the part of employers on the grounds of discrimination based on characteristics unrelated to work productivity, e.g. race, sex, age.

7

Cost–Benefit Rules for Job-Training Programmes

Per-Olov Johansson*

7.1 Introduction

A critical issue when assessing the social profitability of labour market policy measures is the treatment of *market imbalances*. The traditional way to view employment-creating (public sector) projects is highlighted by the following quotation from Musgrave and Musgrave (1973: 161): 'employment effects of particular projects become relevant to benefit evaluation if alternative policies to deal with unemployment are not available. The resulting gain in employment is then an additional benefit, or the opportunity cost of labor is zero.' This well-known partial equilibrium view found in most textbooks is illustrated in Fig. 7.1, where the wage is fixed above the market-clearing level. (In Fig. 1, S is the supply of labour, D denotes the initial demand curve and D^1 the final demand curve for labour, and $\bar{w}$ is the current wage rate.) Obviously, all labour employed in a marginal project can be treated as coming from the unemployment pool. Therefore, a positive shadow price should be attributed to the labour hired only to the extent that households perceive disutility from additional employment. Hence, a zero disutility from work effort produces the rule or result quoted above.

Given this partial equilibrium view, it is perhaps not too surprising that empirical studies often include multiplier effects. The idea behind this is that incomes earned by formerly unemployed people are spent, initiating the multiplier process well known from textbooks on Keynesian macro-economics. This is, of course, equivalent to assuming that there is excess capacity in some sectors

* The author would like to thank V. Bergström, A. Björklund, P. Chen, J. Hamilton, B. Holmlund, M. Johansson, P. Lundborg, K. G. Löfgren, H. Ohlsson, P. Skedinger, and V. Vredin for helpful suggestions and discussions.

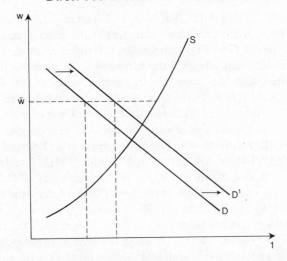

Fig. 7.1. Partial equilibrium illustration of the employment effect of an increase in the demand for labour

of the economy, i.e. unemployment is due to insufficient aggregate demand.

For a long period of time, cost–benefit analysts had difficulty in providing a theoretical justification for their treatment of the macro-economic effects caused by a project.[1] This difficulty arose because of the lack of a satisfactory link between micro-economics and Keynesian macro-economics. Public finance theory uses models based on individual optimization, but it is ill equipped to deal with non-market-clearing situations as these lie beyond its Walrasian equilibrium framework. Macro-economics, on the other hand, focuses on market imbalances, but its micro-economic under-pinnings have often been weak. This lack of micro-economic foundations has made it difficult to directly assess the *welfare* effects of government policies.

In their seminal paper, 'A General Disequilibrium Model of

[1] There is an extensive literature on the foundations of cost–benefit analysis. See Eckstein (1958), McKean (1958), Krutilla and Eckstein (1958), Marglin (1967), Harberger (1969, 1971), Musgrave (1969), Lesourne (1975), Little and Mirrlees (1968), Dasgupta *et al.* (1972), Boadway (1975), Srinivasan and Bhagwati (1978), and Diewert (1983), to mention just a few.

Income and Employment', Barro and Grossman (1971) provided a
link between micro-economics and Keynesian macro-economics.
However, to the best of my knowledge, this link was not discovered
by cost–benefit analysts until the early 1980s. It turns out that the
general disequilibrium approach in general produces cost–benefit
rules which are very different from the partial equilibrium rules presented in earlier models. There are at least two kinds of models that
have been used in deriving disequilibrium cost–benefit rules and in
making welfare evaluations. The early papers (e.g. Bell and Devarajan (1983); Blitzer, Dasgupta, and Stiglitz (1981); Cuddington,
Johansson, and Löfgren (1984); J. H. Drèze (1985); J. P. Drèze
(1982); Fourgeaud, Lenclud, and Picard (1986); Johansson (1982);
Maneschi (1985); and Roberts (1982)), use essentially single-period
models with exogenous private investment. This means that a public
sector project has no adverse effect on the level of investment. The
later models are intertemporal, which allow an explicit treatment of
expectations, and some of them treat private investment as an endogenous variable (see e.g. Johansson (1984); Johansson and Löfgren
(1985, 1988); and Marchand, Mintz, and Pestrieau (1984, 1985)).

The bulk of the aforementioned literature is devoted to cost–
benefit rules to be used when assessing the social profitability of
(state-owned) firms producing goods sold in the market. In contrast,
this paper concentrates on project evaluation rules for job-training
programmes. In order to be able to derive such rules, the paper
develops a disaggregated intertemporal macro-economic model of a
small open economy with endogenous private investment and two
kinds of labour, for simplicity called 'unskilled' labour and 'skilled'
labour. In period 1, unskilled workers are trained to work as skilled
workers in period 2. After having presented the building blocks of
the model in Section 7.2 of the paper, Section 7.3 focuses on general
equilibrium cost–benefit rules. A marginal shift in the volume of
training is used to generate the rules. In Section 7.4, the focus shifts
to general disequilibrium cost–benefit rules and two different kinds
of unemployment are introduced. The first situation, labelled classical unemployment, is characterized by unemployment among
unskilled workers due to excessive real wages. The second situation,
called Keynesian unemployment, refers to a situation where there
are unemployed unskilled workers and (some) firms are unable to
sell all they want to sell due to deficient demand. The social profit-

ability of job-training efforts is investigated under each of these two regimes.

7.2. The Model in the Absence of Quantity Constraints

This section considers a small open economy which can buy and sell tradables without limit in each period at fixed foreign currency prices.[2] Moreover, assuming perfect capital mobility and a single internationally traded bond, the foreign currency interest rate is exogenously fixed at the world level for the small open economy under consideration. The exchange rate, which translates foreign currency prices into domestic currency prices, is assumed to be fixed, while the price of non-traded goods and the wage rates are allowed to adjust so as to achieve equilibrium in the market for non-tradables and the two labour markets.

7.2.1. Production Sectors

There are two 'representative' firms in the model, one producing non-traded goods and the other producing traded goods. Firms use the two kinds of labour and invest part of their own output.[3] The model contains three periods, but the third period is there mainly for technical reasons (see the discussion in Neary and Stiglitz (1983)). The main focus of this paper is on period 1 and period 2, which are often referred to as 'today' and 'the future', respectively.

Within this environment, private firms maximize the present value of profits given prices and the production technology. The profit function, or perhaps better the present value function, is written as

$$\Pi^i(\mathbf{p}^i, \mathbf{w}, \odot^i) = \max_{[\ell^i, I^i]} \{\mathbf{p}^i(\mathbf{y}^i - \mathbf{I}^i) - \mathbf{w}\ell^i + \phi^i(I_2^i, \odot^i) \mid$$
$$y_1^i = F^i(\ell_{11}^i, \ell_{21}^i), y_2^i = H^i(\ell_{12}^i, \ell_{22}^i, I_1^i)\}$$

(1)

[2] The model is in many respects similar to the ones in Neary and Stiglitz (1983) and Johansson and Löfgren (1988). Parts of the presentation of the model draw heavily on Johansson and Löfgren (1988).

[3] The assumption that firms invest out of their own output is introduced just in order to simplify notation and presentation and has no bearing upon the cost–benefit rules.

where superscript $i = x$ refers to producers of traded goods and $i = n$ refers to producers of non-traded goods; $\mathbf{p}^i = (p_1^i, p_2^i)$ is a vector of prices containing the present value price in period $t(t = 1, 2)$; $\mathbf{y}^i = (y_1^i, y_2^i)$ is a vector of gross outputs of goods; $\mathbf{I}^i = (I_1^i, I_2^i)$ is a vector of investments; $\mathbf{w} = (w_{11}, w_{21}, w_{12}, w_{22})$ is a vector of present value wage rates; w_{jt} is the present value wage paid to workers of skill $j(j = 1, 2)$ in period t; $\ell^i = (\ell_{11}^i, \ell_{21}^i, \ell_{12}^i, \ell_{22}^i)$ is a vector of demands for labour, $\phi^i(\cdot)$ denotes profits in all periods beyond the second period as a function of the level of investment in the second period and exogenous expectations $\odot^i$ of future prices, etc.; $F^i(\cdot)$ and $H^i(\cdot)$ are the twice continuously differentiable and strongly concave first-period and second-period production functions, respectively; all prices are domestic currency prices; and notation denoting transposed vectors has been suppressed.

According to (1), firms choose current and future employment levels. In addition, firms may invest part of the output in order to augment productivity of labour in the future. Note that we 'collapse' all periods beyond the second period into a single period, so that $\phi^i(\cdot)$ contains the sum of the present values of expected profits in these future periods.[4]

In later sections, we shall employ the envelope theorem in order to simplify the exposition.[5] For example, the effect of a ceteris paribus change in p_1^i on the present value of profits is equal to

$$\partial \Pi^i(\mathbf{p}^i, \mathbf{w}, \odot^i)/\partial p_1^i = y_1^i(p_1^i, \mathbf{w}_1) - I_1^i(\mathbf{p}^i, \mathbf{w}_2) = x_1^i(\mathbf{p}^i, \mathbf{w}) \quad i = x, n$$
(2)

where $x_1^i(\cdot)$ is the first-period supply of commodity i, i.e. what is produced less what is invested of the commodity; and $\mathbf{w}_t = (w_{1t}, w_{2t})$ for $t = 1, 2$. Thus, by taking the partial derivative of (1) with respect to a price, we obtain the net supply of that commodity.

7.2.2. The Government

To derive cost–benefit rules for labour market training, we shall assume that workers of skill 1 (unskilled workers), are trained in period 1 to become workers of skill 2 (skilled workers), in period 2.

---

[4] The (far from self-evident) assumption that $\phi^i(\cdot)$ is independent of first-period investment is due to Neary and Stiglitz (1983).

[5] See e.g. Varian (1984) for details.

The government pays each job training participant αw_{11} dollars, with $\alpha \leqslant 1$, and buys goods which are used as inputs in the job-training programme. In order to simplify the exposition, the number of teachers and other personnel used for training is treated as independent of small changes in the volume of training. Finally, the government pays β per cent of the wage as unemployment compensation to unemployed (unskilled) workers, if any. Hence, the government budget constraint takes the form

$$T = \alpha w_{11} \ell^q_{11} + \mathbf{p}_1 \mathbf{G}_1 + \sum_{t=1}^{2} \beta w_{1t} \ell^u_{1t} + k \tag{3}$$

where T denotes taxes; ℓ^q_{11} is the number of unskilled workers trained in period 1; $\mathbf{G}_1$ is a vector of traded and non-traded goods used as inputs in the job-training programme; ℓ^u_{1t} denotes unemployed unskilled workers, if any, in period t; and k denotes fixed training costs. The simple specification of the public sector in (3) allows us to concentrate on deriving cost–benefit rules with a minimum of notational clutter.

7.2.3. Households

In order to focus on efficiency considerations while setting aside matters of equity and income distribution, we lump together all households into an aggregate or 'representative' household. This is a standard assumption in cost–benefit analysis. The household consumes both traded and non-traded goods, and supplies both skilled and unskilled labour. In addition, the household is assumed to save in order to be able to consume in periods beyond the second period. This is captured by including as an argument in the utility function the holdings of an asset at the end of the second period.

Both borrowing and lending are allowed at the prevailing interest rate. Once the possibility of borrowing or lending at the prevailing interest rate is introduced, the issue of whether profits are distributed in the period in which they are generated or in the subsequent period becomes less important. In what follows it will be assumed that the sum of current profits from private producers is distributed within the current period. Moreover, in order to simplify the exposition and the derivation of the cost–benefit rules, it is assumed that the household supplies both kinds of labour in fixed amounts.

The budget constraint of the household can be written as

$$M_0 + \Pi + \sum_{t=1}^{2} w_{1t}(L_{1t} - \ell^q_{1t} - \ell^u_{1t}) + \sum_{t=1}^{2} w_{2t}\ell_{2t}$$

$$+ \sum_{t=1}^{2} w_{1t}(\alpha\ell^q_{1t} + \beta\ell^u_{1t}) - T - \mathbf{p}\mathbf{X} - M = M_0 + \Pi$$

$$+ \mathbf{w}\ell - \mathbf{p}_1\mathbf{G}_1 - k - \mathbf{p}\mathbf{X} - M = 0 \qquad (4)$$

where M_0 is initial wealth yielding the international interest rate; $\Pi = \Pi^n + \Pi^x$; L_{1t} is the fixed gross supply of unskilled labour in period t, so that $\ell_{1t} = L_{1t} - \ell^q_{1t} - \ell^u_{1t}$ is the supply of unskilled labour to the private sector (with $\ell^q_{12} = 0$ since there is no training in period 2, and $\ell^u_{1t} = 0$ if wages adjust so as to achieve full employment also for unskilled workers); ℓ_{2t} is the supply of skilled labour to the private sector in period t; $\mathbf{p} = (p^n_1, p^n_2, p^x_1, p^x_2)$ is a vector of goods prices; $\mathbf{X} = (X^n_1, X^n_2, X^x_1, X^x_2)$ is the corresponding vector of demands for goods; M is end of second-period wealth; and $\ell = (\ell_{11}, \ell_{12}, \ell_{21}, \ell_{22})$ is the vector of unskilled and skilled workers supplied to the private sector.

Two comments to the budget constraint (4) are in order. First, the middle expression in (4) is obtained by netting out transfer incomes since these are paid for by (lump-sum) taxes.[6] This way of writing the budget constraint is used in what follows since it saves some notational clutter and highlights the fact that gross income is made up of profits and labour income. Second, since we are thinking of an aggregate household, we can interpret ℓ_{1t}, for example, as the number of unskilled workers supplied to the private sector in year t. Similarly, ℓ^q_{11} can be thought of as the number of unskilled workers who participate in training (expressed on a yearly basis).

The household is assumed to maximize utility subject to its budget constraint. The indirect utility function of the household is defined as

---

[6] In (4), fixed training costs k are assumed to have no wage component. This assumption is used just to simplify notation.

$$\nu(\mathbf{p}, \Pi + \mathbf{w}\ell - \mathbf{p}_1 \mathbf{G}_1 - k + M_0, \odot) = \max_{[\mathbf{X}, M]} \{U(\mathbf{X}, M, \odot) \mid$$

$$M_0 + \Pi + \mathbf{w}\ell - \mathbf{p}_1 \mathbf{G}_1 - k - \mathbf{p}\mathbf{X} - M = 0\} \tag{4'}$$

where $U(\cdot)$ is the twice continuously differentiable and strongly quasi-concave utility function, and denotes exogenous expectations of prices beyond the second period. According to (4'), indirect utility is a function of all prices, exogenous income, and expectations. This indirect utility function has all the properties known from textbooks on micro-economics. For example, by taking the partial derivative with respect to a goods price, one obtains

$$\partial \nu / \partial p_t^i = -\lambda X_t^i \qquad \forall i, t \tag{4''}$$

where λ denotes the marginal utility of exogenous income Y, i.e. $\partial \nu / \partial Y = \lambda$. In other words, by taking the partial derivative of the household's indirect utility function with respect to a goods price, one obtains the corresponding demand function multiplied by $-\lambda$.

7.2.4. Society's Welfare Function

From the point of view of the entire economy, the profits of private sector firms in (4') are functions of prices and wages, i.e. they cannot be treated as exogenous entities as in (4'). Therefore, using the indirect utility function (4), the social welfare function can be written as

$$\nu(\mathbf{p}, Y + M_0) = V(\mathbf{p}, \mathbf{w}, \mathbf{G}_1, k, M_0) \tag{5}$$

where $Y = \Sigma_{i=x}^{n} \Pi^i(\mathbf{p}^i, \mathbf{w}) + \mathbf{w}\ell - \mathbf{p}_1 \mathbf{G}_1 - k$, and notation denoting expectations is suppressed. Implicitly, (5) is also a function of the number of workers in training, as will be explained in the next section.

From the point of view of the entire economy, the expression (4'') is partial since it neglects the fact that Y is a function of all prices. In fact, from (5) and using (2), the derivative $\partial Y / \partial p_t^i$ is equal to

$$\partial Y / \partial p_t^i = \partial \Pi^i / \partial p_t^i - G_t^i = y_t^i - I_t^i - G_t^i = x_t^i - G_t^i \qquad \forall i, t \tag{5'}$$

where $G_t^i = 0$ if $t = 2$ since, by assumption, there is no training in period 2. Therefore, the partial derivative of (5) with respect to p_t^i is equal to

$$\partial v/\partial p_t^i + (\partial v/\partial Y)(\partial Y/\partial p_t^i) = \partial V/\partial p_t^i = -\lambda X_t^i + \lambda(x_t^i - G_t^i)$$
$$\forall i, t \tag{6}$$

where $\lambda = \partial v/\partial Y$.

Thus, by taking the partial derivative of (5) with respect to a price, one obtains the excess supply or demand of the commodity in question (multiplied by λ). Obviously, if all prices and wages correspond to their market-clearing levels, then $\partial V/\partial p_t^i = 0$ in (6) for all i and t. Similarly, $\partial V/\partial w_{jt} = 0$ for all j and t as long as there is equilibrium in all markets. Therefore, if a change in the volume of labour market training affects prices, the induced effects on social welfare through these changes in prices are equal to zero. These are useful results which will simplify considerably the derivations of the cost–benefit rules.

7.3. General Equilibrium Cost–Benefit Rules

Labour market training takes place in the first period. Those unskilled workers (ℓ_{11}) who participate in the training programme will be employed as skilled workers (ℓ_{22}) in the second period.[7] Recall that in this section we assume that all prices and wages adjust continuously so as to create full employment.

To obtain a welfare change measure in monetary terms of a marginal change in the number of trainees, ℓ_{11}^q, we differentiate totally the social welfare function (5) with respect to ℓ_{11}^q and divide through by λ, the marginal utility of exogenous income to obtain

$$(\partial V/\partial \ell_{11}^q)d\ell_{11}^q/\lambda = dV_m = -w_{11}d\ell_{11}^q - \mathbf{p}_1 d\mathbf{G}_1 + (w_{22} - w_{12})d\ell_{11}^q \tag{7}$$

where $d\mathbf{G}_1 = (\partial \mathbf{G}_1/\partial \ell_{11}^q)d\ell_{11}^q$. Dividing through by λ converts the right-hand-side expression of (7) from unobservable units of utility to observable units of money; thus, dV_m denotes the change in social welfare expressed in monetary units. The first term of the right-hand-side expression yields the first-period loss in private sector production as unskilled workers are drawn from their jobs in the

[7] We simply *assume* that a number of unskilled workers are trained, i.e. there is no mechanism in our simple model explaining the decision to participate or not to participate in training. This simplification may seem acceptable, given our purpose to present project evaluation rules. See, however, the appendix at the end of the paper, and the discussion in Freeman (1986).

private sector to training activities. Recall that we in this section assume both full employment and fixed supplies of labour, so that an individual must have been employed if he did not participate in the training programme, i.e. $d\ell_{11}^q = -d\ell_{11}$ in, for example, (4'). Also note that the wage w_{11} reflects the value of the marginal product of such workers in private sector firms since all firms are unconstrained in all markets. The second term of the right-hand-side expression in (7) yields the cost of variable inputs purchased by the government and used in the training programme. Finally, the term within parentheses captures the increase (if any) in future productivity as a trainee is employed as a skilled worker rather than as an unskilled one.[8]

A change in the size of the training programme may affect some or all of the economy's prices and wages; for example, w_{11} must apparently adjust so as to restore equality between private sector firms' first-period demand for unskilled workers and the reduced supply (net of those in training) of such workers. However, given the assumption of continuous market-clearing prices and wages, equations like (6) ensure that any indirect effects through changed prices and wages 'net out'.[9] Therefore, *(7) is a general equilibrium measure*, although it is only valid for 'small' changes in ℓ_{11}^q. In the case of a large or discrete change in the volume of training, one would have to integrate (7) between initial and final values. The problem is that the line integral in question need not be independent of the path of integration.[10] In order to avoid this technical problem and since most real-world job-training programmes are so small that their impact on prices is of second-order magnitude, the rest of this paper concentrates on (infinitesimal) small changes in ℓ_{11}^q.

The small increase in the number of trained workers considered in (7) is socially profitable if (7) has a positive sign. Apparently, the outcome is very sensitive to the size of the difference in expected future productivities between the two skills, as reflected by $(w_{22} - w_{12})$. The larger this difference, the more likely it is that (7) will

---

[8] Note that $d\ell_{11}^q = -d\ell_{11} = -d\ell_{12} = d\ell_{22}$ in e.g. (4'), due to our assumption of fixed supplies of all skills. Thus, the number of skilled workers in period 2 increases from ℓ_{22} to $\ell_{22} + d\ell_{11}^q$ due to the increase in job training.

[9] To illustrate, since $\partial V/\partial w_{11} = 0$, it must also be the case that $(\partial V/\partial w_{11})(\partial w_{11}/\partial \ell_{11}^q) = 0$.

[10] The reader interested in reading more about this well-known path-dependency problem is referred to Johansson (1987) for a detailed treatment.

have a positive sign. Thus, (7) captures and verifies the major theoretical justification for training programmes, namely, that they are assumed to contribute to human capital formation. That is, training is assumed to raise productivity of workers, and is profitable if the investment compensates for earnings forgone.[11]

7.4. Disequilibrium Cost–Benefit Rules

The assumption of continuous market-clearing prices employed above in deriving cost–benefit rules for job-training programmes is a strong one. For practical applications it is important to determine how the shadow-pricing rules are changed by different kinds of market imbalances. In this section it is shown how the model can be used to derive project evaluation or cost–benefit rules for situations where there is quantity rationing due to price stickiness in markets for goods and factors.[12] Since the model contains several commodities and periods, it is possible to construct many disequilibrium variations, but to keep the problem tractable we shall consider only two cases. These examples suffice to illustrate how the model can be used to derive general (dis-)equilibrium cost–benefit rules. The basic idea is to make the important distinction between unemployment caused by excessive real wages and unemployment due to deficient aggregate demand. The first situation, labelled *classical unemployment*, is characterized by excess supply in the market for unskilled workers due to an excessive real wage in both periods, while the wage of skilled workers is free to adjust so as to achieve equilibrium in the

---

[11] It is beyond the scope of the present paper to discuss why real-world markets may not provide the socially optimal level of training, i.e. the level of training for which $dV_m = 0$ in (7). For a discussion of possible reasons for market failures in private markets for training the reader is referred to the Hollister–Haveman paper, 5.2.

[12] For a survey of different reasons for sticky prices, the reader is referred to Cuddington, Johansson, and Löfgren (1984). For earlier attempts to derive cost–benefit rules (usually for state-owned firms) using general (dis-)equilibrium models, the reader is referred to Bell and Devarajan (1983), Blitzer, Dasgupta, and Stiglitz (1981), Cuddington, Johansson, and Löfgren (1984), Cuddington, Johansson, and Ohlsson (1985), Diewert (1983), Drèze (1982), J. H. Drèze (1985), J. P. Drèze and Stern (1987), Fourgeaud, Lenclud, and Picard (1986), Johansson (1982, 1984), Johansson and Löfgren (1988), Marchand, Mintz, and Pestieau (1984, 1985) and Ohlsson (1987).

market for such workers.[13] The second situation, called *Keynesian unemployment*, refers to a situation where there is unemployment among unskilled workers, and producers of non-traded goods are unable to sell all the goods they are willing to sell at the ruling (fixed) market price for such goods. We shall consider first classical unemployment.

7.4.1. *Classical Unemployment*

The fact that there is an excess supply of unskilled workers but no other market imbalances (quantity constraints) means that firms are still unconstrained in all markets. Hence, the maximization problems of firms are those described in Section 7.2.1 above. On the other hand, the (aggregate or representative) household now maximizes its utility function subject to the budget constraint *plus* the first-period and second-period private sector employment constraints for unskilled labourers: $\ell_{11} = \bar{\ell}_{11}$, $\ell_{12} = \bar{\ell}_{12}$.

Straightforward calculations verify that the indirect utility function (5) now can be written as

$$\hat{V} = \hat{v}(\mathbf{p}, \hat{Y} + M_0) \tag{8}$$

where $\hat{Y} = \Pi + w_{11}\bar{\ell}_{11} + w_{21}\ell_{21} + w_{12}\bar{\ell}_{12} + w_{22}\ell_{22} - \mathbf{p}_1\mathbf{G}_1 - k$; Π denotes the sum of profits earned by tradables plus non-tradables firms; and a bar above a variable denotes a quantity constraint. In the market for unskilled labour, the household does the best possible and sells the amount of labour actually demanded by private sector firms, i.e. $\bar{\ell}_{1t} = \ell_{1t}^n + \ell_{1t}^x$ for $t = 1, 2$. On the other hand, in the market for skilled labour it can sell all it wants, i.e. the household is able to sell all of its fixed supplies in period 1 and period 2, respectively. Note also that transfers from the government, i.e. income received while in training plus unemployment compensations, have been netted out from (8) since these transfers are paid for in the form of (lump-sum) taxes.

Consider now a small increase in training. Totally differentiating (8) with respect to ℓ_{11}^q and dividing through by the marginal utility of income, the following cost–benefit rule is obtained:

$$d\hat{V}_m = w_{11}d\bar{\ell}_{11} - \mathbf{p}_1 d\mathbf{G}_1 + w_{22}d\ell_{11}^q + w_{12}d\bar{\ell}_{12} \tag{9}$$

---

[13] In the context of a single goods market, single labour market, and closed economy, Malinvaud (1977) defines classical unemployment as a situation with excess demand in the goods market and excess supply in the labour market.

where $d\bar{\ell}_{11} = d\ell_{11}^n + d\ell_{11}^x$, and $d\bar{\ell}_{12} = d\ell_{12}^n + d\ell_{12}^x$. In order to interpret this monetary welfare-change measure, assume initially that $d\bar{\ell}_{11} = d\bar{\ell}_{12} = 0$. Then (9) reduces to what can be termed the usual partial equilibrium view regarding the effects of labour market training under unemployment. That is, just as in Fig. 1, the trainees are directly or indirectly drawn from the pool of unemployed so there is no loss of production during the period of training beside the one related to the cost of variable inputs G_1 used up in the training programme. Moreover, the income received by a trainee as he is hired as a skilled worker i.e. w_{22}, captures the future, i.e. second-period, net benefit to the society of training an otherwise unemployed worker. Thus, an increase in the size of the training programme is socially profitable if the sum of future present-value incomes received by the trainee as a skilled worker exceeds the cost of inputs used while he is in training.

The partial equilibrium rule just described overlooks the fact that a change in the training programme may affect *demand* for unskilled workers, i.e. $\bar{\ell}_{11}$ and/or $\bar{\ell}_{12}$. Recall that firms still are unconstrained in all markets, so their demand for labour is a function of prices and wages. Now, the government's purchases of goods used as inputs in training activities stimulates aggregate demand.[14] In turn, this may cause demand for unskilled workers to go up. If so, $d\bar{\ell}_{11} > 0$ in (9), implying that this term represents a benefit. On the other hand, since training causes an increase in second-period supply of skilled workers, the equilibrium wage received by such workers will fall, ceteris paribus. One expects this to reduce second-period demand for unskilled workers[15] whose wage, by assumption, is fixed above its market-clearing level. If so, $d\bar{\ell}_{12}$ in (9) has a negative sign, i.e. there is a cost associated with training that the partial equilibrium rule described above overlooks. This is even more pronounced if the second-period wage for unskilled workers is free to adjust so as to

---

[14] One expects this to cause the price of non-traded goods and the wage of skilled workers to go up (while the price of traded goods is fixed, due to the small open economy assumption).

[15] Thus, it is, assumed that $\partial\bar{\ell}_{12}/\partial w_{22} > 0$. Johnson and Layard (1986) seem to make the opposite sign assumption in terms of our model and hence find that training increases demand for unskilled workers. Whether different skills of labour are 'substitutes' or 'complements' is ultimately an empirical issue. See Freeman (1986) for further discussion of this issue.

create full employment for such workers in this period; then $d\bar{\ell}_{12}$ in (9) is equal to minus $d\bar{\ell}^{q}_{1}$, just as in the general equilibrium case considered previously, implying that just a small increase, if any, in productivity (i.e. $w_{22} - w_{12}$) remains.

The reader should also note that the model used in this paper allows for a kind of *time inconsistency*. Since all agents, by assumption, are equipped with rational expectations (perfect foresight), announcements of future policy changes by the government will affect today's behaviour. This can easily be verified by changing, say, the government's second-period purchases of goods in (8) above. Such a change affects today's prices and hence also the current unemployment rate. These effects show up in the cost–benefit rules. However, once we arrive to the second period, today's unemployment level is just a historical datum, i.e. does not show up in the second-period cost–benefit rule. What this example indicates is that a policy that seems optimal for society from today's point of view may nevertheless be profitable to revise once one arrives to period 2. This creates a policy dilemma, since rational agents then have good reasons for questioning the credibility of policy announcements by the government.[16]

7.4.2. Keynesian Unemployment

If both prices and wages are fixed such that there is excess supply of both goods and labour, one speaks of Keynesian unemployment. In this paper, however, the analysis is restricted to a situation where there is unemployment among unskilled workers, and private producers of non-traded goods face a sales constraint for their output in the short run, i.e. in period 1. Firms producing traded goods are assumed throughout to never face quantity constraints. As before, in the long run, represented by period 2, all prices and wages except the wage of unskilled workers are flexible, so that all domestic markets except the market for unskilled workers are in equilibrium.

Private firms producing non-traded goods face a sales constraint

---

[16] We shall not elaborate further on this time inconsistency issue, but the interested reader is referred to Kydland and Prescott (1977) for a detailed discussion. See also sec. 4.1 in Johansson and Löfgren (1988).

$\bar{x}_1^n = y_1^n - I_1^n$. Adding this constraint to the maximization problem (1) for $i = n$ yields a profit function which can be written as

$$\hat{\Pi}^n(\mathbf{p}^n, \mathbf{w}, \bar{x}_1^n) = \Pi^n(\hat{p}_1^n, p_2^n, \mathbf{w}) + (p_1^n - \hat{p}_1^n)\bar{x}_1^n \tag{10}$$

where p_1^n is the market price of non-traded goods in period 1, and $\hat{p}_1^n$ is the virtual price of such goods in period 1. This virtual price is such that the *quantity-unconstrained* supply x_1^n is equal to the quantity constraint $\bar{x}_1^n$ (and all other supply and demand levels remain unchanged). This is illustrated in Fig. 7.2a. Obviously, since the firm is rationed, it must be the case that $p_1^n > \hat{p}_1^n$ (see Neary and Roberts 1980 for details). This implies that the right-hand-side profit function in (10) yields a lower level of profits than the left-hand-side profit function, although $\hat{p}_1^n$ is chosen in such a way that both functions produce the same optimal supply and demand levels. This explains why we add the expression $(p_1^n - \hat{p}_1^n)\bar{x}_1^n$ to the right-hand side of (10).

Taking the partial derivative of (10) with respect to $\bar{x}_1^n$, one obtains

$$\partial\hat{\Pi}^n/\partial\bar{x}_1^n = (\partial\Pi^n/\partial\hat{p}_1^n)(\partial\hat{p}_1^n/\partial\bar{x}_1^n) - \bar{x}_1^n(\partial\hat{p}_1^n/\partial\bar{x}_1^n) + (p_1^n - \hat{p}_1^n) \tag{11}$$

$$= (p_1^n - \hat{p}_1^n) > 0$$

where $\partial\Pi^n/\partial\hat{p}_1^n = x_1^n(\hat{p}_1^n, p_2^n, \mathbf{w}) = \bar{x}_1^n$. According to (11), the increase in profits caused by a small increase in sales is equal to the difference

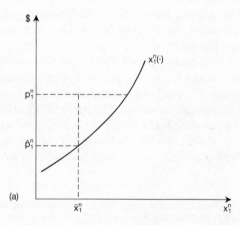

Fig. 7.2a. The 'virtual' supply curve for a rationed good

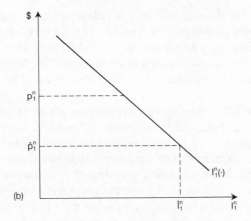

Fig. 7.2b. The investment demand curve

between the ruling market price and the virtual price of non-tradables, as can also be seen from Fig. 7.2a.

Substituting (10) into (8) we obtain, roughly speaking, the social indirect utility function to be used in Keynesian unemployment situations. Taking the total derivative of this function with respect to the policy parameter and dividing through by the marginal utility of income, we obtain the cost–benefit rule to be used in the presence of Keynesian unemployment

$$d\bar{V}_m = w_{11}d\bar{\ell}_{11} + (p_1^n - \hat{p}_1^n)d\bar{x}_1^n - \mathbf{p}_1 d\mathbf{G}_1 + w_{22}d\ell_{11}^q + w_{12}d\bar{\ell}_{12} \quad (12)$$

Note that (12) reduces to (9) if non-tradables firms are not rationed in the output market, since then $p_1^n = \hat{p}_1^n$. However, given that production of non-tradables is now demand-determined, there is a positive difference between the market price and the virtual price of such goods. This difference multiplied by the change in the supply of non-tradables represents an extra benefit that can be ascribed to the change in training efforts.

If the simple balanced-budget theorem, well known from textbooks in macro-economics, were in operation, there would be a one-to-one correspondence between the change in the government's demand for non-tradables, G_1^n, and the change in the first-period production of such goods, $\bar{x}_1^n$. As a consequence, the cost for such goods used for training activities in (12) would be equal to zero.[17] There would still, however, be a real cost for any traded goods used up in the training programme, since producers of such goods, by assumption, are unconstrained in all markets; just as was the case (for all firms) in Section 7.4.1. This cost is equal to $p_1^x dG_1^x$ in (12).[18]

In the model used in this paper, matters are more complicated than in simple 'balanced budget theorem' models, since firms are allowed to adjust their levels of investment following an increase in sales. In fact, demand-constrained firms decrease investment if sales increase. The reason is, loosely speaking, that the opportunity cost of investment increases when the demand constraint is relaxed. This result can be obtained by shifting $\bar{x}_1^n$ to the right in Fig. 7.2a, noting that this increases $\hat{p}_1^n$, and reading off the new lower level of investment in Fig. 7.2b. This result confirms the popular belief among some economists that labour market measures such as job training aimed at reducing short-run unemployment tend to crowd out private investment.

As a consequence, one would overestimate the social profitability of training efforts under Keynesian unemployment if the social cost of inputs used in the training programme is set equal to zero. In (12), the increase in government demand, for non-tradables, G_1^n, exceeds the increase in sales of such goods, $\bar{x}_1^n$, and the marginal cost or virtual price of non-tradables $\hat{p}_1^n$, exceeds the wage w_{11} paid to unemployed unskilled workers hired for the expansion in the level of production of non-tradables. Using these results in (12), the reader can easily verify that the social cost of inputs used in the training programme is strictly positive.[19]

These results imply that one should not, in general, expect training efforts to be very much more profitable under (first-period)

[17] Strictly speaking, the cost is positive if skilled workers are needed to produce non-traded goods since then $\hat{p}_1^n d\bar{x}_1^n > w_{11} d\ell_{11}^n$. Thus, given that $p_1^n d\bar{x}_1^n = p_1^n dG_1^n$, the three first terms in (12) reduce to: $w_{11} d\bar{\ell}_{11} - \hat{p}_1^n d\bar{x}_1^n - p_1^x dG_1^x$, where $w_{11} d\bar{\ell}_{11} = w_{11} d\ell_{11}^n + w_{11} d\ell_{11}^x$.

[18] If the demand for unemployed unskilled workers by producers of tradables is affected, this effect shows up in the cost–benefit rules since, in (12), $w_{11} d\bar{\ell}_{11} = w_{11} d\ell_{11}^n + w_{11} d\ell_{11}^x$, and $w_{12} d\bar{\ell}_{12} = w_{12} d\ell_{12}^n + w_{12} d\ell_{12}^x$. See also Sec. 7.4.1 and n. 12.

[19] Strictly speaking, this is a claim, since the author has not gone through all the necessary calculations. However, for a similar result the reader is referred to Johansson and Löfgren (1988).

Keynesian unemployment than under classical unemployment.[20] In point of fact, if Keynesian unemployment is expected to prevail also in the future, i.e. in period 2, there would not be much room for training activities. Basically, trained workers would *displace* unskilled ones, implying that *the cost–benefit rule would be very similar to the one valid in a full employment situation.* Intuitively, 'supply-side' measures like job training have little effect on affecting aggregate demand for goods (which is, of course, an endogenous variable in the model employed in this paper). Thus, one would expect large displacement effects, i.e. that skilled workers replace unskilled ones, just as in the full employment case considered in Section 7.3. This result is contrary to the popular belief that almost all labour market policy measures stimulate aggregate demand under Keynesian unemployment. However, training basically results in firms using more skilled labour and less unskilled labour, i.e. incomes are redistributed from one group to another. Hence, the effect on aggregate demand and employment will be of second-order magnitude. What is needed instead under Keynesian unemployment in order to raise aggregate income and employment are measures such as fiscal policy and monetary policy which directly stimulate aggregate demand.

Finally, the reader should note that the trade balance does not show up in the cost–benefit rules derived in this paper. This is so because there are no tariffs, import quotas, or constraints on external borrowing. In other words, in the absence of such distortions/constraints, the cost–benefit practitioner need not worry about the training programme's impact on the trade balance. This is so regardless of whether exchange rates are fixed or flexible. The sets of project evaluation rules specified in equations (7), (9), and (12) are general (dis-)equilibrium rules. Hence, they include all effects of a training programme on social welfare, implying that it would mean a kind of 'double counting' to include the effect on the trade balance.

7.5. Concluding Remarks

This paper has shown how a macro-economic model can be used to derive cost–benefit rules to be used to assess the social profitability

---

[20] Unless wages to unskilled workers constitute a considerable share of the marginal cost of producing non-tradables, as can be seen by examining (12).

of training efforts. By contrasting these rules to simple partial equilibrium rules of thumb, the paper hopefully illustrates the need for using carefully derived general (dis-)equilibrium project evaluation rules.

In order to keep the model as simple as possible, some important issues have been set aside. For example, the income distribution issue has not been dealt with. Similarly, the tax scheme imputed to the government, although the one generally employed within the field, is very simple, implying that some important effects, for example relating to incentives, may have been overlooked. For discussion of these and many other complications, the reader is referred to the Hollister–Haveman paper.

Appendix

This appendix presents a simple model explaining the decision to participate or not to participate in labour-market training. The basic feature of the model is that the individual does not know his future income with certainty. In other words, he does not know for sure whether training will increase his utility (ex post). The model used below is extremely simple and (perhaps) unrealistic, but is nevertheless useful in illustrating the main ideas.

Let $V(\mathbf{p}, y_1 + T_1)$ be the (cardinal and smooth) indirect utility function *conditional* on a decision to participate in labour market training, and $V(\mathbf{p}, y_0 + T_0)$ the indirect utility function when no training is selected. The future (present value) real labour incomes y_1 and y_0 are uncertain, while goods prices p and transfer incomes T from the government are assumed for simplicity to be known with certainty.

An individual elects to participate in training if

$$\Delta V = E[V(\mathbf{p}, y_1 + T_1) - V(\mathbf{p}, y_0 + T_0)] > 0 \tag{A1}$$

where the expectation is taken with respect to the joint distribution of labour incomes. Equation (A1) simply states that the individual elects to participate if the expected utility of training exceeds the expected utility of no training. Taking second-order Taylor series expansions around the points $(\mathbf{p}, \bar{y}_1 + T_1)$ and $(\mathbf{p}, \bar{y}_0 + T_0)$, respectively, and suppressing higher-order terms yields

$$E[V(\mathbf{p}, y_i + T_i)] = V(\mathbf{p}, \bar{y}_i + T_i) + V_{yy}^i(\mathbf{p}, \bar{y}_i + T_i) \cdot \sigma_i^2 \quad i = 0, 1 \tag{A2}$$

where a bar denotes an expected income, $V_y^i = \partial V(\cdot)/\partial y_i$, $V_{yy}^i = \partial^2 V(\cdot)/\partial y_i^2$, $E(y_i - \bar{y}_i) = 0$, and $\sigma_i^2 = E(y_i - \bar{y}_i)^2$ is the variance. Substituting (A2) into (A1) and rearranging terms one obtains

$$\Delta V = V(\mathbf{p}, \bar{y}_1 + T_1) - V(\mathbf{p}, \bar{y}_0 + T_0) + V_{yy}^1 \sigma_1^2 - V_{yy}^0 \sigma_0^2. \qquad (A3)$$

Thus, in this model, expected incomes ($\bar{y}$) as well as forecast error variances (σ^2) affect the decision whether or not to participate in training. Reasonably, the higher the expected income $\bar{y}_1$ relative to the expected income $\bar{y}_0$, the more likely it is that the individual elects to participate in training. Similarly, if the individual is *risk-averse*, i.e. if $V_{yy}^i < 0$, greater uncertainty in y_1, i.e. a larger variance σ_1^2, reduces the probability that he or she participates in training. (If the individual is *risk neutral* (i.e. $V_{yy} = 0$) or there is no uncertainty, the two final terms in (A3) vanish, and the model becomes similar to the one used in the main text.)

Equation (A3) can be estimated using, for example, logit or probit techniques. Given that appropriate time-series data on incomes for trained and non-trained workers are available, (A4) provides an illustration of a (logistic) relationship that can be estimated:

$$\ell n(\pi/(1 - \pi)) = \alpha + \beta_1(\bar{y}_1 + T_1) + \beta_2(\bar{y}_0 + T_0) + \beta_3 \sigma_1^2 + \beta_4 \sigma_0^2 + \epsilon \quad (A4)$$

where π is the proportion of workers participating in labour market training in a given year, and ϵ is a random variable whose expected value is equal to zero. The forecast error variances in (A4) can be calculated by using e.g. an autoregressive integrated moving-average (ARIMA) process (see e.g. Johansson 1987). In principle, panel data can also be used to estimate (A4). This is the case if the respondents are asked to estimate $\bar{y}_i$ as well as σ_i^2 for $i = 0, 1$.

8

Labour Market Training: The Lesson from Swedish Evaluations

Anders Björklund

A major difference between the United States and Western Europe in the field of labour market policy is the ambition to evaluate the policies and learn from the experience. Whereas American policy initiatives generally have been relatively small in size, the attempts to evaluate them have been much more systematic than in Western Europe. An 'evaluation industry' has grown up, with research organizations like Mathematica, Manpower Demonstration Research Corporation (MDRC), and Abt Associates having resources to do the field work for data collection and running demonstrations as well as the subsequent analysis of the data at a high scientific level. In addition, many labour economists at the best universities have been active in improving the evaluation methodology and in applying the techniques on the data collected for evaluation purposes. Robinson Hollister and Robert Haveman's contribution is a very informative and pedagogical exposition of the lessons from evaluations in the United States.

Even though many European countries have spent relatively more resources on labour market policy, the American evaluation industry has no counterpart on the opposite side of the Atlantic. There is, however, an embryonic evaluation industry in Sweden, which to a large extent has been stimulated by the methodological development in the United States. In this comment I shall present the results from three recent studies of the Swedish labour-market training programme[1] and conclude by discussing the implications for future research.

---

[1] A similar presentation of evaluations of other measures can be found in Björklund (1990).

8.1. Three Studies of Training

8.1.1. Edin (1988)

Edin studied the effect of training for a sample of workers made redundant due to the closing of a pulp plant in Kramfors in northern Sweden in 1977, using data on earnings and labour market activities for the period 1969–80.

The model estimated was (slightly simplified) the following:

$$Y_{it} = \mu_i + \gamma_1 a_{it} + \gamma_2 a_{it}^2 + \beta_{11} U_{it-1} + \beta_{12} U_{it-2}$$
$$+ \beta_{13} U_{ip} + \beta_{21} T_{it-1} + \beta_{22} T_{it-2}$$
$$+ \beta_{23} T_{ip} + \beta_{31} R_{it-1} + \beta_{32} R_{it-2} + \beta_{33} R_{ip}$$
$$+ \beta_{41} H_{it-1} + \beta_{42} H_{it-2} + \beta_{43} H_{ip}$$
$$+ \beta_{51} S_{it-1} + \beta_{52} S_{it-2} + \beta_{53} S_{ip} + v_{it}$$

where Y_{it} = log weekly earnings relative to average industrial weekly earnings for individual i in year t; μ_i = an unobserved individual permanent effect; a_{it} = age; U_i = weeks of unemployment; T_i = weeks of labour market training; R_i = weeks in public relief work; H_i = weeks of sickness; S_i = weeks spent in regular education; and v_{it} is an error term.

Time spent in unemployment, training, etc. can affect earnings with lags of one and two years. All past time spent in one of those states is denoted with subscript p and is interpreted as the permanent effect on earnings. The sample excludes individuals who left the labour force during the period. Hence the coefficient on any of the variables in the equation should be interpreted as the effect of time spent in the specific state instead of being employed. Edin uses panel data to eliminate the individual permanent effects and allows the error term v_{it} to be serially correlated.

All three training coefficients are negative, i.e. labour market training reduces weekly earnings compared to employment. The effect during the first year is −9 per cent and significant, but the permanent effect and the effect after two years are smaller and insignificant. More relevant is to compare the training and the unemployment coefficients, because unemployment is often considered as the alternative to participation in training programmes. It turns out that the drop during the first year is stronger for training than for unemployment, and significantly so. Hence, the study suggested a negative (though barely significant) first-year effect of training, but no positive long-term effects. Edin also found a significant negative second-year coefficient for relief work. On the other hand, participation in relief work was not significantly worse than being unemployed.

An interesting methodological finding in Edin's study was that the estimated effects were very sensitive to the introduction of serially correlated error terms.

8.1.2. Björklund (1989a)

This study focuses on the effect of training during the period 1976–80. The sample analysed was representative for the whole country. In this respect the results are more general than those obtained by Edin. On the other hand, the periods spent in various labour market states (employment, training, unemployment, out of the labour force, etc.) were not equally well documented in the data, which introduces some uncertainty about the interpretation of the training coefficient.

The research strategy was to estimate several models to see whether the results are sensitive to the specification of the model. Effects on hourly wage rates, employment, and yearly earnings were also estimated. The results are presented in Table 8.1.

In general pattern, the effects of training were positive but weakly significant. The only exception is the effect on hourly wage rates using a state dependence model which is estimated to be negative (though not significantly different from zero). The self-selection model provided a significant positive average effect on participants' wage rates whereas the effect for marginal new participants was negative.

Two problematic patterns can be found in the results: the standard errors are very large, and the estimated effects are quite sensitive to the choice of model. The latter indicates the need for some model selection procedure which can discriminate between alternative model specifications.

8.1.3. Axelsson (1989)

This is a study of vocational labour-market training courses which were completed in the fourth quarter of 1981. A longitudinal data

TABLE 8.1. *Results from Björklund (1989b)*

A. Effects of training during 1976–1980 on employment and hourly wages rates in 1981

	State dependence model	First-diff. model	Self-Selection model
Relative effect on hourly wage in 1981	− 0.049* (0.028)	+ 0.051 (0.039)	0.105** (marginal effect negative)
Effect on percentage employed at the time of the survey	+ 0.055* (0.031)	+ 0.080** (0.039)	—

B. Effects of training during 1976–1982 (first six months of 1982) on employment and income in 1983

	State dependence model	First-diff. model
Effect on percentage employed anytime during the year	+ 0.009 (0.024)	+ 0.013 (0.034)
Relative effect on yearly earnings during the year	+ 0.044 (0.080)	+ 0.186* (0.097)

Notes: Standard errors in parentheses.
*Significantly different from zero at the 10% level
**Significantly different from zero at the 5% level
***Significantly different from zero at the 1% level

Source: Björklund (1989b)

base was constructed for the purpose of evaluation. In particular, register information on yearly income from employment ((*inkomst av tjänst*), including a number of taxable transfers), was collected for the years 1980–3 both for training participants and a comparison group of unemployed job-seekers.

First-difference models—i.e. the change in income from 1980 to 1982 and from 1980 to 1983—were estimated with training participation and a set of background variables describing local labour market conditions and personal characteristics as independent variables.

Axelsson obtained significantly positive effects for both 1982 and 1983 (SEK 6,600 and 9,000 respectively with *t*-values greater than five). Since the average yearly incomes in these years were just below SEK 40,000, the relative impacts were rather high. However, he did not check the robustness of the results to alternative model specifications. On the other hand, he did allow the training coefficient to interact with the other explanatory variables. It appeared that the effect of training was much (and significantly) higher for foreign citizens than for Swedes: over SEK 12,000 higher. Furthermore, the effect was higher for women than for men, higher for handicapped than for others, and higher for those who lacked previous vocational training than for those who had such training. Taking the interactions at face value, one can find groups of Swedish citizens for whom the point estimate of the training effect was negative.

The extremely large effect for foreign citizens leads to doubts about the model specification. It cannot be ruled out that many trainees of foreign citizenship in Sweden in 1980 had unusually low registered income. This is particularly likely since it is common to participate in labour market training during the first years in Sweden. The first-difference model might then overstate the effects for this group.

8.2. Implications for Future Research

It appears that the results from these studies are too uncertain to allow firm policy conclusions about the effectiveness of training as a manpower policy instrument. In particular, there is uncertainty about the proper model specification. In this respect, the results from the Swedish studies are similar to the American results reported by Hollister and Haveman. We therefore have to address ourselves to how future research should proceed to reach more reliable conclusions.

Basically, there are two alternatives. One is to conduct classical experiments where prospective participants are randomly assigned to an experimental and to a control group, and the other is to expand the non-experimental methodology. An example of a successful classical experiment which has permitted rather firm conclusions is the National Supported Work experiment presented by Hollister and Haveman. The policy instrument tested in this experiment was a new one, however, whereas the Swedish labour market training programme is an ongoing one, and experiments on ongoing programmes are more problematic. To evaluate the present Swedish training programme, for example, both the experimental group and the control group must be representative of those who normally participate. However, as for several years there has been idle capacity in the Swedish training centres, with very few exceptions all those who apply for a course are allowed to participate.[2] If both the experimental and the control groups must be chosen from the population of training applicants, some of those who would normally have been allowed to participate must become part of the control group, and hence withheld services they would otherwise have received. This is an ethical problem. Another problem is organizational: because some of those who would normally participate must be controls, some training slots cannot be used during the experiment and classrooms and teachers can become redundant. In sum, classical experiments are problematic to undertake for evaluations of the present Swedish training system.

The other alternative is to improve the non-experimental methodology. Two improvements are needed. First, the standard errors of the programme effects from each specific model must be improved considerably. This requires better data both on outcome and explanatory variables. Second, the uncertainty about correct model specification must be reduced. Hollister and Haveman seem very pessimistic on this point, although it should be noted that Heckman, Hotz, and Dabos (1987) have a more optimistic assessment: the estimator they selected using a new model selection procedure to discriminate between alternative panel data estimators proved quite successful in replicating the results from the National Supported Work experiment. A drawback, however, is that the test procedure requires additional waves of panel data.

---

[2] With the terminology of Björklund (1988), this is a demand-constrained case. The opposite case is the supply-constrained one where there are more willing participants than training slots at the training centres, and the programme authorities must effect rationing among the applicants.

References for Part I

Adams, C., Cook, R., and Maurice, A. (1983). 'A Pooled Time-Series Analysis of the Job-Creation Impact of Public Service Employment Grants to Large Cities', *Journal of Human Resources*, 18: 283–94.

Ashenfelter, O. (1978). 'Estimating the Effect of Training Programs on Earnings', *Review of Economics and Statistics*, 60: 47–57.

Axelsson, R. (1989). *Svensk Arbetsmarknadsutbildning: En kvantitativ analys av dess effekter*, (Swedish labour market training: A quantitative analysis of its effects), Umeå University.

Azariadis, C. (1979). 'Implicit Contracts and Related Topics: A Survey', in Z. Hornstein (ed.), *Economics of Labor Markets*. London: HMSO.

Baily, M.N., and Tobin, J. (1977). 'Macroeconomic Effects of Selective Public Employment and Wage Subsidies', *Brookings Papers on Economic Activity*.

Balkenhol, B. (1979). 'Marginal Employment Subsidies: Issues and Evidence', World Employment Program Research, Working Paper WEP 2–24/WP.15. Geneva: ILO.

—— (1980). 'Direct Job Creation Schemes in Industrialized Countries: Issues and Evidence', World Employment Program Research, Working Paper WEP 2–24/WP.17. Geneva: ILO.

Barnow, B. (1987). 'The Impact of CETA Programs on Earnings', *Journal of Human Resources*, 22: 149–93.

Barro, R.J., and Grossman, H.I. (1971). 'A General Disequilibrium Model of Income and Employment', *American Economic Review*, 61: 82–93.

Bassi, L. (1984). 'Estimating the Effects of Training Programs with Nonrandom Selection', *Review of Economics and Statistics*, 66: 36–43.

Bassi, L., and Ashenfelter, O. (1986). 'The Effect of Direct Job Creation and Training Programs on Low Skilled Workers', in S. Danziger and D. Weinberg (eds.), *Fighting Poverty: What Works and What Doesn't*. Cambridge: Harvard University Press, 1986.

Bell, C., and Devarajan, S. (1983). 'Shadow Prices for Project Evaluation under Alternative Macroeconomic Specifications', *Quarterly Journal of Economics*, 98: 457–77.

Bendick, M., and Devine, J. (1982). *Workers Dislocated by Economic Change: Do They Need Federal Employment and Training Assistance?* National Commission for Employment Policy, Seventh Annual Report Washington, DC: NCEP.

Betsey, C., Hollister, R., and Papageourgiou, M. (1985). *Youth Employment and Training Programs: The YEDPA Years*. Washington, DC: National Academy of Sciences Press.

Bishop, J., and Haveman, R. (1979). 'Employment Subsidies: Can Okun's Law be Repealed?', *American Economic Review*, 62: 124-30.

Björklund, A. (1988). 'What Experiments Needed for Manpower Policy?', *Journal of Human Resources*, 23/2: 267-77.

—— (1989). 'Evaluation of Labor Market Training Programs: The Swedish Experience', The Industrial Institute for Economic and Social Research (Industries Utredningsinstitut), Stockholm. Mimeo.

—— (1990). 'Evaluations of Swedish Labor Market Policy'; *Finnish Economic Papers*, 3/1: 3-13.

Blitzer, C., Dasgupta, P., and Stiglitz, J. (1981). 'Project Appraisal and Foreign Exchange Constraints; *Economic Journal*, 91: 58-74.

Bloch, F., ed., (1979). *Research in Labor Economics*: Evaluating Manpower Training Programs. Greenwich, Conn.: JAI Press.

Bloch-Michel, C., *et al.* (1983). 'Création d'enterprises par les demandeurs d'emploi', Bilan de l'Emploi, 1982, Ministère des Affaires Sociales et de la Solidarité Nationale, 1983. (Cited in Casey and Bruche 1985).

Bloom H., and McLaughlin, M. (1982). *CETA Training Programs: Do They Work for Adults*? Washington, DC: US Congressional Budget Office.

Boadway, R.W. (1975). 'Cost-Benefit Rules in General Equilibrium; *Review of Economic Studies*, 42: 361-73.

Bosworth, B. (1986). 'Comment by Barry Bosworth', in Butkiewicz, Koford, and Miller (1986).

Bosworth, B., and Rivlin, A. (1987). *The Swedish Economy*. Washington, DC: Brookings Institution.

Brown, R. (1979). 'Assessing the Effects of Interview Non-Response on Estimates of the Impact of Supported Work', Princeton, NJ: Mathematica Policy Research.

Bulow, J.L., and Summers, L.H. (1986). 'A Theory of Dual Labor Markets with Applications to Industrial Policy, Discrimination and Keynesian Unemployment', *Journal of Economic Literature*, 4.

Burdett, K., and Hool, B. (1982). 'The Effects on the Inflation-Unemployment Trade-Off', in Haveman and Palmer (1982).

Burtless, G. (1984). 'Manpower Policies for the Disadvantaged: What Works?', *The Brookings Review*, 3/1: 18-22.

—— (1985). 'Are Targeted Wages Subsidies Harmful? Evidence from a Wage Voucher Experiment', *Industrial and Labor Relations Review*, 39: 105-14.

Butkiewicz, J.L., Koford, K., and Miller, J.B., eds. (1986). *Keynes' Economic Legacy*. New York: Praeger.

Cain, G. (1968). 'Benefit–Cost Estimates for Job Corps', Discussion Paper No. 9–68, Institute for Research on Poverty, University of Wisconsin–Madison.

—— (1976). 'The Challenge of Segmented Labor Market Theories to Orthodox Theory', *Journal of Economic Literature*, 14: 1215–57.

Cain, G., and Hollister, R. (1983). 'Evaluating Social Action Programs', in Haveman and Margolis (1983).

Casey, B., and Bruche, G. (1985). 'Active Labor Market Policy: An International Overview', *Industrial Relations*, 24: 37–61.

Centre for Employment Initiatives (1985). *The Impact of Local Enterprise Agencies in Great Britain*. London: Centre for Employment Initiatives.

Clark, K., and Freeman, R. (1980). 'How Elastic Is the Demand for Labor?', *Review of Economics and Statistics*, 62: 509–20.

Corson, W., and Nicholson, W. (1981). 'Trade Adjustment Assistance for Workers: Results of a Survey of Recipients in the Trade Act of 1974', in R. Ehrenberg (ed.), *Research in Labor Economics*, vol. iv. Greenwich, Conn.: JAI Press.

Crane, J., and Ellwood, D. (1984). 'The Summer Youth Employment Program: Private Job Supplement or Substitute?', prepared for the US Department of Health and Human Services at Kennedy School, Harvard University.

Cuddington, J.T., Johansson, P.O., and Löfgren, K.G. (1984), *Disequilibrium Macroeconomics in Open Economies*. Oxford: Basil Blackwell.

Cuddington, J.T., Johansson, P.O., and Ohlsson, H. (1985). 'Optimal Policy Rules and Regime Switching in Disequilibrium Models', *Journal of Public Economics*, 27: 247–54.

Dasgupta, P., Sen, A., and Marglin, S.A. (1972), *Guidelines for Project Evaluation*. Vienna: UNIDO.

Denmark (1985), *Hovedelementer I den danske arbejdsministers indlaeg. Konference on Teknologi og Beskaeftigelse ivendedie Den.* ('The main arguments put forward by the Danish Minister of Labor. Conference on Technology and Trade . . .') 10–11 Apr.

Dickinson, K., Johnson, R., and West, R. (1986). 'An Analysis of the Impact of CETA Programs on Participants' Earnings', *Journal of Human Resources*, 21: 64–91.

Diewert, W.E. (1983). 'Cost–Benefit Analysis and Project Evaluation: A Comparison of Alternative Approaches', *Journal of Public Economics*, 22: 265–302.

Drèze, J.H. (1985). 'Second Best Analysis with Markets in Disequilibrium: Public Sector Pricing in a Keynesian Regime', *European Economic Review*, 29: 263–301.

Drèze, J.P. (1982). 'On the Choice of Shadow Prices for Project Evaluation', Discussion Paper No. 16, Indian Statistical Institute, New Delhi.

Drèze, J.H., and Modigliani, F. (1981). 'The Trade-Off between Real Wages and Employment in an Open Economy (Belgium)', *European Economic Review*, 15: 1–40.

Drèze, J.P., and Stern, N. (1987). 'The Theory of Cost–Benefit Analysis', in A.J. Auerbach and M. Feldstein, (eds.), *Handbook of Public Economics*, ii. Amsterdam: North-Holland.

Eckstein, O. (1958). *Water Resource Development.* Cambridge, Mass.: Harvard University Press.

Edin, P.-A. (1988). *Individual Consequences of Plant Closures*, Uppsala University.

Ellwood, D. (1986). 'Targeting "Would-Be" Long-Term Recipients of AFDC', Mathematica Policy Research, Princeton, NJ.

Farkas, G., Smith, D.A., Stromsdorfer, E.W., Trask, G., and Jerrett, R., III (1982). 'Impacts for the Youth Incentive Entitlement Pilot Projects: Participation, Work, and Schooling over the Full Program Period', New York: Manpower Demonstration Research Corporation.

Fraker, T., and Maynard, R. (1987). 'The Adequacy of Comparison Group Designs for Evaluations of Employment-Related Programs', *Journal of Human Resources*, 22: 194–228.

Fourgeaud, C., Lenclud, B., and Picard, P. (1986). 'Shadow Prices and Public Policies in a Disequilibrium Model of an Open Economy', *European Economic Review*, 30: 991–1012.

Freeman, R.B. (1986). 'Demand for Education', in O.C. Aschenfelter and P.R.G. Layard (eds.), *Handbook of Labor Economics*, i. Amsterdam: North Holland.

Freeman, R. (1988). 'Evaluating the European View that the US Has No Unemployment Problem', National Bureau of Economic Research, Working Paper No. 2562, Cambridge, Mass.

Gould, W., Ward, M., and Welch, F. (1982). 'Measuring Displacement: An Econometric Approach', Report to the US Department of Labor, Los Angeles: Unicorn Research Corporation.

Grossman, J., Maynard, R., and Roberts, J. (1985). 'Reanalysis of the Effects of Selected Employment and Training Programs for Welfare Recipients'. Mathematica Policy Research, Princeton, NJ.

Gueron, J. (1986). 'Work Initiatives for Welfare Recipients', Manpower Demonstration Research Corporation, New York City.

Hamermesh, D. (1976). 'Econometric Studies of Labor Demand and Their Application to Policy Analysis', *Journal of Human Resources*, 11: 507–25.

Harberger, A.C. (1969). 'The Opportunity Cost of Public Investment Financed by Borrowing', in P.R.G. Layard (ed.), *Cost–Benefit Analysis*. Baltimore, Maryland: Penguin Books.

Harberger, A.C. (1971). 'Three Basic Postulates for Applied Welfare Economics: An Interpretative Essay', *Journal of Economic Literature*, 9: 785–97.

Haveman, R., and Krutilla, J. (1967). *Unemployment, Excess Capacity and the Evaluation of Public Investments*. Baltimore: Johns Hopkins.

Haveman, R., and Margolis, J., eds. (1983). *Public Expenditures and Policy Analysis*, 3rd edn. Chicago: Rand McNally.

Haveman, R., and Palmer, J., eds. (1982). *Jobs for the Disadvantaged*. Washington, DC: Brookings Institution.

Heckman, J.J., Hotz, V.J., and Dabos, M. (1987). 'Do We Need Experimental Data to Evaluate the Impact of Manpower Training on Earnings?', *Evaluation Review*, 11/4: 395–427.

Helliwell, J.F. (1988). 'Comparative Macroeconomics of Stagflation', *Journal of Economic Literature*, 26: 1–28.

Hollister, R., Kemper, P., and Maynard, R., eds. (1984). *The National Supported Work Demonstration*. Madison: University of Wisconsin Press.

Hollister, R., Kemper, P., and Wooldridge, J. (1979). 'Linking Process and Impact Analysis: The Case of Supported Work', in T. Cook and C. Reichardt (eds.), *Qualitative and Quantitative Methods in Evaluation Research*, i. Beverly Hills, Calif.: Sage.

ILO [International Labour Office] (1981). 'Termination of Employment at the Initiative of the Employer', Report 7/1, International Labour Conference, 67th session. Geneva: ILO. *Industrial Relations*, 24/1 (Winter 1985).

Johansson, P.O. (1982). 'Cost–Benefit Rules in General Disequilibrium', *Journal of Public Economics*, 18: 121–37.

—— (1984). 'Disequilibrium Cost–Benefit Rules for Natural Resources', *Resources and Energy*, 6: 355–72.

—— (1987). *The Economic Theory and Measurement of Environmental Benefits*. Cambridge: Cambridge University Press.

Johansson, P.O., and Löfgren K.G. (1985). *The Economics of Forestry and Natural Resources*. Oxford: Blackwell.

—— (1988). 'Disequilibrium Cost–Benefit Rules: An Exposition and Extension', in H. Folmer and E. van Ierland (eds.) *Evaluation Methods and Policy-Making in Environmental Economics*. Amsterdam: North Holland.

Johnson, G.E. (1979). 'The Labor Market Displacement Effect in the Analysis of the Net Impact of Manpower Training Programs', in Bloch (1979).

—— (1980). 'The Theory of Labour Market Intervention', *Economica*, 47.

—— (1983). 'Potentials of Labour Market Policy: A View from the Eighties', *Industrial Relations*, 22/2: 283–97.

Johnson, G.E., and Layard, P.R.G. (1986). 'The Natural Rate of

Unemployment: Explanation and Policy', in O. Ashenfelter and P. R. G. Layard (eds.), *Handbook of Labor Economics*, vol. ii. Amsterdam: North-Holland.

Johnson, G. E., and Tomola, J. (1977). 'The Fiscal Substitution Effect of Alternative Approaches to Public Service Employment', *Journal of Human Resources*, 12: 3–26.

Keifer, N. (1979). 'The Economic Benefits from Four Government Training Programs', in Bloch (1979).

Kemper, P. (1980). 'Supported Work Evaluation Supplementary Paper: Indirect Labor Market Effects in Benefit–Cost Analysis', Mathematica Policy Research, New York City.

Kemper, P., and Long, D. (1981). 'The Supported Work Evaluation: Technical Report on Value of In-Program Output and Costs', Manpower Demonstration Research Corporation, New York City.

Kesselman, J. (1978). 'Work Relief Programs in the Great Depression', in Palmer (1978).

Killingsworth, M. (1985). 'Substitution and Output Effects on Labor Demand: Theory and Policy Applications', *Journal of Human Resources*, 20: 142–52.

Krueger, A., and Summers, L. H. (1987). 'Reflections on the Inter-Industry Wage Structure', in K. Lang and J. S. Leonard (eds.), *Unemployment and the Structure of Labor Markets*. Oxford: Basil Blackwell, 1987.

Krutilla, J., and Eckstein, O. (1958). *Multiple Purpose River Development*. Baltimore, Md: Johns Hopkins University Press.

Kulik, J., Smith, D. A., and Stromsdorfer, E. (1984). 'The Downriver Community Conference Economic Readjustment: Final Evaluation Report', Abt Associates, Washington, DC.

Kydland, F. E., and Prescott, E. C. (1977). 'Rules Rather than Discretion: The Inconsistency of Optimal Plans', *Journal of Political Economy*, 85: 473–93.

LaLonde, R. (1986). 'Evaluating the Economic Evaluations of Training Programs with Experimental Data', *American Economic Review*, 76: 604–20.

Lang, K., and Dickens, W. T. (1987). 'Neoclassical and Sociological Perspectives on Segmented Labor Markets', National Bureau of Economic Research, Working Paper No. 2127, Cambridge, Mass.

Lawrence, R., and Schultze, C., eds. (1987). *Barriers to European Growth*. Washington, DC: Brookings Institution.

Layard, P. R. G., and Nickel, S. J. (1980). 'The Case for Subsidizing Extra Jobs', *Economic Journal*, 90: 51–73.

Lesourne, J. (1975). *Cost–Benefit Analysis and Economic Theory*. Amsterdam: North-Holland.

Little, I. M. D., and Mirrlees, J. A. (1968). *Manual of Industrial Project Analysis in Developing Countries*, i. Paris: OECD.

Lucas, R. E. (1978). 'Unemployment Policy', *American Economic Review*, 68: 353–7.

Lundberg, E. (1985). 'The Rise and Fall of the Swedish Model', *Journal of Economic Literature*, 23: 1–36.

McKean, R. N. (1958). *Efficiency in Government through Systems Analysis*. New York: John Wiley & Sons.

Malinvaud, E. (1977). *The Theory of Unemployment Reconsidered*. Oxford: Basil Blackwell.

Mallar, C., Kerachsky, S., Thornton, C., and Long, D. (1982). 'Evaluation of the Economic Impact of the Job Corps Program: Third Follow-Up Report', Mathematica Policy Research, Princeton, N J.

Maneschi, A. (1985). 'The Shadow Pricing of Factors in a Multicommodity Specific-Factors Model', *Canadian Journal of Economics*, 18: 843–53.

Marchand, M., Mintz, J., and Pestieau, P. (1984). 'Shadow Pricing of Labor and Capital in an Economy with Unemployed Labor', *European Economic Review*, 97: 239–52.

—— (1985). 'Public Production and Shadow Pricing in a Model of Disequilibrium in Labor and Capital Markets', *Journal of Economic Theory*, 36: 237–51.

Marglin, S. (1967). *Public Investment Criteria: Benefit–Cost Analysis for Planned Economic Growth*. Cambridge, Mass.: M I T Press.

Maynard, R., and Maxfield, M. (1986). 'A Design of a Social Demonstration of Targeted Employment Services for A F D C Recipients', Mathematica Policy Research, Princeton, N J.

Maynard, R., *et al.* (1985). 'An Impact Evaluation of the Buffalo Dislocated Worker Demonstration', Mathematica Policy Research, Princeton, N J.

Meyer, R., and Wise, D. (1982). 'High School Preparation and Early Labor Force Experience', in R. Freeman and D. Wise (eds.), *The Youth Labor Market Problem: Its Nature, Causes, and Consequences*. Chicago: University of Chicago Press.

Musgrave, R. (1969). 'Cost–Benefit Analysis and the Theory of Public Finance', *Journal of Economic Literature*, 7: 797–806.

Musgrave, R., and Musgrave, P. B. (1973). *Public Finance in Theory and Practice*. London: McGraw-Hill.

Nathan, R., Cook, R., Rawlins, V. L., and associates (1981). *Public Service Employment: A Field Evaluation*. Washington, DC: Brookings Institution.

Neary, J. P., and Roberts, K. W. S. (1980). 'The Theory of Household Behaviour under Rationing', *European Economic Review*, 13: 25–42.

Neary, J. P., and Stiglitz, J. E. (1983). 'Toward a Reconstruction of Keynesian Economics: Expectations and Constrained Equilibria.' *Quarterly Journal of Economics*, 98 (Supplement): 199–228.

Nichols, D. (1982). 'Effects on the Non-inflationary Unemployment Rate', in Haveman and Palmer (1982): 131–55.

Ohlsson, H. (1987). 'Cost–Benefit Rules in a Regionalized Disequilibrium Model', *Scandinavian Journal of Economics*, 89: 165–82.

OECD[Organization for Economic Cooperation and Development] (1980). *Direct Job Creation*. Paris. OECD.

—— (1983). *Marginal Employment Subsidies*. Paris.

—— (1984). *Community Business Ventures and Job Creation*. Paris.

—— (annual). *Employment Outlook*. Paris.

Palmer, J., ed. (1978). *Creating Jobs: Public Employment Programs and Wage Subsidies*. Washington, DC: Brookings Institution.

Perloff, J. (1982). 'Micro- and Macroeconomic Effects', in Haveman and Palmer (1982): 95–123.

Phan-Thuy, P.N. (1979). 'Controversies on Marginal Employment Premiums as an Anti-Inflationary Job Promotion Measure in Industrialized Countries: A Preliminary View', World Employment Program Research, Working Paper WEP 2-24/WP.14. Geneva: International Labour Office.

Rehn, G. (1985). 'Swedish Active Labor Market Policy: Retrospect and Prospect', *Industrial Relations*, 24: 62–89.

Rivera-Casale, C., Friedman, B., and Lerman, R. (1982). 'Can Employer or Worker Subsidies Raise Youth Employment? An Evaluation of Two Financial Incentive Programs for Disadvantaged Youth', Centre for Employment and Income Studies, Brandeis University, Waltham, Mass.

Roberts, K. (1982). 'Desirable Fiscal Policies under Keynesian Unemployment', *Oxford Economic Papers*, 34: 1–22.

Schmid, G. (1982). 'Zur Effizienz der Arbeitsmarktpolitik: Ein Plädoyer fur einen Schritt zurück und zwei Schritte vor', Discussion Paper IIM/LMP 82-3, Wissenschaftszentrum, Berlin, 1982. Cited in Casey and Bruche (1985).

Schwanse, P. (1982). 'European Experience', in Haveman and Palmer (1982): 297–324.

Skidmore, F. (1984). 'The Impacts of Supported Work on Former Drug Addicts', in Hollister, Kemper, and Maynard (1984).

Srinivasan, T.N., and Bhagwati, J.N. (1978). 'Shadow Prices for Project Selection in the Presence of Distortions: Effective Rates of Protection and Domestic Resource Costs', *Journal of Political Economy*, 86: 96–116.

Starr, G. (1981). *Minimum Wage Fixing*. Geneva: International Labour Office.

Stiglitz, J. (1986). 'Theories of Wage Rigidity', in Butkiewicz, Koford, and Miller (1986).

US Congress, Office of Technology Assessment (1986). *Technology and*

Structural Unemployment: Reemploying Displaced Adults. Washington DC: US Government Printing Office.

US General Accounting Office (1984). 'Federal Economic Development Assistance Programs: An Econometric Analysis of Their Employment Effects, 1974–78', GAO/OCE–84–85, Washington, DC.

—— (1986). 'Emergency Jobs Act of 1983; Funds Spent Slowly, Few Jobs Created', GAO/HRD–87–1, Washington, DC.

Varian, H.R. (1984). *Microeconomic Analysis*, 2nd edn. New York: Norton.

Vernez, G., and Vaughan, R. (1978). *Assessment of Countercyclic Public Works and Public Service Employment Programs.* Santa Monica, Calif.: Rand Corp.

Wachter, M. (1974). 'Primary and Secondary Labor Markets: A Critique of the Dual Approach', *Brookings Papers on Economic Activity*, No. 3.

Walker, G., *et al.* (1986). *An Independent Sector Assessment of the Job Training Partnership Act.* New York: Grinker, Walker & Associates.

Whitely, J.D., and Wilson, R.A. (1983). 'The Macroeconomic Merits of a Marginal Employment Subsidy', *Economic Journal*, 93: 862–80.

Wilensky, H. (1985). 'Nothing Fails like Success: The Evaluation Research Industry and Labor Market Policy', *Industrial Relations*, 24/1.

Zimmerman, D. (1980). 'A Study of the Value of Output of Participants in the Summer Youth Employment Program', Draft Final Report, Mathematica Policy Research, Princeton, NJ.

PART II

The Economics of Unemployment Insurance: The Case of Sweden

9

Introduction

Unemployment has risen sharply over the past fifteen years in most European countries. This development has challenged many conventional views among economists as well as policy-makers. New explanations of unemployment have appeared in the economics literature, and new policies to combat unemployment have come to the fore. The development has also brought about a new interest in the role of unemployment insurance (UI). This interest has been driven by different concerns; some people have emphasized the financial burden for government budgets of the rising expenditure on unemployment benefits, others have been concerned about income losses for the long-termed unemployed, and some economists and politicians have seen high unemployment benefits as one of the major factors behind the rise in unemployment.

Sweden's unemployment experience differs radically from what has happened in most other European countries. Unemployment in Sweden has fluctuated between 1 and 3.5 per cent since the early 1960s, and there is only a weak trend increase; the cyclical peaks in the 1960s involved lower unemployment than the peaks in the 1970s and the 1980s, and the same holds for the slumps.

Despite Sweden's excellent unemployment record, there are reasons for concern about a clear trend increase in the duration of unemployment. In the late 1960s, the average duration of a completed spell of unemployment was seven weeks; in the mid-1980s, the unemployment who have remained so was about twice as long. The fraction of the labour force unemployed for a year or more has not exceeded 10 per cent, however, and this is very low by European standards.

We have benefited from many useful comments and suggestions from Villy Bergström, Gary Burtless, Paul Chen, Rob Hollister, Per Lundborg, Karl-Gustaf Löfgren, Günther Schmid, Hans Tson Söderström and Anders Vredin. The work on this paper started while the authors were at the Industrial Institute for Economic and Social Research (IUI) in Stockholm.

The increase in the duration of unemployment has occurred simultaneously with various extensions of the Swedish UI system. Real benefits for insured workers have increased faster than real wages, the maximum benefit periods have increased, a growing fraction of the unemployed has been covered by UI, and a new type of benefit has been introduced. It is natural to ask whether there is some causal link between the marked extensions of the Swedish UI system and the increase in unemployment duration, and this is one of the objectives of this study.

The essay has two main purposes. The first is to offer a nontechnical review of the literature on unemployment insurance, and the second is to examine the Swedish UI system in the light of this literature. The issues involved are positive as well as normative. An overwhelming fraction of the literature has dealt with various positive issues concerning incentive effects of UI, but very few studies have undertaken serious investigations about the welfare economics of UI. This is also reflected in our essay.

The essay is organized as follows. Chapter 10 discusses some central problems relevant for all insurance markets, but particularly for the market for UI; we focus primarily on the rationale for government intervention. Chapter 11 proceeds to a detailed investigation of the Swedish system. We describe the institutional framework and examine how well the UI benefits cover income losses for unemployed workers.

Chapter 12 deals with incentive effects. We offer a brief survey of relevant theoretical and empirical literature and explore the consequences of a generous treatment of seasonal unemployment. Chapter 13 attempts to make a tentative evaluation concerning the effects of the Swedish UI system on income distribution. In Chapter 14 we return to the normative issues and offer a discussion of the properties of an optimal UI system. Chapter 15 concludes the study itself, and Chapters 16 and 17 are devoted to comments by Gary Burtless and Eskil Wadensjö, respectively.

10

Problems in Insurance Markets

Underlying the demand for unemployment insurance, as for all other kinds of insurance, is risk aversion. The presence of risk aversion implies that a *certain* income stream is preferred to an *uncertain* income stream even if the average or expected income is equal in both cases. The term 'uncertain income stream' refers not to an uneven flow but rather to one that cannot be predicted with certainty, for example, due to the risk of being laid off. Thus, a risk-averse person who runs a certain risk of becoming unemployed would willingly pay some regular insurance premium in order to receive compensation for lost income in the event of unemployment.

An insurance solution is normally preferable to other methods, such as private savings, for smoothing a risky stream of income. This has been shown by Baily (1978). The intuitive explanation is as follows. With insurance, there is a guaranteed income regardless of whether the person happens to become unemployed or not. If the expected unemployment is estimated at 1 per cent of the work time, a premium of 1 per cent of the income will guarantee an even stream of income. Suppose instead that the person saves 1 per cent of his income to have at his disposal in case of unemployment. This choice gives the same outcome as that of insurance only if the person is unemployed exactly 1 per cent of the time. If he manages to avoid unemployment totally, he would be much better off, while the reverse is true if he suffers an unexpectedly high amount of unemployment. Consequently the savings alternative is an uncertain one. Risk aversion implies that the certain insurance alternative is preferred to the uncertain savings alternative.

It follows, of course, that in the matter of an income stream which is uneven but predictable with certainty, for example certain types of seasonal work, the insurance alternative is no longer preferable.

The demand for unemployment insurance is thus relatively obvious in real-world labour markets where workers are facing lay-off risks. Problems occur, however, in devising methods to meet this demand. One problem arises when the insured can affect the probability that the event against which he is insured will occur. This problem, generally called *moral hazard*, clearly exists in this field. A person can affect the probability of becoming unemployed in several ways. A worker can voluntarily quit, or he can affect the probability of getting a new job once he has become unemployed, even if his entry into unemployment is totally involuntary. The probability of becoming re-employed normally depends on the intensity of search and the criteria set by the worker for accepting a job offer. Both search intensity and acceptance criteria are obviously affected by the job seeker.

The problem of moral hazard can be treated in at least two different ways, which are not mutually exclusive. The first is to choose a type of insurance which gives only *partial coverage* for the loss in income. Complete coverage may require prohibitively high insurance premiums. The best solution for both the buyer and the seller of insurance in such markets is therefore one in which the insured shares part of any fall in income, but in return pays significantly lower insurance premiums than what would otherwise be the case. The partial coverage also reduces the insured's incentive to stay in unemployment, which then leads to lower premiums. The second approach is to set certain requirements for the behaviour of the insured and then try to enforce these requirements. The cheaper the means of enforcement are, of course, the more enforcement one will choose, and the higher will be the optimal level of coverage. The control mechanism in the Swedish unemployment insurance system is that the unemployed person who wishes to receive compensation must apply at the employment office and accept 'suitable work'.

The problem of moral hazard faces a public as well as a private insurance system, and by itself constitutes no strong argument for government-provided UI. On the other hand, Pauly (1974) has pointed out that in a private system with many insurance companies, it would be possible to obtain full insurance by purchasing from several companies. In this way, the incentive to prevent unemployment disappears, and the optimal ratio between 'prevention protection' and 'insurance protection' would not be reached. This misuse would not occur in the case of state monopoly. However, as Shavell (1979) points out, such a phenomenon could probably be avoided even in a system of private companies. Nor is there anything which prevents private insurance companies using a public employment office as a mechanism of enforcement.

Another important obstacle in meeting the demand for unemployment insurance is that of *adverse selection*. This problem arises if individuals differ markedly with respect to risk of unemployment. It further requires that those potentially insured are conscious of their own risk, while the insurance companies can only estimate the average risk in the market. It is thus a problem of information, more specifically of asymmetric information.

In such circumstances, the insurance company cannot differentiate premiums according to each person's risk, but rather must charge according to the average risk of the group. In this case insurance is very advantageous for those with high risk and to the same degree disadvantageous for those with low risk. The latter group can very well choose not to buy insurance or to significantly reduce the amount of insurance purchased. It is this exit of potential insurance buyers which is called adverse selection. As a consequence of this, the opportunity for the high risk group to insure itself will obviously be reduced or disappear. In extreme cases of this kind of information problem, the private market may cease to exist.

Since adverse selection is based on an information problem, it affects private as well as public markets. There is no reason to believe a priori that a public system is preferable to a private one with respect to treating the information problem itself. But this problem has motivated state intervention to assure that unemployment insurance can be obtained at all. This can be accomplished if the government provides unemployment insurance. It then becomes a matter of obligatory insurance. The premiums may, however, be differentially applied in various ways. The government may also intervene via subsidies to support UI schemes run by private firms or organizations.

Is there reason to believe that an obligatory system is superior to the system, or lack of a system, that a 'free market' would result in? This question has been discussed somewhat in the theoretical literature on insurance. This literature, based on some rather special models, indicates that it is possible to achieve welfare gains with an obligatory system if the adverse selection problem exists.

Akerlof (1978) has formulated a model which leads to adverse selection. Diamond and Rothschild (1978) claim that social welfare (the sum of utilities or welfare for all individuals) increased if an obligatory insurance scheme is introduced in Akerlof's model. The winners' gains are thus larger than the losers' losses.

Pauly (1974) has constructed an example in which an obligatory system, with a premium based on the average risk, results in an improved situation for both low and high risk groups. A presumption for this noteworthy result is, however, that the low risk group will demand some amount of insurance even in the absence of the obligatory system.

Jones (1986) has investigated whether public provision of unemployment insurance can improve welfare in the aggregate. An appealing property of the study is that the issue is analysed in a model which explicitly generates unemployment; both Akerlof and Pauly are considering unspecified insurance markets. Jones's model deals with involuntary unemployment generated by an efficiency wage model. Workers are risk-averse and have heterogeneous abilities and reservation wages. Firms are risk-neutral and offer a uniform wage to all workers, because they cannot distinguish between types of workers.

The private outcome of the model does not involve provision of unemployment insurance, which is rather surprising since one can expect that firms can reduce labour costs by offering insurance against the involuntary unemployment which occurs in those models. On the other hand, public provision of unemployment insurance will increase total welfare, i.e. the sum of welfare for both participants and non-participants.

A third problem in the market for insurance is that the insurance company may have difficulties offering insurance on reasonable terms since unemployment often occurs at the same time for many of the insured, i.e. during economic recessions. An insurance company's opportunity to pool risks across subscribers is reduced if the risks are positively correlated (see Hirschleifer and Riley 1979). A private unemployment insurance company would face large problems during a recession. Thus, the larger the uncertainty is regarding the recession's depth and length, the smaller the company's commitments can be.

Because the government's stabilization policies affect the business cycle, the opportunities of insuring oneself against unemployment are affected by the government's actions. It is thus reasonable to argue that the government should take a more comprehensive responsibility regarding unemployment insurance.

In addition to the *efficiency* arguments for government contribution to unemployment compensation, *equity* arguments may also be made. The risk of unemployment is in general highest among those who have a weak position in the labour market due to poor schooling or training, or lack of work experience. Government support of unemployment insurance should therefore function as a subsidy for a good which is particularly demanded by people in lower earnings categories. Boadway and Oswald (1983) have shown that the optimal solution in terms of equity and efficiency might be a combination of progressive income taxation and subsidized unemployment insurance schemes.

One might thus offer efficiency as well as equity arguments for government intervention. But, paradoxically enough, it is doubtful if such arguments are consistent. If the risk of unemployment is strongly related to, for example, poor schooling, there exists no problem of adverse selection. The insurance premiums could then be related to the variables that capture the unemployment risk.

Unemployment risks can probably be quite well detected for groups which have been active on the labour market a relatively long time. Conversely, the problem of adverse selection is likely to be greater among entrants to the labour market. They have not had the opportunity to reveal the strength of their position in the labour market and thus their risk of unemployment.

With these general problems in insurance markets in mind, we turn to a presentation of the Swedish system.

11

The Swedish System

11.1 Introduction

The government in Sweden has, for a long time, actively contributed
to various forms of unemployment compensation. In 1935, the
government began to subsidize those unemployment insurance
funds (UI funds) which satisfied certain requirements, known as the
certified unemployment funds. Although the funds are formally
associated with labour unions, it is the government which has
determined the most important regulations, including rules for the
benefit levels and criteria for receiving benefits. Furthermore, the
proportion of the payments made by these funds which is covered by
government contributions has increased significantly over time,
which means that the government plays a very important financial
role in this field.

Outside of the UI system administered by the labour unions, the
government carries the responsibility for a secondary compensation
system which is designed largely for new entrants in the labour
market, who are not usually covered by the unemployment funds'
operations. This programme is called cash benefit assistance
(*kontant arbetsmarknadsstöd*, or KAS).

In the area between the system of unemployment compensation
and that of pensions lies a government programme for 'early retirement motivated by labour market objectives'. Unemployed workers
above 60 years old may, under certain conditions, receive early
retirement benefits if there is a lack of job opportunities.

Gross government expenditure with respect to UI funds, KAS,
and early retirement for labour market reasons, are given in Table
11.1. Since 1974 the expenditure as a fraction of GNP has risen
markedly, reflecting in part the rising unemployment but also higher
government share of total paid-out benefits. In the peak years 1982
and 1983, the fraction was 0.9 per cent of GNP.

TABLE 11.1. *Gross government expenditure for unemployment benefits (in million SEK)*

Year	Subsidies to UI funds	Cash benefits	Early retirement for labour market reasons	Total	% of GNP
1974	543	64	n.a.	607	0.2
1975	524	67	n.a.	591	0.2
1976	628	105	n.a.	733	0.2
1977	905	181	n.a.	1,086	0.3
1978	1,412	255	n.a.	1,667	0.4
1979	1,559	283	n.a.	1,842	0.4
1980	1,593	321	n.a.	1,914	0.4
1981	2,423	409	240	3,072	0.5
1982	3,486	521	280	4,287	0.9
1983	5,057	797	310	6,165	0.9
1984	5,587	557	420	6,564	0.8
1985	5,765	389	720	6,874	0.8
1986	6,426	341	1,123	7,890	0.8
1987	7,078	347	1,128	8,553	0.9
1988	6,313	270	1,130	7,713	0.7

Sources: Labour Market Board (AMS), National Social Insurance Board and Statistics Sweden.

11.2. Different Forms of Compensation

11.2.1. Unemployment Insurance

The most important type of unemployment compensation in Sweden is unemployment insurance. This is, in principle, voluntary for individual employees. For most labour unions, however, membership in the UI fund is obligatory for union members, so that the voluntary nature is to some extent circumscribed. On the other hand, union membership is not compulsory for members of UI funds. Anyone who works in a field covered by a UI fund has the right to become a member; entry is restricted only by an age limit (over 15 and under 64) and a lower limit on working hours (17 hours per week).

Currently, the majority of the Swedish labour force (16–64 years old) belongs to some unemployment fund. Approximately 78 per cent were members as of 1 July 1985; membership for 1980, 1975, and 1970 was 72 per cent, 64 per cent, and 56 per cent respectively.

Permanent U I funds first appeared in the beginning of the 1890s with the establishment of the typographers' union in 1892. During the following decades, and particularly during the years 1912–20, many new funds were created. Requests for government assistance to the U I system became common quite early. After a long debate (which is analysed in an economic history dissertation by Edebalk 1975), Swedish parliament voted for a system in which the government would contribute to voluntary unemployment insurance funds, beginning in 1935. However, in order to qualify for government contributions the funds had to be certified; this has implied that parliament to a large extent decides the system of regulation. The unemployment funds themselves retained primarily overseeing and administrative functions.

Since 1935, the government's share of U I funds' expenses has had an increasing trend, as shown in Table 11.2. More than 90 per cent of the expenses are covered by the government, and the contribution from fees paid by the members has declined in proportion. Even though the membership fees are low in absolute terms, the relative variation between U I funds is considerable: in 1986 the *yearly* fees ranged from SEK 60 to SEK 550[1]. This is mainly a reflection of unemployment differentials between the industries and occupations covered by funds.

Of the government's contribution to the U I funds, 65 per cent is covered by a special payroll tax (*arbetsmarknadsavgiften*) which is equal for all firms. This payroll tax also covers 65 per cent of the costs for KAS benefits and some labour market policies. The rest of the contribution is financed from general taxes.

U I compensation is paid according to a daily benefit level (*dagpenning*), which, since 1974, has been considered as taxable income. Compensation is made for five days per week. Previously there was a mandatory five-day waiting period for which no compensation was made, but parliament decided to abolish this waiting period with effect from 1 January 1989.

Benefits can be received for 300 days, i.e. 60 weeks; persons over 55 years of age may collect benefits for 450 days, i.e. 90 weeks. The maximum benefit period was extended in 1968 and 1974. Individuals

---

[1] The average hourly wage rate for manufacturing workers in 1986 was approximately SEK 55.

TABLE 11.2. *Income and expenses of the UI funds (SEK millions)*

Year	Income			Expenses		Surplus	Government share of expenses
	Members	Government	Interest	Compensation	Administration		
1935–9	—	—	—	—	—	—	0.39
1940–4	—	—	—	—	—	—	0.46
1945–9	—	—	—	—	—	—	0.46
1950–4	—	—	—	—	—	—	0.46
1955–9	—	—	—	—	—	—	0.57
1959/60– 63/4	—	—	—	—	—	—	0.53
1964/5– 68/9	—	—	—	—	—	—	0.62
1969/70– 3	—	—	—	—	—	—	0.67
1974	226	543	60	678	44	107	0.75
1975	243	524	46	653	48	112	0.75
1976	263	628	55	763	53	131	0.77
1977	253	905	67	1,015	56	154	0.85
1978	251	1,412	85	1,542	69	138	0.88
1979	241	1,559	85	1,690	87	108	0.88
1980	245	1,593	125	1,730	94	138	0.87
1981	251	2,423	145	2,595	108	115	0.90
1982	319	3,486	138	3,880	132	− 68	0.87
1983	431	5,058	113	5,328	157	118	0.92
1984	459	5,587	117	5,863	169	130	0.93
1985	551	5,765	169	6,066	196	222	0.92
1986	587	6,426	159	6,760	213	199	0.92
1987	617	7,078	154	7,455	246	149	0.92
1988	637	6,313	174	6,713	273	138	0.90

Source: Labour Market Board (AMS), Insurance Unit.

under 55 had benefit periods of 150 days before 1974, whereas workers aged 55 or more had this benefit period before 1968. On 1 July 1968 the benefit period was extended to 450 days for all unemployed over the age of 60, and for some over 55. (The National Labour Market Board (AMS), could extend the benefit period if unemployment was caused by a firm's closure or a permanent reduction of personnel, *omställningsbidrag*.)

The qualification requirements for receiving benefits are numerous, complicated, and difficult to evaluate without a thorough study of how they are applied in practice. Part of the requirements aim at excluding groups with a temporary attachment to the labour market: if compensation had to be made also for those only temporarily 'visiting' the labour market, the total level of payments could obviously be very high. To avoid this problem, a 'membership requirement' is imposed: to qualify for benefits, the claimant must have paid membership dues to the U I fund for at least 12 months prior to the claim. Furthermore, there is a minimum requirement of 5 months' gainful employment during the 12 months preceding the period of unemployment. This is referred to as the 'work requirement'.

Another group of conditions depend on the unemployed person's search intensity and work requirements. The first of these is that the person must be registered at the employment office as seeking work. The unemployed individual has in general been required to contact the employment office regularly in person. During these visits he or she has had to show up a special card and get it signed in order to receive benefits. However, this requirement has gradually been reduced. In the 1930s, visits had to be daily. From the late 1970s till 1986, the requirement was one contact in every four-week period. During 1987 even this requirement was gradually eliminated, and now it is the task of the personnel at the employment office to contact the people seeking benefit. The main motivation for this change was the considerable resources needed to handle the card-signing.

Secondly, an offer of 'suitable' work must be accepted. The law (SFS 1973:370) formulates this requirement in the following way:

The job offer shall be considered suitable if, within the bounds of existing job opportunities, adequate consideration is taken of: 1) the person's work background and suitability for the particular kind of work as well as personal aspects of the job, 2) whether the wages and benefits are comparable to those determined by a collective agreement, or, if no collective agreement applies, are reasonable in comparison to those earned in equivalent jobs at comparable firms, 3) that no legal conflict (strike or lock out) is ongoing at the workplace, 4) and that the working conditions meet the requirements set in law and by the authorities.

The employment offices are responsible for implementing the work test. In doing this they use a handbook issued by the National

Labour Market Board in which this general formulation is made more specific. If the employment office finds that a claimant has turned down a suitable offer, a report is sent to the unemployment insurance fund for final decision, and the claimant may be denied benefits for 4 weeks. (From 1 July to 31 December 1982, the denial period was 6 weeks.) Violations of other conditions lead to shorter denial periods. If it becomes clear that the unemployed person will not accept offers of suitable employment—for example, if he or she repeatedly turns down offers—the U I fund may deny further benefits until the person has worked for a period of 30 days (prior to 1 July 1982, 20 days). In certain cases, 'suitable work' may include special job-training programmes as well as temporary jobs (relief works) provided by the Labour Market Board.

There is no information easily obtainable regarding the practical application of these rules and how the requirements have varied over time. However, the Labour Market Board collects statistics regarding the number of benefit denials which have occurred during the year and these are presented in Table 11.3. It appears that the number of yearly benefit denials has been between 1,750 and 4,530 since 1970. As a fraction of all who receive U I benefits during a year, this amounts to approximately 1 and 2 per cent. This indicates that the rules about job refusals are not mere formalities: the risk of losing benefits cannot be ignored by U I recipients who refuse to accept 'suitable work' or abstain from active search efforts.

The time pattern reveals two interesting features. First, the number of denials increased during the cyclical upturns 1972–4, 1977–80, and 1984–8. The most likely explanation is that the work test is more difficult to implement during recessions when the availability of jobs is scarce. The second feature is that the percentage of denials displays a trend decline. The reasons for this are unclear: it may be that the work test was enforced less strictly, or it may be that the unemployed have become more willing to accept job offers.

Similar disqualification rules apply to workers who are dismissed for failure to perform their job and those who leave their jobs voluntarily. For those who quit in connection with migration due to a spouse's change of job, a less stringent rule may be applied.

Special rules pertain to part-time unemployment. A person who searches for a full-time job and is working part-time can receive U I benefits to compensate for the loss of income because of part-time

TABLE 11.3. *Number of benefit denials*

Year	Unemployment insurance (UI)		Cash benefits (KAS)		
	No. of denials	% of total beneficiaries during year	No. of denials	% of total beneficiaries during year	No. of vacancies (thousands)
1970/1	2,920	—	—	—	—
1971/2	3,670	—	—	—	—
1972(Sept.)/ 1973(Aug.)	4,530	—	—	—	—
1974	4,210	—	1,900	3.4	49
1975	2,670	—	1,550	2.9	50
1976	2,340	—	1,310	2.1	46
1977	1,750	1.3	1,370	1.7	38
1978	2,240	1.3	1,490	1.5	35
1979	3,620	2.1	1,950	1.9	49
1980	4,180	2.3	1,860	1.8	54
1981	3,600	1.4	1,550	1.3	30
1982	2,850	0.9	1,110	0.8	20
1983	2,890	0.9	1,110	0.7	21
1984	2,880	0.8	560	0.4	29
1985	2,910	0.9	360	0.4	36
1986	3,240	0.9	276	0.4	39
1987	3,500	1.0	275	0.5	46
1988	4,250	1.3	200	0.5	52

Source: Labour Market Board (AMS), Insurance Unit.

unemployment. Through 30 June 1984, such complementary benefits could be received only for a limited period. The maximum period was defined in terms of daily benefit payments: the equivalent of 50 daily benefit payments could be collected. Hence, a half-time unemployed could collect benefits for 100 days (or 20 weeks). The unemployment insurance fund was, however, allowed to extend the period to an equivalent of 150 daily benefit payments.

From 1 July 1984, the rule about a maximum period was abandoned. It is a general opinion among civil servants working with the UI system that the number of part-time unemployed collecting benefits increased substantially at this time. However, there are no reliable statistics on this. The government reintroduced a maximum period equivalent to 150 daily benefit payments with effect from 1 July 1987.

11.2.2. Cash Benefits (KAS)

The rules which apply to unemployment insurance mean that a large number of unemployed persons are not entitled to benefits. Accordingly, in 1974 a complementary system of cash benefits was set up, KAS, which is financed entirely by the government. The annual expenses for KAS have amounted to about 10–15 per cent of the total government expenditure on unemployment compensation.

To qualify for cash benefits, either a work or a schooling requirement must be fulfilled. The former requires 5 months of work within the last 12 months. The schooling requirement means that those who have completed 12 months' full-time studies above the compulsory level or 5 months in the labour market training system (*arbetsmarknadsutbildning*) are eligible for benefits. A special qualifying period of 3 months is required for school leavers. In addition to those groups, persons over 60 years old who have exhausted their UI benefits are eligible for KAS compensation.

The maximum benefit period for KAS is 150 days (30 weeks). Those who are older than 55 years can receive payments for 300 days, and over-60s are entitled to payments for 450 days. (Before 1 July 1984 the benefit period was unlimited for those over 60 years of age.) During the 1980s the minimum age to qualify for KAS was raised twice: from 16 to 18 years of age on 1 January 1983, and to 20 years of age on 1 July 1985. For these groups KAS was replaced by guarantees of a job or schooling.

Like UI benefits, KAS compensation takes the form of daily benefits that are taxable, but the level of benefits is much lower than that of the UI funds. The same requirements regarding registration at the employment office and acceptance of suitable work apply, although the final decisions about benefit refusals for KAS are made by the county labour market boards. Data on such denials presented in Table 11.3 show that they exhibit a cyclical pattern similar to that for UI benefits. The strong decline during the 1980s was probably caused by the increased age limits for KAS compensation. The rules about compensation for part-time unemployed are also similar to those for unemployment insurance.

When KAS was set up in 1974, it replaced a system run by the local governments with partial financial support from the central government. However, this system covered only a very small fraction of the unemployed (see SOU 1971:44, p. 7). Therefore the introduction of KAS represented an extension of unemployment compensation to those who are not covered by UI funds.

11.2.3. Early Retirement

The early retirement programme is a government compensation system which is related to unemployment in several respects. Since 1 January 1974, early retirement benefits can be paid to all unemployed persons over 60 years old who have collected benefits from either the insurance funds or KAS for the maximum allowable time. This programme includes both general pension benefits and supplementary pensions (ATP).

This kind of early retirement is usually entitled 'early retirement based on purely labour market considerations' (*förtidspension på rent arbetsmarknadsmässiga grunder*). During the 1980s the number of early retirees has increased rapidly. As shown in Table 11.4, there were more retirees than unemployed aged 60–64 during the late 1980s. It is not likely that those who receive early retirement pensions continue to be counted as unemployed.

The formal requirement for this kind of early retirement is that the individual has collected UI benefits (and hence been registered at the employment office as a job searcher) for 90 weeks. However, it has become common that informal agreements about early retirement are reached between the laid-off individual, the firm, and the officers at the employment offices at the time of the lay-off. Because of the length of the benefit period, 58 years and 3 months is the critical age when decisions about early retirement can be taken. The possibility to reach such agreements has made early retirement an alternative when a firm wishes to reduce its personnel (see Nilsson and Stenkula 1978 and Hellberg and Wrethem 1978).

The major part of early retirement benefits are paid to disabled people; it is required that working capacity is permanently reduced by at least one-half. There is considerable informal evidence that the disability requirements are enforced less strictly for workers threatened by unemployment. Early retirement for disability reasons has increased rapidly over the past two decades (Wadensjö 1984).

TABLE 11.4. *Stock of unemployed, number of new retirees for labour market reasons, and stock of retirees, 60–64 years of age*

Year	Stock of unemployed	Yearly inflow of new retirees	Stock of[a] retirees
1977	4,900	1,700	n.a.
1978	7,200	2,050	n.a.
1979	7,300	2,600	n.a.
1980	5,800	3,600	5,000
1981	8,100	3,500	5,500
1982	12,700	3,700	5,900
1983	16,800	5,500	7,600
1984	20,400	9,100	12,000
1985	16,900	10,500	15,800
1986	14,000	7,500	16,500
1987[b]	7,000	5,900	15,500
1988[b]	5,600	5,400	14,600

[a] As of 31 Dec.
[b] New definition of unemployment.
Source: Statistics Sweden (SCB) and National Social Insurance Board (Riksförsäkringsverket).

11.2.4. Severance Pay

Outside of the government-administered and government-supported compensation systems, the labour market organizations have made certain agreements to compensate the older unemployed. Through agreement between the SAF (the Swedish employers' federation) and the LO (Swedish trade union confederation), special severance allowances have existed since 1965, and in 1967 a benefit system was established—the AGB system (*avgångsbidrag*), administered by the Labour Market Insurance Company (AFA).[2]

Severance pay can be claimed by persons 40 to 64 years of age. It is furthermore required that the person's employment is terminated due to personnel reduction, and that he has been employed by the dismissing employer for a certain time (until 1969 this requirement was 10 years, from 1969 to 1984 it was 5 years, and from 1985 it has

2 More detailed information about AGB is given in Edebalk and Wadensjö (1987).

been 3 years). Exceptions to this last requirement are made for certain groups—for example construction workers, painters, and seamen, where the requirement is a minimum of 5 years within the industry.

Compensation can be made in two stages. The first, an 'A' payment, is made upon dismissal in the form of a lump-sum payment of SEK 5,200 plus SEK 250 for each year of age exceeding 40 (applies to 1985). This means that a 50-year-old worker receives approximately one month's salary in severance pay. The payment is taxable, but is paid in addition to regular UI benefits.

Those who remain unemployed for longer and are 'actively searching' for a new job or have gone through retraining can receive an additional amount (the 'B' payment), which varies from SEK 6,000 to 27,000 and is not taxable. Half a year of unemployment is required for the highest amount. AGB may also be paid to those who had to leave jobs due to reasons of health. The minimum age limit in this case is 50 years. An additional requirement is that the latter claimant either obtains new work or begins searching through the employment office. Only 'A' payments are made in such cases.

From 1979 to 1985, between 4,000 and 13,000 insurance claimants have received AGB payments each year. More than half of these cases have also received 'B' payments. The total payments have reached 45 to 320 million SEK. For employers covered by the SAF–LO agreement, the fees for the insurance are determined as a proportion of the wage bill (0.3 per cent in 1985).

Agreements regarding severance compensation (AGE) to white-collar workers have been in operation since the end of the 1960s. A 1974 agreement on security of employment between SAF (Swedish employers' federation) and PTK (private white-collar workers' unions) has resulted in the majority of the white-collar workers in the private sector being included. The operation set up by the agreement is administered by a board called Trygghetsrådet SAF–PTK. The information presented here is based on the board's publications and annual reports.

In order to obtain benefits, the reason for the termination of employment must be a permanent lay-off. On the other hand, severance pay may be made without prior termination notification if the firm, local union, and the employee have agreed upon early retirement. In such cases, compensation can be made to the firm as partial financing for early retirement. Furthermore, it is required that the employee is at least 40 years old and has been employed by the firm for five years or more.

These severance benefits are made in several instalments. The first is paid at the day of job termination and amounts to one month's salary. It is taxable and is paid even to those who can get a new job immediately. If the period of unemployment becomes extended, further payments can be made. These are based partially on the local labour market situation, and are tax free up to a certain level.

Between 1978 and 1981, between 1,400 and 4,600 white-collar workers received severance benefits. Between SEK 30 and 65 million were made in payments. In addition, between SEK 36 and 370 million were accorded annually in early retirement benefits to between 300 and 2,300 white-collar workers. The payments were financed by a levy on the wage bill for white-collar workers (0.9 per cent in 1984), which is paid by the employers.

Taken together, these two types of severance pay were paid to between 6,000 and 18,000 blue- and white-collar workers during 1979–85. A crude estimate of the yearly inflow into unemployment indicates that between 10 and 20 per cent of all those above 40 years of age who became unemployed received severance pay in addition to the regular unemployment benefits. The total payments, including the early retirements of white-collar workers, were between SEK 140 and 760 million. In the peak year (1983), these payments amounted to around 12 per cent of the government's expenditure on UI, KAS, and early retirement.

11.2.5. Advance Notification of Lay-Offs

An additional administrative measure related to severance compensation should also be mentioned: the rules about advance notification of lay-offs. According to the law on employment protection (*Lagen om anställningsskydd*, LAS), an employer must issue notice of termination of employment at least one month in advance. This required notification period increases with the age of the employee; for example, it is two months for persons aged 25–30 years old and six months for persons of 45 or older. During the notification period, the employee has the right to draw his normal salary, regardless of the extent to which the job still exists. In the case that the firm declares bankruptcy, the 'notification' salary is protected by a government guarantee.

The regulations regarding 'notification' salaries and 'regular' unemployment benefits taken together can sometimes lead to a maximum compensation period of considerable length. It should also be observed that the employee has the right to visit the employment office, or in other ways search for work, during the notification period.

11.3. Compensated and Uncompensated Unemployment

The number of conditions that the unemployed must satisfy in order to receive some form of unemployment compensation is such that many unemployed do not qualify for benefits. It is therefore important to identify the coverage of each of the various forms of compensation.

Detailed information about this is obtainable from the unemployment statistics ('registered unemployment') produced by the employment exchange offices. Even though there is a slight discrepancy between registered unemployment and the more widely used unemployment data from the surveys conducted by Statistics Sweden, the two data sources reveal the similar cyclical and structural pattern.

The data given in Table 11.5 reveal that among all those unemployed in the period 1978–88, the proportion receiving no

TABLE 11.5. *Percentage of unemployed receiving some unemployment compensation by age-group and duration of unemployment*

Year	No. of unemployed	% receiving compensation			No. of unemployed	% receiving compensation		
		UI	KAS	None		UI	KAS	None
	Total Unemployed Population				*Unemployed Women Only*			
1978	102.6	45	14	41	51.8	39	17	44
1980	94.6	46	16	38	51.7	42	18	40
1982	161.3	50	14	36	81.8	45	17	38
1983	178.3	51	15	34	87.5	47	17	64
1984	159.3	58	11	31	79.1	55	13	32
1985	139.4	61	9	30	70.7	60	10	30
1986	133.5	63	8	29	67.2	63	8	29
1988	88.7	69	7	24	43.7	68	7	25

TABLE 11.5.   *Cont.*

Year	No. of unemployed	% receiving compensation			No. of unemployed	% receiving compensation		
		UI	KAS	None		UI	KAS	None
		< 19 years (both sexes)				*20–24 years* (both sexes)		
1978	18.5	9	26	65	19.6	37	19	44
1980	18.0	8	31	61	18.5	40	21	39
1982	26.7	12	27	62	31.8	47	20	33
1983	28.0	10	32	58	35.4	47	22	31
1984	10.4	9	11	80	34.5	49	22	30
1985	7.7	9	4	87	31.6	54	17	29
1986	7.4	12	1	87	31.7	57	13	30
1988	4.7	13	0	87	19.7	61	11	28
		25–54 years (both sexes)				*55 years and over* (both sexes)		
1978	46.8	49	10	41	17.7	77	9	14
1980	39.8	51	10	39	18.2	79	8	13
1982	76.1	56	10	34	26.7	76	7	17
1983	79.9	56	10	34	34.9	78	6	16
1984	75.0	57	10	33	39.4	80	5	13
1985	65.5	61	9	30	34.5	78	5	17
1986	65.5	65	8	27	28.9	78	4	18
1988	45.8	70	7	23	18.5	88	4	8
		Unemployed <3 months (both sexes)				*Unemployed >3 months* (both sexes)		
1978	61.5	37	13	50	41.1	56	17	27
1980	59.9	38	15	47	34.7	59	17	24
1982	95.9	44	14	42	65.4	59	15	26
1983	103.4	45	15	40	74.9	60	15	25
1984	92.0	48	13	39	67.3	71	9	20
1985	75.5	55	9	36	63.9	68	9	23
1986	70.1	58	8	34	63.4	68	8	24
1988	52.7	63	7	29	36.0	77	6	17

Source: Labour Market Board (AMS). Officers of the Board report that some of those who are reported as UI recipients might not actually receive benefits because of the waiting periods which existed in the system during the period. Hence, the percentage of unemployed who receive no compensation is underestimated.

compensation at all varied between 24 and 41 per cent. Furthermore even though there has been a clear decline in the percentage without compensation, a substantial number of unemployed none the less obviously lack economic compensation. It further appears that 7–16 per cent of the unemployed have received KAS, and 45–69 per cent have received unemployment insurance compensation.

The other parts of Table 11.5 give some breakdowns by sex, age group, and duration of unemployment. Unemployed women have been slightly less likely than men to receive unemployment compensation and more likely to receive KAS or no compensation. The share of unemployed without compensation falls with age. Similarly, KAS has been more frequent among the young. Finally, the short-term unemployed are more likely to lack compensation than the long-term unemployed.

Data availability for the period prior to 1978 is less satisfactory. Since the early 1960s, however, the Labour Force Survey has included a question to the unemployed about membership of a certified UI fund. Most of the members probably receive unemployment compensation. The exceptions would be mostly those who do not satisfy the membership and work requirements, those affected by the waiting-period rules, and those who have exhausted their benefits. It is therefore possible to obtain a crude estimate of the coverage of this type of compensation.

The data are presented in Table 11.6. The proportion of the unemployed who are members, and hence probably receive compensation, has risen sharply during the last decades. During the mid-1960s around 25 per cent of the unemployed were members of certified funds; in 1985 the figure had increased to 63 per cent. At the same time, 78 per cent of all labour force participants were members of a fund.

It is unlikely that unemployed individuals not covered by UI or KAS receive other forms of compensation, such as severance pay or early retirement benefits. Persons eligible for severance pay are most likely to be eligible for UI as well, and early retirees have typically left the labour force.

Unfortunately, we do not know to what degree those who lack unemployment compensation receive public welfare payment. There is also a lack of information about combined benefits (unemployment compensation and welfare payments). Our empirical knowledge about the income situation of the unemployed is con-

TABLE 11.6. *Percentage of unemployed persons who are members of UI funds, by sex and age group*

Year	Both sexes		Men	Women
	16–74	16–24	16–74	16–74
1963	21	—	34	07
1964	28	—	42	08
1965	25	—	40	08
1966	31	—	48	11
1967	33	—	45	18
1968	36	—	46	19
1969	37	—	49	21
1970	41	—	52	27
1971	41	—	52	27
1972	40	—	49	29
1973	40	—	50	28
1974	39	—	46	32
1975	40	—	50	31
1976	41	—	47	35
1977	43	—	49	39
1978	50	—	53	45
1979	48	32	52	44
1980	48	36	53	43
1981	54	41	60	48
1982	55	39	60	50
1983	57	42	62	50
1984	63	50	65	60
1985	63	50	64	62
1986[a]	65	58	66	64
1987[b]	64	—	65	63
1988[b]	61	—	62	60
1989[b]	59	—	60	59

[a] 16–64 years.
[b] 16–64 years, new definition of unemployment.
Source: Statistics Sweden (SCB), Labour Force Surveys (AKU).

sequently rather deficient. Further, it is important to understand which *types* of unemployment are covered by compensation and which are not—as shown above, UI benefits may be paid for radically different kinds of unemployment—for example, involuntary dismissal, short-term lay-offs, and voluntary quits. Information of this kind would be valuable for an analysis of the distributional and incentive effects of unemployment insurance, but the data available are deficient in spite of the fact that the unemployment funds receive such data as part of their normal operation: each claimant of UI benefits must present a report from their former employer stating the reason for leaving the job. The UI funds can in principle store and publish this information, but in fact only a few white-collar insurance funds do so. Table 11.7 presents some of these data for the period 1980–6. Among the mining and manufacturing white-collar workers, 31–46 per cent of the unemployed persons had their employment terminated by the employer. Note that roughly 15–30 per cent of unemployed white-collar workers quitted voluntarily.

11.4. Rules Affecting Temporary Lay-offs[3]

Special rules pertain to *'permitteringar'* which are temporary lay-offs lasting in general a couple of weeks: such temporary lay-offs are not considered to terminate the formal job contract between the employer and the employee.

Some groups, such as all white-collar workers and some LO groups, have reached agreements with the employers that do not allow temporary lay-offs at all, but for most blue-collar workers they are permissible. The rules which affect these lay-offs are determined both by law and by agreements.

The laws have changed several times during the last decades. The general trend has been that the employers have been forced to pay 'temporary lay-off wages' during successively longer periods of lay-offs. The government, via subsidized UI benefits has covered successively shorter periods. Thus, the degree of 'experience rating'—the term used about a system which forces the individual firm to pay the costs of the lay-offs it causes—concerning temporary lay-offs has consequently increased in Sweden during the last decades.

The laws which were in effect during the period 1974 to 1984 made a distinction between continuous temporary lay-offs and recurrent ones (e.g. every other week, a couple of days per week, or a shorter

---

[3] This section draws heavily on Edebalk and Wadensjö (1986).

TABLE 11.7. *Reasons for unemployment within some white-collar UI funds (%)*

	1980	1982	1984	1986
Mining and manufacturing white-collar workers (Industritjänstemännen)				
Number of persons	2,048	3,836	5,301	5,229
Fraction job-losers (reorganization, personnel reduction)	40	46	43	31
Voluntary quits	30	22	15	19
Studies	4	5	9	8
Other	26	27	33	42
Government white-collar workers (Statstjänstemännen)				
Number of persons	1,490	2,676	4,488	7,000
Termination of temporary job	58	72	74	75
Job losers (reorganization, personnel reduction)	12	6	7	7
Fraction who quit voluntarily and moved with spouse	11	8	7	6
Other voluntary quits	19	16	12	12
Local government white-collar workers (Kommunaltjänstemännen)				
Number of persons[a]	4,246	7,634	11,646	14,763
Termination of temporary job	70	80	84	86
Voluntary quits	27	18	15	13
Whereof quit voluntarily and moved with spouse	12	10	12	n.a.
Other	3	2	1	1

[a] Number of spells of compensation per year.
Source: Enegren (1988).

work day). In the case of a *continuous lay-off*, the law forced the employer to pay temporary lay-off wages, almost equal to the ordinary wage, from the third week onwards. UI benefits were allowed during the second week but not during the first, due to the one-week waiting period, but an agreement between unions and employers forced the employer to pay temporary lay-off wages during this week.

In the case of *recurrent lay-off*, U I benefits were to be paid during 5 effective weeks per calendar year. The first effective week and all periods of temporary lay-off in excess of 6 weeks (30 days) were to be covered by temporary lay-off wages paid by the employer. Consequently, U I benefits could be used for longer periods in case of recurrent lay-offs. Hence, the degree of experience rating was lower for recurrent lay-offs during 1974–84.

The new laws from 1985 onwards are slightly more complicated, although the distinction between continuous and recurrent temporary lay-offs has been abandoned. Furthermore, U I benefits can no longer be paid to temporarily laid off workers.

The new laws require that the employer pays temporary lay-off wages during the whole period, but the government compensates the employer for parts of his costs. Fig. 11.1 shows the division of costs between the employer and the government. It can be seen that the government covers most of the costs for certain effective days of temporary lay-offs (3–10, 13–20, and 23–30) and the rest is paid by the individual firm.

It is hard to say how the degree of experience rating has been affected by this change in the rules. However, it is clear that the

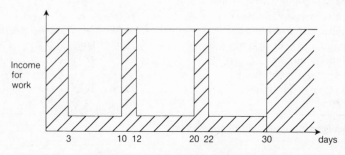

Fig. 11.1. The employer's and the government's share of costs for temporary lay-offs according to the new rules from 1985

Note: The areas with diagonal lines indicate what is compensated by the employer. The empty areas indicate what the government pays. Days means 'effective work days'.

Source: Edebalk and Wadensjö (1986).

relatively generous treatment of recurrent lay-offs in comparison with continuous lay-offs has been eliminated.

Unfortunately, the statistical information about the number of temporary lay-offs in the Swedish labour market is very meagre. The available information, which must be treated as 'indicative', shows that temporary lay-offs, as would be expected, have decreased in magnitude as the degree of experience rating increased.

In the early 1980s the total number of temporary lay-offs was low by international standards; including part-time (recurrent) lay-offs, they probably amounted to no more than a couple of per cent of total unemployment.

11.5. Benefit Levels and Replacement Ratios

Unemployment benefits are typically related to the unemployed worker's income when employed; this permits specification of a *replacement ratio*, the ratio of net income if unemployed to that in work. Measures of replacement ratios are widely used in empirical studies of the effects of unemployment compensation.

Calculations of replacement ratios involve a number of different problems. One is how a worker's expected income if employed should be specified. The answer depends on which labour force category we focus on. For instance, unemployed individuals have in general lower potential earnings than those in work, women have lower earnings than men, and young workers face lower expected wages than adult employees.

Replacement ratios are also affected by the duration of the unemployment spell. This is partly due to the one-week waiting period, during which no benefits are paid out; it is also a consequence of the interaction between the U I system and the progressive income tax system. The waiting period causes the replacement ratio for a spell of unemployment, referred to as the 'average' replacement ratio, to increase with the duration of the spell.

Progressive income taxes causes the average tax rate to fall as the duration of unemployment increases. The after-tax replacement ratio is therefore greater than the replacement ratio before taxes. However, for short spells, the difference between replacement ratios calculated before and after tax are negligible; the reason is simply that short spells entail little loss in yearly income and therefore a negligible reduction in the average tax rate.[4]

The average replacement ratio gives a measure of the relative income compensation during an unemployment spell of a given length. The 'marginal' replacement ratio is based on a different concept. It relates income if unemployed one additional week to potential income $_t$ if employed during this week. For a worker who just has passed his one-week waiting period, the marginal replacement ratio is (roughly) given by the ratio between benefits and earnings. (Income tax effects are not important, since the individual's marginal tax rate if unemployed one extra week will be roughly the same as the marginal tax rate if employed.) For a worker who has exhausted his benefits, the marginal replacement ratio is obviously zero.

Marginal and average replacement ratios are linked to different theoretical frameworks. The marginal replacement ratio has its orientation towards search theory, where job acceptance decisions are made on the basis of a comparison between the value of an offer and the value of continued search. The average replacement ratio, on the other hand, has links to classical labour supply models of voluntary unemployment. The average replacement ratio shows a worker's incentive to take, or retain, a job instead of spending a given number of weeks in unemployment. In some models, including models of union wage setting, the benefit level, rather than the replacement ratio, appears as a crucial variable that influences unemployment.

It is obvious that a tax system which is tied to the calendar year causes the rate of compensation to depend on how a certain period of unemployment is distributed across the year. Compare, for example, the situation of two otherwise identical individuals who each experience a period of unemployment of one year, but the first becomes unemployed at the beginning of the year and the other in the middle of the year. The average replacement ratio will be higher

---

[4] The after-tax average replacement ratio is given by the expression

$$R = \frac{B(D-1)(1-t')}{D \cdot W(1-t)}$$

where B is the weekly benefit level, D is unemployment duration in weeks, W is weekly earnings, t' is the average income tax rate if unemployed D weeks, and t is the tax rate if not unemployed. For short spells of unemployment, t is approximately equal to t'.

for the former individual, simply because income tax rates will be lower.

11.5.1. Trends in Benefit Levels and Replacement Ratios

Real benefits for insured workers (i.e. members of UI funds) have increased substantially since the mid-1960s. Fig. 11.2 shows the development of real, after-tax, benefit levels for a worker receiving the average granted amount of UI compensation. The purchasing power of benefits displayed an upward trend from 1965, and by the early 1970s it was around 50 per cent higher than it was in the mid-1960s. This trend was broken, however, in the late 1970s.

Replacement ratios for 'average unemployed workers' are shown in Fig. 11.3. (Details of the calculations are given in the Appendix to Chapter 15.) The calculations recognize the trend increase in UI

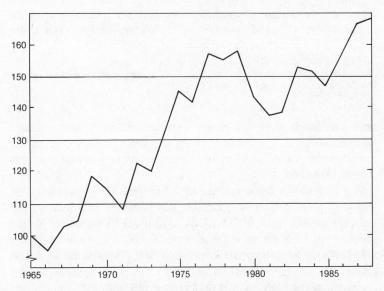

Fig. 11.2.   The development of real after-tax benefits for insured workers, 1965–1988 (Index: 1965 = 100)

Note: The benefit level is the average benefit granted (*tillförsäkrad dagpenning*). The income tax rate applied presupposes three months of unemployment. Benefits were not taxable before 1974.

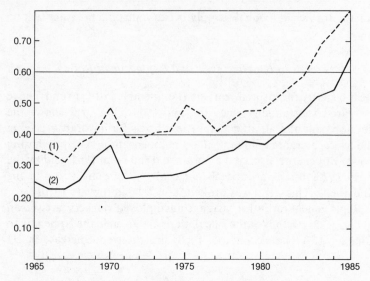

Fig. 11.3. Percentage of unemployment days per year covered by UI compensation (1), and average (after-tax) replacement ratios for unemployed workers (2), 1965–1986

Note: Unemployment spells of average lengths are assumed. Details of the calculations are given in the Appendix.

coverage; unemployed workers are much more likely to receive compensation in the 1980s than in the 1960s, partly due to the introduction of KAS in 1974 and partly due to the growing membership in UI funds.

Fig. 11.3 shows replacement ratios for spells of average lengths. The strong upward trend is notable and is caused primarily by the growing membership in UI funds. Around 30 per cent of weeks spent in unemployment were covered by UI compensation in the mid-1960s, and twenty years later the coverage had risen to above 60 per cent. On average, unemployed workers could expect to receive 20–30 per cent of lost income in the late 1960s, but more than 50 per cent in the mid-1980s.

Average replacement ratios for insured workers are displayed in Fig. 11.4. Female replacement ratios are above those of males because of lower female earnings. Because male wage rates have

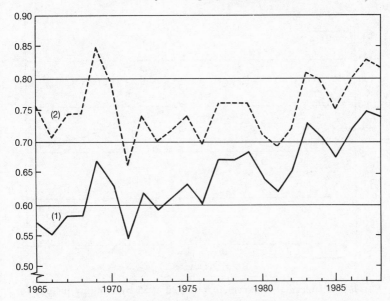

Fig. 11.4. Average replacement ratios among insured male (1) and female (2) blue-collar workers, 1965–1988

Note: Unemployment spells of three months' duration are assumed.

grown slower than female wages, male replacement ratios have increased faster than replacement ratios for women.

Benefit levels have an upper limit in nominal terms, with the restriction that no more than 91.7 per cent of previous income can be covered (90 per cent from 1 July 1989). Replacement ratios are therefore falling with a worker's expected income if employed. Consider a worker who has passed his waiting period of one week and who compares his income next week if unemployed to his prospective income in work during this week. Fig. 11.5 shows how this marginal replacement ratio varies with potential earnings for workers with U I compensation and K A S. A male blue-collar worker with average earnings faces a marginal replacement ratio of 75–80 per cent. A male white-collar worker with the average manu-facturing salary faces a marginal replacement ratio of around 50–60 per cent. Workers with K A S experience much lower marginal (and average) replacement ratios.

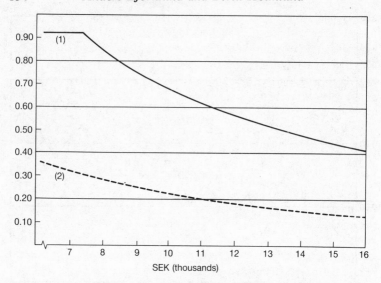

Fig. 11.5. Marginal replacement ratios in 1985 by monthly income for workers with UI compensation (1) and KAS (2)

Note: The calculations are based on daily benefits of SEK 315 (UI compensation) and SEK 100 (KAS), respectively.

In conclusion, the Swedish UI system has become successively more generous since the mid-1960s. The maximum benefit periods have increased substantially, and there is also a marked trend increase in UI coverage, partly due to the introduction of KAS and partly due to the growing membership in UI funds. Real net benefits for insured workers have increased by 50 per cent since 1965; real wages have increased at a slightly slower pace, and replacement ratios for insured workers have thus risen.

As noted in Chapter 3, other improvements have also taken place for workers threatened with unemployment. Older workers can receive severance pay on terms set in agreements between labour unions and the employers' federation. And the legislation on employment protection—involving, *inter alia*, advance notification rules—has facilitated on-the-job search before job loss actually occurs.

A caveat is in order, however, regarding the calculations presented above. They are based on various hypothetical characteristics of unemployed individuals. Unfortunately, we do not have much information from household survey data on *actual* replacement ratios. The diversity of the circumstances of the unemployed (stressed by e.g. Atkinson and Micklewright 1985), can of course not be illuminated without access to such data.

11.6. The Relationship to Labour Market Policy

Sweden is famous for emphasizing 'active' measures to help unemployed to get jobs or training rather than 'passive' help by means of unemployment compensation. The relationship between the arsenal of active labour market policies and the unemployment compensation system is so close that the latter system is not adequately described without the active measures. The causal relationship goes in both directions: many unemployed enter various labour market programmes, and participation in such programmes can make individuals eligible for new spells of unemployment compensation.

First of all, the unemployed can receive free services from the employment offices. Since the late 1970s, it has been compulsory to notify employment offices of all vacancies; these offices are available all over the country and provide nationwide information about vacancies as well as counselling of various sorts. The services include coverage of travelling costs to visit employers at places other than the home town.

In addition, all unemployed (plus those who run the risk of becoming unemployed) who move to another place for a job are eligible to mobility grants, which cover the direct mobility costs plus an extra amount which equals approximately two monthly salaries.[5] Retraining courses are also available, the trainee receiving a stipend which in general equals (but sometimes exceeds) the unemployment benefit.

For many years, more resources have been spent on subsidizing such activities than on cash payments. Some data are presented in Table 11.8.

---

[5] The extra amount (*starthjälpen*) was abolished on 1 July 1987.

TABLE 11.8.   *Expenditures on cash payments and various labour market policies in Sweden (SEK millions)*

Year	Cash payments	Employment offices	Mobility grants	Retraining	Temporary jobs
1979/80 (cyclical peak)	1,870	832	165	3,714	3,131
1982/3 (cyclical downturn)	4,525	1,022	146	3,810	4,299

Source: SOU 1984:31.

It is important to emphasize that the work test in the UI system is also enforced by the employment offices. Hence, the employment offices are simultaneously providing labour market information; implementing labour market policy measures, like training, mobility grants, and certain wage subsidies; and enforcing the work test. It is likely that the availability of such measures makes it easier to implement the work test.

Job creation programmes have also been targeted for employment of registered unemployed. The most important programme is the *beredskapsarbete* (temporary job or relief job) which in general lasts for five or six months. The number of persons employed in this way has varied cyclically between 0.5 and 1.5 per cent of the labour force during the 1970s and 1980s.

The possibility to escape unemployment by entering a labour-market programme was strengthened in October 1983 when UI recipients were given the right to a temporary job (*beredskapsarbete*) at the end of the benefit period. At first this did not apply to people over the age of 60, but from July 1984 the right was extended to all recipients of UI.

As very few applicants for such temporary jobs have been denied a job in practice this has introduced a job guarantee for the long-term unemployed. Because the typical length of a temporary job equals the length of the work requirement to be eligible for another period of UI benefits—5 months—it is in principle also an income guarantee; up to 60 weeks of unemployment compensation can be followed by a temporary job for 5 months which is followed by another period of UI benefits, etc. Not very much is known about the way this job guarantee works. During the first half of 1984, the National Labour Market Board carried out a follow-up study in three counties. This showed that about one-third of those who could apply for a temporary job did so.

The right to a job lasting 5 months, which equals the work requirement for a new benefit period illustrates that there also is a causal link *from* labour market policies *to* unemployment. Participation in training programmes can also make a person eligible for future unemployment benefits. Until June 1986, 2 months of training could be counted as work to fulfil the work requirement for UI- or KAS benefits. From July 1986 onwards, all (completed) training has been counted as work. Until June 1984, the educational requirement to receive KAS was fulfilled after 3 months in AMU training (5 months from June 1984 to June 1986). Since July 1986 this rule has been irrelevant since training can be counted as work.

12

Incentive Effects

12.1. Introduction

The past two decades have seen considerable theoretical and empirical interest in understanding the incentive effects of UI. This interest has partly been driven by new perspectives on unemployment associated with concepts such as the 'natural' or 'equilibrium' unemployment rate. The new interest in natural rate theories reflects new theoretical contributions. Three theoretical perspectives are of particular relevance here, namely (*a*) search theory, (*b*) contract theory, and (*c*) bargaining and trade union theory. These different frameworks have all something to say about the way UI may influence unemployment.

Job search theory was worked out and refined during the 1970s, and has focused on the behaviour of the individual unemployed worker. The theory provides a natural extension of the conventional static labour supply model to deal with a situation where the worker has to search for a wage rather than simply adjust work hours to the prevailing wage. Although the theory has been elaborated in various directions, it is fair to say that it remains as essentially a supply-side micro-theory.

Search theory may be less relevant when it comes to cases where workers are temporarily laid off from their employer. During a short spell of temporary lay-off, the worker may have rather weak incentives to search for jobs elsewhere; he may prefer just to sit and wait for a recall from his employer. The importance of temporary lay-offs differs widely between different countries, for example between Sweden and the United States; whereas temporary lay-offs have accounted for only a few per cent of total unemployment in Sweden, the corresponding figure for the United States has been in the range of 10–20 per cent. The theoretical work on employment contracts emerging during the 1970s has shed new light on the determinants of temporary lay-offs and on the role of UI and its financing in that respect.

The 1980s have seen a rather dramatic increase in studies of trade union behaviour and wage bargaining. This interest is influenced by a desire to understand the sources of real-wage stickiness, which is thought to be crucial for the behaviour of unemployment. UI benefits play a role in these union and bargaining models, a role that is very natural given the models' basic assumptions.

We feel that the different theoretical perspectives complement each other and provide important insights into the role of UI in determining unemployment. We proceed in Section 12.2 by offering a brief survey of some of the key predictions from the different theories. Section 12.3 reviews the empirical work in the field and discusses the Swedish experience.

12.2. Theoretical Issues

12.2.1. Job Search and Labour Supply

The basic content of the micro-theory of labour market search is by now well known, but it might be useful to summarize some major points. The standard model portrays an unemployed individual searching for acceptable offers. The worker's objective is often taken to be maximization of lifetime income, but may in more general models be maximization of lifetime utility. In the simplest model, the worker draws in each period a wage offer from an exogenous and known wage offer distribution. Optimal behaviour is characterized by a reservation wage rule that separates acceptable offers from unacceptable ones. If the escape rate from unemployment is denoted by μ, the offer distribution by $F(\cdot)$, and the reservation wage by w^*, we have

$$\mu = 1 - F(w^*). \tag{1}$$

It is straightforward to show that the worker's reservation wage is increasing in the benefit level, so a higher benefit level will reduce the escape rate (increase the duration of unemployment) through a lower acceptance probability.

There are, however, other and perhaps more important avenues through which benefits may influence the pace at which workers exit from unemployment. The impact on *search effort* is one example. Indeed, it seems quite plausible that workers may have to search for job openings *per se*, rather than just having to choose, at a fixed search cost, between 'good' and 'bad' offers. There is thus a case for incorporating endogenous search effort into any model that attempts to capture the real world. Such models have been worked out, and they predict, as should be expected, that an increase in the benefit level reduces the worker's optimal search effort. (Burdett and Mortensen, 1978; Albrecht *et al.* 1986.) It is natural to think in terms of a function that generates offers, and we denote this function by $\theta(\cdot)$; it may be interpreted as the probability of receiving an offer during a short time-interval. The function $\theta(\cdot)$ is increasing in search effort (s), and it may be influenced by various other characteristics (Z) specific to the individual or the labour market. The exit rate thus takes the form

$$\mu = \theta(s, \mathbf{Z})[1 - F(w^*)] \qquad (2)$$

and both search effort and the reservation wage are now endogenous choice variables, influenced by variables like unemployment benefits but also by variables in the $\mathbf{Z}$ vector. For example, an improvement in the worker's labour market—a larger flow of offers or a rightward shift of the offer distribution—will in general affect both search effort and the reservation wage. A common empirical procedure expresses (2) as a reduced-form equation where the choice variables are substituted out.

Real-world U I systems have typically a fixed maximum duration for benefit payments; we noted above that the Swedish system now involves benefit exhaustion after 60 or 90 weeks. A rise in the maximum length of benefit payments can be expected to have effects similar to those produced by a rise in the benefit level; the escape rate is likely to fall as workers become more choosy or reduce their search effort. U I systems with a fixed maximum duration period may also produce falling reservation wages over the spell of unemployment, and therefore lead to 'positive duration dependence'; the probability of leaving unemployment would then increase as the duration of the spell increases. Although newly laid-off workers will raise their reservation wages when the benefit level is increased, it can also be shown that workers close to benefit exhaustion will *reduce* their reservation wages when the benefit level is raised. Workers take future separation probabilities into account in their job acceptance decisions, and a higher benefit level makes it therefore more advantageous to have a job; workers near the end of the benefit period react by becoming less choosy. (Mortensen 1977 and Burdett 1979 deal with these issues.)

Research on incentive effects of U I has also paid some attention to 'entitlement effects'. How does a higher benefit level affect the behaviour of unemployed individuals for whom unemployment compensation is not available? Search theory predicts that higher benefits will make it *more* attractive to accept offers and thereby qualify for benefits in the future. Unemployment duration should therefore fall among individuals not entitled to benefits. In the Swedish context, this may be relevant for new entrants to the labour market who do not receive regular U I compensation or K A S.

In Sweden, a large part of the available jobs are temporary in the sense that the termination date is fixed in advance. The job-seeker knows in such cases that the work will cease after, say, 6 months. A higher benefit level makes the uninsured worker more inclined to accept such temporary jobs and thereby qualify for future benefits.

The effects of U I on job search behaviour is closely related to how the work test is enforced. The standard job search model assumes that job refusal does not mean benefits are withdrawn, but this is of course what a strict work test is supposed to do. Although it is difficult to obtain information about how the work test is applied in practice, it is clear that unemployed persons in Sweden can to some extent refuse offers without losing their benefits, for example if they are overqualified for a certain job or are regarded as being locationally tied. Offers may also be received and rejected outside the employment offices.

Unemployment compensation can be perceived as a subsidy of labour market work, and this brings up a possible link between U I benefits and labour supply. Since labour force participation is associated with certain risks of unemployment, the reduction in the cost of unemployment will raise the relative earnings from work in the labour market. Changes in the benefit system may thus increase labour force participation (Hamermesh 1979, 1980).

U I benefits are to some extent tied to previous income; for example, the daily benefit-pay rises with a shift from part-time to full-time work. By working more weeks (or more hours per week), the employed person can thus affect the level of his future hypothetical unemployment benefits. Higher replacement ratios may therefore increase labour supply among employed workers (Yaniv 1982).

Our discussion so far has ignored the obvious fact that U I benefits have to be financed in one way or another. Financing U I benefits by income or payroll taxes is likely to reduce the worker's net real wage, and this may induce additional labour supply effects. General equilibrium analysis of this problem is however almost non-existent in the literature. (McLure 1977 and Barron *et al.* 1986 are among the few exceptions.)

The standard search models discussed above have little to say about how U I affects the distribution of wage offers. Higher benefits may affect wage setting, for example through higher reservation wages among job searchers. A satisfactory equilibrium model of unemployment cannot ignore wage determination, and this has been brought up in a number of recent studies to which we now turn.

12.2.2. *Wage Determination*

Higher reservation wages imply longer spells of unemployment so long as the wage offer distribution remains unaffected. One can, however, reasonably argue that changes in workers' reservation wages will influence firms' wage setting. Few papers have addressed these issues within a search equilibrium framework; the exceptions include Albrecht and Axell (1984) and Lang (1985). A general result in these papers is that the U I-induced increase in equilibrium unemployment is less than what partial supply-side models suggest. One mechanism driving this result is that a higher benefit level brings about a reallocation of firms in the wage structure. Low-wage firms find it more difficult to recruit workers when reservation wages increase, and they therefore raise their wage offers. But when the frequency of low-wage firms decline, it may take a shorter time for job-seekers to find acceptable offers.

Unemployment benefits may influence wage-setting in various other ways, aside from the possible mechanism mentioned above. U I benefits play a significant role in the rapidly growing literature on wage bargaining and trade union behaviour. A popular approach portrays the union as attempting to maximize the individual worker's expected income (or expected utility). A prediction from standard models is that higher benefits will raise the union's desired wage rate by reducing the marginal cost of a wage increase. Since higher benefits reduce the income (or utility) differential between employment and unemployment, the union becomes more inclined to push for higher wages, thereby reducing employment by moving up on the labour demand curve. This result follows from models of a monopoly union, where the wage rate is unilaterally set by the union, but also from models with bargaining over wages (Oswald 1985; Holmlund 1989).

Like most search models, union models have typically ignored how an increase in benefits is financed. An exception is Oswald (1982), who explicitly deals with how a rise in the benefit level affects wages if it is financed by taxes on workers or firms. It is shown that, under reasonable assumptions, higher benefits still tend to raise wages.

The union wage response to an increase in unemployment benefits may be crucially dependent on the extent to which the union perceives a direct link between its own wage choice and the taxes needed to finance benefits. If the union perceives no such link, it may react by pushing up wages for two reasons: in addition to the benefit-induced wage push, there may also be a wage response to the higher tax that is needed to finance the higher benefit level.

The Swedish arrangement, with heavily subsidized union-affiliated UI funds, adds new aspects to the financing issues. The subsidy is linked to unemployment in the fund; the higher is unemployment, the higher are subsidies to the UI fund. It can be shown that a less progressive UI subsidy system will reduce the union's desired wage (Holmlund and Lundborg 1988). The 'price' of employment-reducing wage hikes increases if union members, through higher UI premiums, have to finance a larger fraction of increases in benefits.

Again, this result is sensitive to the bargaining environment. If wage setting takes place at the firm level, UI premiums will be exogenous to the negotiated wage outcome in the single firm. A reduction in government subsidies will then be equivalent to higher taxes on workers, and this may well lead to a positive wage response and hence lower employment.

Unemployment benefits may also influence wage setting according to efficiency wage models. Firms may have incentives to pay a wage exceeding the market-clearing wage, for example in order to reduce quits or improve work morale. Quits into unemployment become more attractive if unemployment compensation is generous, and the cost of being fired is also lower in an economy with high UI benefits. Efficiency wage models therefore predict a positive relationship between the equilibrium unemployment rate and the level of benefits (Johnson and Layard 1986).

12.2.3. Temporary Lay-offs

We noted in Chapter 11 that Swedish firms have to pay a worker on temporary lay-off his ordinary wage provided that the lay-off period extends beyond a certain number of weeks. The Swedish system thus involves an element of experience rating, with some features in common with the US system. US firms have to pay a UI tax that is dependent on the firm's lay-off behaviour. Experience rating is imperfect, however, in the sense that the firm is typically not liable for the full amount of benefit payments to its ex-employees.

Feldstein (1976) argued in an influential theoretical paper that imperfect experience rating was a crucial explanation of temporary lay-offs in the US; an increase in experience rating would lead to fewer lay-offs, according to Feldstein's analysis. The framework Feldstein used was contract theory. The model considers the behaviour of a single firm with a pool of 'attached' workers. There is uncertainty about product demand, and the firm and its workers have to agree on a contract that specifies employment, wages, and perhaps work hours for every possible realization of demand. For example, the contract specifies wages and employment for booms as well as slumps. The number of laid-off workers in each state is simply given by the difference between the number of attached workers and the number of employed ones.

In Feldstein's analysis there is an unambiguous relationship between experience rating and lay-offs: an increase in experience rating reduces lay-offs. Imperfect experience rating may be viewed as a subsidy that can only be realized if some workers are laid off. A lower subsidy should therefore reduce lay-offs.

Although the intuition behind Feldstein's result seems straightforward, its general validity has been questioned. For example, Burdett and Hool (1983) demonstrate that the result is somewhat sensitive to assumptions about workers' attitude towards risk. Feldstein assumed risk-neutral workers, but the negative relationship between lay-offs and experience rating does not necessarily carry over to the case where workers are risk-averse.

Most contributions to contract theory have taken the number of workers attached to the firm as exogenous. Burdett and Wright (1987) present a model where the number of workers attached is endogenous. This turns out to have important implications for the analysis of experience rating. It holds that higher experience rating reduces lay-offs, but also reduces the number of attached workers. The intuitive explanation is that higher experience rating increases labour costs, and this is bound to reduce the number of workers that the firm is willing to hire. The effect on average employment is in general ambiguous, reflecting the lower lay-off rate as well as the lower number of attached workers; under certain relatively plausible conditions it can be shown that average employment falls as experience rating is increased.

12.2.4. Resource Allocation

U I benefits and the way they are financed also have implications for resource allocation. Suppose that an individual has to choose between working in two different industries, A and B, which are differentiated with respect to wages and patterns of demand. The demand for labour in industry A is stable throughout the year and/or business cycle, while employment in the other industry shows seasonal and/or business cycle fluctuations. An acceptance of a job offer in industry A implies a small risk of unemployment, while the choice of industry B bears a larger probability of being unemployed during some period.

Suppose that the individual's decision depends on a comparison of the expected net incomes of the two alternatives. It is clear that a higher level of unemployment benefits makes the industry with fluctuating unemployment more attractive. Unemployment benefits financed by general taxes is equivalent to an industry-specific wage subsidy in which the subsidy is paid to the employees instead of the employers. The labour supply facing industry A is reduced at the same time as that facing B increases.

In the above discussion, we have assumed that the individual has complete knowledge of employment fluctuations between industries as well as about the way in which these affect his own chances of unemployment. We may also allow for the existence of differences in uncertainty with regard to the income and employment outcomes between industries. In a competitive market for unemployment insurance (if such could exist), the insurance premiums would become differentiated with respect to the risk differentials (see Beenstock and Brasse 1986). Unemployment benefits financed by general taxes would therefore be a subsidy for the risky industries and a tax for the low-risk industries. Resource allocation would be distorted.

In conclusion, a UI system with liberal rules on seasonal unemployment, as well as where risk differences are not reflected in the contributions to the costs of the system, leads to distortions of resource allocation similar to those of direct, industry-specific subsidies. It is not easy to state the order of magnitude of these effects in the Swedish case; that would require information on the wage elasticities of the demand for labour across industries as well as labour supply elasticities with regard to the expected income differences between industries. Some estimates of the implicit wage subsidies are given in the following discussion of Swedish experiences.

12.3. Empirical Evidence

12.3.1. From Theory to Empirical Work

Empirical studies of the effects of UI on unemployment have been guided by different theoretical frameworks. The new contributions to search theory in the 1970s have been very influential; virtually all empirical studies of unemployment duration draw more or less explicitly on search theory foundations. The growing interest in contracting models seen in the 1970s has analogously contributed to a number of studies concerned with the effects of UI and experience rating on temporary lay-offs. The emergence of a variety of trade union and bargaining models during the past ten years have been followed by a growing number of empirical studies where there is a role for unemployment benefits in wage-setting equations.

Empirical work in this field has typically not been directly preoccupied with the ultimate effects of UI on unemployment. Researchers have in general focused on some components of unemployment, such as the duration of unemployment spells or the extent of temporary lay-offs, or on some variable that is thought to be causally related to unemployment, such as labour costs. Most of the studies are based on British or US data, but there are also some studies from other countries, including Sweden. Most US studies have been micro-econometric, using cross-sectional or longitudinal data pertaining to unemployed individuals with varying benefit levels. The British studies have, on the other hand, often exploited time series on benefits, unemployment, unemployment outflow, or wages.

The use of time-series modelling in this field has its pros and cons. We have already noted that it may be misleading to use partial, supply-side models as a basis for policy conclusions about the impact of unemployment compensation; results from partial models do not necessarily carry over to a general equilibrium framework. Micro-econometric studies have typically explored variations in duration among unemployed workers with varying benefit levels; at best, these studies may capture pure supply responses, but they do not inform about the total impact on unemployment.

Time-series models may, from this point of view, appear more appropriate than models based on cross-sectional data. A macro-econometric model explaining, for example, labour demand, labour force participation, and wage setting is conceivable; from such a model one might derive and compute the total effects of higher benefits. This approach has also been pursued in several British studies, where an increase in the benefit level is assumed to raise wages and thereby reduce the demand for labour. Unfortunately, the effects estimated from time-series models appear extremely sensitive to the choice of sample period and exogenous variables.

12.3.2. Evidence from Britain and the United States

The evidence obtained from various empirical studies is summarized below.

(1) Evidence from time series. The set of British time-series studies include Gujarati (1972), Maki and Spindler (1975), Sawyer (1979), Junankar (1981), Nickell and Andrews (1983), Minford (1983), and Layard and Nickell (1985, 1986). In the studies by Nickell and Andrews, Minford, and Layard and Nickell, the effect of unemployment compensation on unemployment operates via wage equations. The estimates of the elasticity of unemployment with respect to (real) benefits range from zero (or even negative numbers) to Minford's

elasticity of 4. The well-known paper by Layard and Nickell (1986) produces a benefit elasticity of 0.7, using data for the period 1954–83. (Note that this elasticity is not directly estimated but computed from the three equations of the Layard–Nickell model, i.e. the price equation, the wage equation, and the labour demand equation.) It is safe to conclude that the time-series studies have so far not converged to anything near a consensus regarding the impact of benefits on unemployment.

(2) Micro-econometric evidence: unemployment duration. A number of micro-econometric studies of the relationship between unemployment duration and benefits have been carried out in Britain and the United States. (Löfgren and Engström 1989 contains a recent survey.) Both of these countries have in common with Sweden a work test: an unemployed worker can be denied benefits if he refuses to accept a job offer. The extent to which this work test actually is enforced in the different countries is, however, by and large an open question.

Early micro-econometric British studies (Lancaster 1979); Nickell 1979a, 1979b found an elasticity of duration with respect to benefits of around 0.6. (See Atkinson *et al.* 1984 for a critical evaluation.) Effects of a roughly similar magnitude emerged from US studies from the 1970s; evaluations and summaries of those studies are given by Danziger *et al.* (1981), Gustman (1982), and Burtless (1987).

The British study by Narendranathan *et al.* (1985) uses longitudinal data on the first unemployment spell experienced by a male sample from 1978–9, with direct observations on unemployment benefits receipts; earlier British studies used imputed rather than actual benefit levels. The study finds an elasticity of expected duration with respect to benefits in the range of 0.30–0.35. This elasticity shows a marked age variation, ranging from 0.8 for teenage males to 0.4 for men aged 25–44 and zero for men over 45.

Narendranathan *et al.* also test whether the effects of unemployment benefits vary with elapsed duration, suggesting that because of the 'small (or negative) increase in utility from prolonging unemployment for men already unemployed for some months, one might expect that the reservation wage for such men will have fallen sufficiently for the probability of accepting a job offer to approach unity'. This conjecture is not rejected by the tests; benefits had no effect on expected duration for males unemployed over 6 months, except for teenagers. This finding is consistent with the theoretical predictions from search models incorporating a limited duration of UI benefits; recall that higher benefits may increase the probability of job acceptance as the worker approaches benefit exhaustion.

UI benefits may prolong job search by raising reservation wages among insured workers. Feldstein and Poterba (1984) have shed light on this issue by using a sample of unemployed workers with reported reservation wages. They explore the determinants of a worker's reservation-wage ratio, i.e. the ratio of the reported reservation wage to the wage in the worker's last job. They find that a rise in the net replacement ratio—the ratio of benefits to net earnings—by one percentage point raises the reservation-wage ratio by 0.1 points for workers on lay-off, by 0.4 points for other job losers, and by 0.3 points for voluntary job-leavers.

Standard search models predict that higher benefits will raise the worker's re-employment wage, since the induced rise in the reservation wage raises the worker's mean acceptable offer. Several empirical studies have examined this possible effect. Most studies have been undertaken in the United States, and the typical finding, although not universal, is that higher UI benefits involve significant earnings gains for insured workers (Ehrenberg and Oaxaca 1976; Burgess and Kingston 1976; Holen 1977; Classen 1977 and 1979).

(3) Temporary lay-offs and labour supply. A few US studies have addressed how government-subsidized UI benefits affect the frequency of temporary lay-offs, and the empirical evidence has, on the whole, supported the theoretical predictions. Feldstein (1978), using micro-data, explained the probability of being on temporary lay-off by, *inter alia*, the UI replacement ratio. Feldstein's estimates indicate very strong effects; UI benefits appear to cause around 50 per cent of all temporary lay-off unemployment in the United States. However, the estimates capture the effects of higher benefits on firms' lay-off behaviour as well as workers' search behaviour. Generous benefits may prolong unemployment among workers on lay-off by reducing search efforts and raising reservation wages; by implication, the likelihood of finding a worker on temporary lay-off at a point in time is increased.

Feldstein's study does not inform about the role of experience rating in affecting unemployment. This issue is addressed by Topel (1983), who measures the extent of UI subsidization across different

US states, Topel's estimates imply that incomplete experience rating accounts for as much as 30 per cent of all spells of temporary lay-off unemployment. Non-subsidized benefits appear to have a negligible impact on lay-offs.

While many studies have investigated the responses of insured workers to changes in benefits, very few papers deal with 'entitlement' effects. For individuals currently out of the labour force, an increase in benefits raises the likelihood of labour force participation, and uninsured workers in the labour force will reduce reservation wages as a response to higher benefits, thereby reducing the duration of unemployment spells.

Two studies by Hamermesh (1979, 1980) have addressed these issues, and found empirical support in favour of the entitlement hypothesis. For example, easier UI eligibility requirements induce more weeks worked among adult women. Clark and Summers (1982), using data on labour force transitions, find similar results. The probability of moving from employment to non-participation is significantly reduced as a result of UI benefits. Taking all labour force transitions into account (i.e. transitions between unemployment, employment, and non-participation), Clark and Summers find that total elimination of UI in 1978 would have reduced the unemployment rate by 0.6 percentage points, but also reduced the employment/population ratio by 0.6 points. The study thus indicates that UI benefits tend to increase unemployment and employment and reduce non-participation.

12.3.3. The Swedish Experience

We have noted that the Swedish UI system has several unique features. The close association between UI and trade unions is found only in Sweden and a few other countries, including Denmark and Finland. It is also noteworthy that Sweden has practised relatively stiff experience rating rules regarding temporary lay-offs.

We have also shown that unemployment compensation in Sweden has become successively more generous since the mid-1960s. There have been increases in the length of the maximum benefit periods, and a marked trend increase in UI coverage. Replacement ratios have shown an upward trend, a new type of benefit (KAS) has been introduced, and early retirement for labour market reasons has become widespread.

The political ambitions to offer more generous unemployment compensation have not been moderated by much concern over adverse incentive effects. By and large, the efficiency aspects have had second-order priority relative to equity considerations in policy discussions on these matters. The fact that there are rather few Swedish empirical studies in this field may to some extent reflect a lack of political demand for thorough evaluations of actual and planned extensions of the U I system.

The extensions of unemployment compensation in Sweden have been accompanied by a clear trend increase in unemployment duration. The average duration of a completed unemployment spell was around 7 weeks in the late 1960s but had risen to 15 weeks during the first half of the 1980s. There has also been a trend decline in unemployment inflow during the last two decades (see Table 12.1). A few studies have tried to identify possible relationships between the rise in unemployment duration and the extensions of U I, and we now turn to a discussion of these studies.

(1) Time-series evidence: unemployment, unemployment duration and wage setting. There are three published Swedish studies that deal with the effects of U I compensation on unemployment and unemployment duration, namely Ståhl (1978), Björklund (1978), and Björklund and Holmlund (1989). Ståhl explored whether variations in the benefit level had influenced unemployment among members of U I funds during the period 1963–73. The other two

TABLE 12.1 *Incidence and duration of unemployment*

| | Unemployment as % of labour force (u) | Weekly inflow into unemployment as % of labour force (f) | Duration of unemployment in weeks (D) | | | |
| | | | By age group | | By U I fund membership | |
			16–64	55–64	Members	Non-members
1965–9	1.8	0.265	6.8	14.2	10.8	7.6
1970–4	2.2	0.191	11.5	24.2	16.0	10.7
1975–9	1.9	0.165	11.5	23.9	14.9	11.5
1980–4	2.9	0.187	15.5	38.8	16.6	16.5
1985–6	2.7	0.174	15.5	42.2	16.3	17.2

Note: The duration of unemployment (D) has been calculated from data on u and f, using the formula $u = f \cdot D$.

studies tried to explain changes in unemployment duration by using quarterly data on unemployment outflow.

Ståhl (1978) could not find any significant relationship between unemployment and unemployment benefits. Both Björklund (1978) and Björklund and Holmlund (1989) found that unemployment benefits had some adverse effects on unemployment duration, but the estimated effects were not quantitatively important.

Björklund (1978) used time-series for unemployment outflow and investigated whether the increase in the duration of unemployment during the period 1965–76 could be explained by the increases in benefits during that time. He identified the important changes during this period as the extension of the benefit period, first for older workers in 1968 and then for other UI fund members in 1974; and the introduction of KAS in 1974. Such an effect can be identified in 1968 for the older workers, but no corresponding effect can be found in 1974 for the other groups. However, there is a clear trend increase in the duration of unemployment for older as well as younger workers over the entire period.

Björklund and Holmlund (1989) used essentially the same kind of data as Björklund (1978), but extended the period of investigation to include the period 1965–85. They used two kinds of variables capturing changes in the UI system, namely, (*a*) dummies to account for the increases in benefit periods that took place in 1968 and 1974, and (*b*) a computed series on replacement ratios. The ratio between the total number of vacancies and unemployment was used to capture labour market tightness, and separate estimations were done for several different categories of unemployed individuals: disaggregations were done with respect to age, UI fund membership, and elapsed duration.

Björklund and Holmlund found some evidence suggesting that extended UI may have contributed to an increase in unemployment duration. The quantitative effects were small, however, suggesting that the quite substantial extensions cannot have been a major factor behind the increase in unemployment duration.

Search theory suggests that higher unemployment benefits will increase unemployment duration, in part through a fall in search effort. The Swedish experience does not sit easily with this theoretical prediction. Using information in the Swedish labour force surveys it is possible to calculate the average number of search methods used by unemployed workers. Table 12.2 presents some

TABLE 12.2   *Use of multiple job-search methods by unemployed workers (as percentage of unemployed workers)*

	No. of methods				Av. no. of methods used		% using employment office
	0	1	2	3			
Members of UI-funds							
1963–66	9	76	13	2	1.05	(1.15)[b]	82
1967–70	11	81	7	1	99	(1.11)[b]	83
1971–74	11	77	10	2	1.01	(1.13)[b]	84
1975–78	7	82	9	2	1.08	(1.16)[b]	89
1979–82	4	76	15	5	1.21	(1.26)[b]	92
1983–86	2	77	14	6	1.23	(1.26)[b]	95
Non-members							
1963–66	20	66	13	1	96	(1.20)[b]	52
1967–70	17	69	12	2	99	(1.19)[b]	56
1971–74	10	71	16	3	1.13	(1.26)[b]	69
1975–78	6	76	15	3	1.15	(1.22)[b]	74
1979–82	4	73	18	5	1.25	(1.30)[b]	80
1983–86	3	72	17	8	1.29	(1.33)[b]	85

[a] This is basically an 'others' category, but it includes some people temporarily laid-off with salary plus unemployed who were waiting to start a job within 30 days.
[b] Excluding those identified in n. *a* as using no method of job-search.
Note: The search methods asked about were visiting employment offices, answering advertisements, and contacting employers.
Source: Labor Force Surveys, Statistics Sweden.

basic information. There is a trend increase in the average number of search methods used, and this trend is primarily accounted for by the fact that unemployed persons outside the UI funds have become more inclined to register at the employment offices. The introduction of KAS has almost certainly made it more attractive to search via the employment offices; benefit recipients have been required to visit the employment offices in order to be eligible for KAS or regular UI benefits. In this way the introduction of KAS as well as the growth of UI coverage may have contributed to an increase in search effort that might explain why the adverse incentive effects appear to be so small.

Very little empirical work has been done in Sweden on the role of unemployment benefits in wage determination. Holmlund (1989) and Calmfors and Forslund (1990) use wage-bargaining models as guides for estimations of real-wage equations for Sweden. Holmlund investigates wage-setting in mining and manufacturing and finds some weak support for the hypothesis that wages are pushed up by higher benefits; the benefit elasticity of real wages is, however, very small (around 0.05). Calmfors and Forslund, by contrast, are unable to detect any significant role for unemployment benefits in their estimations of real-wage equations for the Swedish business sector.

The studies discussed above face the multicollinearity problems that are usually found in aggregate time-series. The estimated UI coefficients are, in general, sensitive to the inclusion or exclusion of other variables. One might therefore hope that more reliable results should be available from micro-econometric studies, and we now turn to this work.

(2) Evidence from micro-data. A few Swedish studies have explored the effects of UI by using data on single individuals and their unemployment experiences. Björklund (1981) investigated variations in unemployment duration in cross-sectional data of unemployed individuals with and without UI benefits. Individuals who collected benefits had neither longer spells of unemployment nor higher wages in subsequent jobs than unemployed workers with UI (when controlling for other factors, such as age, sex, and education).

Heikensten (1984) used micro-data from the Swedish labour force surveys (AKU), and explored whether transitions from unemployment were influenced by membership in UI funds, *inter alia*. He found that the probability of remaining unemployed one quarter after unemployment entry was higher for UI-fund members; individuals with UI compensation thus experienced longer spells of unemployment. This effect was due, however, to a lower probability of leaving the labour force; the probability of moving from unemployment to employment was not significantly affected by UI fund membership. This study thus indicates that UI compensation tends to increase unemployment duration by reducing labour force withdrawals.

Holmlund (1986) investigated transitions to employment among unemployed youth (age 16–24) in the Stockholm area. He used a data set where transitions between labour force states are recorded week by week. The conditional probability of leaving unemployment was explained by a number of personal and other characteristics, including income sources during unemployment. Individuals with UI compensation were found to experience significantly longer spells of unemployment; the estimated difference in duration between otherwise identical persons with and without UI compensation was 7 weeks. Individuals with KAS did not show significantly different behaviour from those who did not receive KAS or UI compensation.

(3) Seasonal unemployment. The Swedish UI funds generally adhere to the traditional occupational and industrial classifications. Table 12.3 shows the average compensation per member for some of the funds, after deduction of employees' contributions. This net compensation, which is roughly equivalent to the government contribution per member, expresses the implicit wage subsidies of

TABLE 12.3. *Average UI subsidies per member and per year for some UI funds, 1976-1981 (in SEK after deduction of employees' contributions)*

	1976	1977	1978	1979	1980	1981
Agricultural workers	806	909	1,374	1,096	1,869	2,302
Forestry workers	1,090	1,375	1,729	2,267	2,591	2,743
Clothing workers	547	991	1,611	1,835	1,319	1,873
Metal workers	219	349	96	615	551	1,013
Construction workers	839	1,251	2,113	1,855	1,519	2,789
Painters	384	465	875	903	700	1,010
Longshoremen	276	1,019	1,399	1,512	1,802	2,684
Seamen	115	492	975	888	699	1,485
Swedish fishermen	2,733	3,063	2,984	4,311	3,685	3,672
Total	180	266	434	478	479	742

Note: Numbers indicate amounts before tax.
Source: Labour Market Board (AMS), Insurance Unit.

the UI system. The chief recipients of an income supplement in the form of subsidized unemployment benefits are Sweden's fishermen, who receive an amount equivalent to more than 5 per cent of the average worker's income. Relatively high amounts of compensation are also paid to construction workers, as well as to workers in agriculture and forestry.

Thus, Table 12.3 suggests that the current system treats seasonal unemployment rather generously: construction, agriculture, forestry, and fishing can be assumed to be especially prone to seasonal fluctuations in the demand for labour. This finding is supported by Table 12.4, which shows the variation in unemployment across a year for some UI funds. Seasonal swings are

TABLE 12.4.   *Index of seasonal variation of unemployment for some UI funds, 1976–1979 (index 100: yearly average)*

	Forestry workers	Metal workers	Construction workers	Swedish fishermen	Total unemployment
Jan.	143	109	161	196	122
Feb.	138	102	162	280	118
Mar.	133	103	147	227	112
Apr.	121	100	116	92	99
May	75	91	75	38	88
June	54	95	55	26	85
July	67	101	55	21	88
Aug.	57	100	61	28	89
Sept.	59	96	61	43	89
Oct.	90	98	72	43	91
Nov.	123	99	90	78	101
Dec.	139	105	143	123	118
Average unemployment 1976–9 (%)	5.0	1.5	4.4	2.7	1.4
Coefficient of variation for monthly unemployment rates 1976–9	0.36	0.27	0.48	0.96	0.21

Note: Unemployment figures are published by AMS in their series *Arbetsmarknadsstatistik* (Labour market statistics).

most apparent within fishing; unemployment during the winter months is ten to fifteen times as high as during the summer. Seasonal variation is also strong within forestry and construction.

Edebalk and Wadensjö (1978) have studied the seasonal variation of unemployment mostly within the construction workers' UI fund. The availability of unemployment benefits to seasonal unemployment increased considerably in 1964, and Edebalk and Wadensjö investigated whether seasonal fluctuations in unemployment also increased at this point. They found an effect in the expected direction, but the level of statistical significance was relatively low so the results must be interpreted cautiously. Seasonal fluctuations in unemployment showed a trend decrease during the period under investigation (1956–75), which means that the new rules could, at most, have slowed up this development.

In summary, the indications are that seasonal unemployment is treated generously in the Swedish UI system. This means that industries which have predictable seasonal patterns in demand or production conditions are subsidized at the expense of industries which have a relatively stable level of activity across the year. The number of employed within, for example, fishing, forestry, and construction is higher, and the number employed in the engineering industry is lower, than would be the case in a system which did not subsidize seasonal unemployment. Note also that in this way, the system probably also raises the total level of unemployment.

12.3. Concluding Remarks

Theoretical work during the past fifteen years or so has identified many mechanisms through which UI may affect labour markets. Search theory has delivered clear predictions about how UI affects search effort and reservation wages among insured and uninsured workers; contract theory has identified relationships between UI and firms' lay-off behaviour; bargaining and efficiency wage models have offered support for the hypothesis that higher UI benefits may raise unemployment through higher wages.

Despite rich theoretical contributions and a large number of empirical studies, there are reasons to emphasize the fragility of our current knowledge. On the theory side, it is unfortunate that most results are derived from partial equilibrium models without much allowance made for general equilibrium effects. Although it has been established, perhaps beyond reasonable doubt, that unemployed workers with high benefits experience longer unemployment spells than those with low benefits, we do not know to what extent these results carry over to a general equilibrium setting. Sweden's labour market performance underlines these caveats. Despite substantial extensions of the UI system, it is hard to find much evidence of strong adverse effects on unemployment. This may reflect imperfect econometric methods, but it also highlights how limited our knowledge is.

Two neglected issues have relevance for interpretations of the Swedish experience. Firstly, Sweden's ambitious labour market programmes have presumably offset part of the unemployment increase that otherwise might have been caused by extended UI. Secondly, the importance of the work test has not been seriously addressed in theoretical or empirical work. We simply do not know much about how the work test has been implemented over time, and how it is practised in different parts of the country.

Is it then always a good thing to reduce unemployment? Not necessarily; we shall return to normative issues in Chapter 14. Suffice it here to say that UI may entail unambiguous welfare gains to workers even if it brings some increase in unemployment.

13

Unemployment Insurance and Income Distribution[1]

A fundamental argument for government intervention in the unemployment compensation system is that information costs and lack of opportunities for individuals to pool their unemployment risks restrict the supply of unemployment insurance on the private market. The insurance literature has pointed to the efficiency gains of various kinds by government support of the system.

It is unlikely that no one loses in this intervention; that is, it is unlikely that the government's actions in this area are Pareto-efficient. The government's expenditures are financed primarily by payroll taxes paid by the employers. These contributions are probably paid by all workers in the form of lower wages in the long run. Since many employees have decided not to pay the fee for membership in an unemployment insurance fund, they probably lose in the current situation. They are forced to contribute to the cost by way of wages forgone but do not have access to the benefits in case of unemployment.

Which groups win in the Swedish unemployment insurance system? Does the system contribute to a more even income distribution? In order to answer these questions, one must be able to compare the actual distribution of income with the hypothetical distribution which would result if the government subsidization were taken away or reduced. This is obviously a difficult task. It is likely that a number of changes would occur in the labour market if the government support were withdrawn. Certain private or co-operative insurance systems would probably arise. The structure of contracts in the labour market might be changed, etc. This would, in turn, affect even those who did not encounter unemployment in the current system.

Without a developed model of these indirect effects, we can, as a

---

[1] This chapter is based on Björklund (1986).

first approximation, investigate the direct effects. We first postulate that each employee contributes to the financing of the government subsidies to unemployment compensation by sacrificing a fraction of the wage. This means that we assume a backward shifting of the payroll tax. Second, we assume that the winners are those who actually receive the benefits.

What redistribution would be expected a priori? First of all, we can expect negligible transfers to high income earners, because we know the risk of unemployment is lower among the more highly skilled workers (see Björklund 1981; Holmlund 1981). On the other hand, we can also expect that a rather small amount is distributed to individuals with very low incomes, who probably have weak attachment to the labour force; those may include many people who are handicapped or have long-term illnesses, but also youths and women who work on a temporary basis.

One can point to some arguments for part of the subsidy going to workers who lie relatively high on the wage scale. One argument is that unemployment benefits are paid for temporary lay-offs which occur in industries with relatively high wages, such as the engineering, paper, and steel industries. Here it is a matter of a relatively small loss of income, which in the current situation is compensated partially by lay-off supplements and partially by unemployment benefits. How large a part of insurance payments are made for lay-offs is not known since the relevant data are lacking.

Another argument is that a large part of the transfers go to families with relatively high total incomes. A family with two income earners has a better chance to obtain benefits than a family with a single income. We also saw above that in the white-collar workers' funds, a not insignificant amount went to persons who had quit work voluntarily to move with their spouses.

In the following, we present an empirical analysis of the distributional impact of unemployment compensation, based on data from the Level of Living Survey (see Eriksson and Åberg 1987). Table 13.1 gives a picture of the distribution of unemployment benefits across different income groups in 1980. The first part of the table shows the location of KAS recipients within the income distribution. Not surprisingly, they can mainly be found on the lower half of the income scale: 93 per cent of the recipients of KAS belong to the lowest half (see the first row of the table). However, KAS recipients are not highly concentrated in the lowest decile, which is

TABLE 13.1   *Unemployment benefits by income class and distribution of earned income in population (ages 18–65), 1980*

	Decile 1	Quartile 1	Quartile 2	Quartile 3	Quartile 4
			KAS Benefits		
Proportion of all KAS recipients	0.09	0.49	0.44	0.05	0.02
Proportion of total KAS benefit paid	0.12	0.59	0.35	0.04	0.02
Benefits as a percentage of claimant's total income	0.52	0.17	0.06	0.04	0.03
			Unemployment Insurance		
Proportion of all UI recipients	0.03	0.11	0.50	0.28	0.11
Proportion of total UI benefits paid	0.03	0.10	0.57	0.22	0.11
Benefits as a percentage of claimant's total income	0.95	0.38	0.22	0.11	0.11
			Distribution of Earned Income		
	0.002	0.05	0.17	0.30	0.48

Note: The income distribution has been estimated using total yearly income before taxes from all sources of taxable income (including unemployment benefits). Earned income excludes sick-pay and unemployment benefits.
Source: Own computations from the Level of Living Survey.

probably dominated by persons who do not participate in the labour force at all.

The second row shows that benefits are more highly concentrated at the lower end of the income scale than recipients are. Whereas 49 per cent of all persons who receive KAS belong to the first quartile, it appears that 59 per cent of all benefits are paid to the individuals in the lowest quartile. This indicates that unemployment duration is longer among KAS recipients with low total income.

The third row reveals that KAS benefits amount to 52 per cent of total income for the recipients of KAS in the lowest decile, but to much lower fractions among high-income earners.

The second part of Table 13.1 provides the equivalent information about UI benefits. It appears that those benefits are paid to individuals at a higher level in the income scale than KAS benefits are. Even so, 67 per cent of all benefits are paid to individuals in the lower half of the distribution. A negligible fraction of all benefits—3 per cent—is paid to the individuals in the lowest decile, and 11 per cent to those in the highest decile. Another difference between the two types of benefits is that UI benefits constitute a larger fraction of the recipient's total income than KAS benefits do.

The third part of Table 13.1 shows the distribution of earned income. Because of the assumption above that the payroll taxes used to finance the benefits are shifted backwards into lower wages, this row describes which income classes contribute most to the costs of unemployment benefits. Comparing the location of the 'contributors' and the 'recipients' of the benefits shows that UI clearly redistributes income from the high income classes to the lower income classes. Unemployment compensation in Sweden is not only an insurance system within certain income classes, but also provides redistribution between income classes.

However, it is important to emphasize that this conclusion relies on analysis of data for individuals during a single year. It is not obvious that the same pattern would emerge if the corresponding analysis were extended to household income, or income over more than one year. In particular, the low-income profile of the KAS benefits would probably be changed if such analyses were done. This is because KAS recipients are quite young, and in many cases still living at home with their parents. This can be seen in Table 13.2: the average age of KAS recipients is 24.5 years; 32 per cent are living with their parents, and their average total income is low compared to the population as a whole.

We next turn to another distributional issue. In Chapter 11 we noted that around 30 per cent of all unemployed in Sweden receive no unemployment compensation at all. It is then natural to ask whether this is to be considered a serious distributional problem. Tables 13.2 and 13.3 shed some light on the issue. It appears that the unemployed who receive no compensation are older than the KAS recipients, but on average slightly younger than all individuals in the sample. Very few are living with their parents. Furthermore, it can be seen that the duration of unemployment is not short, indicating

TABLE 13.2 *Profile of KAS recipients, UI recipients, unemployed persons receiving no compensation and total population aged 18-65 (1980 data)*

	KAS recipients	UI recipients	Unemployed without compensation	Total population
Age, years	24.5	36.1	32.2	39.8
Unemployment 1980, weeks	14.2	18.2	16.0	17.2
Married, %	41	61	59	71
Living with parents and paying less than 100 SEK rent/month, %	22	4	6	4
Average total income in 1980, SEK	35,400	54,300	38,700	57,700

Source: Own computations from the Level of Living Survey.

TABLE 13.3. *Percentage of unemployed receiving no compensation and distribution of earned income by income class, 1980 (for ages 18-65)*

	1st decile	1st quartile	2nd quartile	3rd quartile	4th quartile
Unemployed without compensation	22	50	22	19	9
Distribution of earned income	2	5	17	30	48

Source and notes: See Table 13.1

that the income losses can be substantial. Average total income during the year is far below the average: 72 per cent of this group of unemployed belong to the lower half of the income distribution. It cannot be ruled out that the incomplete coverage of the existing unemployment benefits system is a distributional problem, in the sense that the unemployed without compensation have a very low standard of living.

14

Aspects of Optimal Unemployment Insurance

14.1. Alternative Modes of Financing Benefits

We have already shown that Swedish UI funds have become increasingly subsidized by the government. More than 90 per cent of the funds' expenditures have since 1983 been covered by government grants. The subsidies have typically been of two kinds, a proportional 'basic grant' (*grundbidrag*) and a progressive grant (*progressivbidrag*). According to the law during the period 1984–8, the basic grant amounted to 80 per cent of total UI benefits paid out by the fund. The progressive grant applied to the difference between UI benefits and the basic grant, and was an increasing function of the unemployment rate among members of the UI fund. Government subsidies were thus increasing, at an increasing rate, with unemployment in a UI fund. There was, however, an upper limit to the progressive grant: it was fixed at 0.9 if the number of yearly benefit days was 22 or more.

Government subsidies as a share of the total amount of benefits have varied between 80 per cent and 98 per cent. UI funds with low unemployment (e.g. white-collar workers with higher education) typically faced a subsidy rate of 80 per cent; benefits to unemployed workers in construction, or unemployed forestry workers, were often subsidized at a rate of 98 per cent.

New legislation concerning the financing of UI was decided by the Swedish parliament in 1988. According to the new rules, in effect from 1 January 1989, government grants will cover 100 per cent of paid out UI benefits; members' premiums will therefore cover only the administrative costs.

Several alternative modes of financing benefits may be contemplated. One alternative involves a general reduction in government subsidies and a concomitant increase in premiums paid by members of UI funds. Such a policy has sometimes been recommended as a device to influence wage setting. The argument goes as follows. A UI fund is an integral part of a union, and the union's wage demand has a decisive effect on the outcome of a wage negotiation. In the extreme case, the union simply picks its desired point on the labour demand curve. The optimal wage is determined through maximization of some well-defined objective function, with wages and employment as arguments.

Suppose that a union attempts to maximize the members' welfare, recognizing that a wage increase will reduce employment but also raise the UI premiums paid by the members. The desired mix of wages and premiums is influenced by, *inter alia*, the subsidy system. If union members have to finance a larger share of increases in benefits paid out, the marginal cost of a wage increase is raised. It can be shown that an income-maximizing union will respond by reducing the wage; employment therefore increases, since firms are on their labour demand curves (Holmlund and Lundborg 1988).

Suppose, alternatively, that benefits are in part financed by industry-specific UI taxes on firms' profits or value added. An industry-wide union then perceives a direct link between its own wage choice and the size of the tax base. A higher wage may increase wage income (depending on the elasticity of labour demand), but it always reduces profits (or value added). At a fixed UI tax rate, a wage hike involves higher premiums through a reduced size of the tax base (i.e. lower profits or value added). It can be shown that schemes with industry-specific UI taxes on profits or value added (involving a direct link between the UI fund's revenues and the taxes paid by employers) will raise employment by reducing wage rates. The policies raise employment by increasing the elasticity of workers' net income with respect to the wage (Holmlund and Lundborg 1989).

It would be premature to draw strong policy conclusions from our current meagre knowledge in this field. The welfare economics of economies with union power in wage determination is not well developed; researchers have typically taken it for granted that employment-increasing devices are welfare-improving. So long as this presumption is correct, it is of interest to note that union wage demands can be influenced by means of changes in UI financing. Of course, such taxes involve a number of considerations that have been ignored in our brief discussion. The existence of several unions within the same industry is one complication. Another issue is the relationship between the structure of wage bargaining and the structure of UI taxes. Wages in Sweden are typically negotiated at three levels—economy-wide, industry-wide, and at the level of the firm—and it is not obvious how U I taxes should be designed so as to influence local wage setting.

In conclusion, there may be a case for reduced subsidies to the U I funds as a device to influence wage setting. There is clearly a case for more experience-rating as a means to reduce allocational distortions associated with cross-subsidization of industries. But reduced government subsidies to the U I system may also have adverse distributional consequences, as shown in Chapter 13. As is often the case, a trade-off between efficiency and equity has to be recognized.

Issues pertaining to the financing of U I benefits have also been addressed by Pissarides (1983). His framework is an equilibrium-matching model, where a non-degenerate wage distribution exists because of variations in the efficiency of job–worker matches. The model implies a positive relationship between unemployment and the benefit level, since higher benefits raise workers' reservation wages. (The wage offer distribution is not affected by changes in benefits in this model.) The increase in unemployment can, however, be completely eliminated by financing U I benefits by a progressive income tax. A more progressive tax reduces the rewards of prolonged search. Low-wage jobs become more attractive, and better-paying jobs become less rewarding to hold out for. The progressive tax reduces the dispersion in after-tax wage offers, and this implies weaker incentives to reject job offers.

14.2. Unemployment Benefits and Efficiency

The efficiency properties of search market equilibria are closely related to efficiency aspects of U I. If, for example, it can be shown that the 'natural rate' of unemployment is too low from an efficiency viewpoint, there is a case for introducing a U I scheme as a device to increase unemployment.

These efficiency issues have been addressed in papers by Pissarides (1984a, 1984b) Diamond (1981) Albrecht and Axell (1984) and Mortensen (1983). Few clear-cut results have emerged, but the analyses have identified various externalities in economies where jobs are allocated through search. In general, the equilibrium outcome may involve too little or too much job rejection. In the former case, U I may be introduced as a device to improve social efficiency by making workers more selective in their job acceptance decisions. An example of this mechanism is given in Albrecht and Axell (1984), where increases in UI benefits bring about a reallocation of workers to more productive firms. Too little job rejection may also occur when the contact probabilities of searching firms and workers depend on the aggregate number of unemployed and vacancies. A job match decision between a worker and a firm will negatively affect the probability that the remaining unemployed will find suitable matches with vacancies.

Mortensen (1983) and Boadway and Oswald (1983) have dealt with the question of what the UI benefit level *should* be. In a standard implicit contract model, the optimal benefit level involves full insurance as long as there is perfect experience rating; the benefit level should be set so as to equalize the worker's marginal utility of income across employment and unemployment. This is also the outcome, however, if private UI arrangements are allowed in implicit contract models; profit-maximizing, risk-neutral firms have incentives to offer full insurance to their risk-averse workers without any government intervention. The fact that private UI systems of this kind are rare suggests that the assumptions underlying the contract models are not met in practice.

A troublesome feature of standard models is the absence of permanent job separations. As noted by Sherwin Rosen (1985), a contract 'must embody a delicate balance of encouraging mobility in response to permanent changes in demand and discouraging it for temporary shocks. Full insurance discourages mobility by subsidizing leisure and reducing job search intensity.'

14.3. Severance Pay versus Daily Benefits

As shown above, Swedish benefit payments are constant during the benefit period (with the exception of the initial waiting period). This is obviously not the only potential time profile for the level of compensation. The Ministry of Labour in Sweden proposed in 1981 that benefit levels be substantially lowered during the first 30 days of unemployment (Arbetsmarknadsdepartementet 1981). The response to this proposal was relatively critical, and it was dropped from the legislative proposal passed by the parliament in the spring of 1982. The debate has, however, prompted several quite different suggestions with respect to policy; Grassman *et al.* (1978), for example, proposed the opposite time profile, namely a single payment in the form of a lump-sum severance payment instead of continuing benefits.

What are the consequences of these different payment profiles with respect to efficiency and distribution? Several researchers have attempted to treat these questions, including Baily (1977 and 1978), Flemming (1978), Shavell and Weiss (1979), Sampson (1978), and Hamermesh (1977). The normative issues are addressed using a framework analogous to the theory of optimal taxation.

The theoretical structure is basically the following. Assume that the government has a specified amount to spend on unemployment benefits, and that the unemployed person chooses the search intensity and reservation wage which maximize his expected utility, given the existing rules governing compensation. What is the time profile of benefit payments which, under these assumptions and constraints, provides the maximum expected utility for workers who become unemployed? The focus is thus solely on the duration of unemployment, and the analysis ignores the question of whether the time profile affects the probability of becoming unemployed.

Such a formulation of the problem implies a comparison between two different desired goals. On the one hand, an employed person with risk aversion prefers a constant level of benefit payments, all else equal. On the other hand, it is important to create incentives to quickly find and accept an offer of employment. This reduces the duration of UI payments and makes it possible to be more generous per day spent in unemployment. The limited resources can, in this case, be used to provide higher benefit levels during the benefit period. This is an argument against an even time profile for benefits and in favour of a declining one, and in the extreme case a once and for all payment. As an incentive to find and accept work, it is the future benefits which are relevant. Since these are lower with a declining profile of payments (or a once and for all payment), the incentive to search more intensively and to accept offers rises. Thus it becomes possible to raise the benefit level per day spent unemployed.

The literature in this field gives some indication about which factors affect the choice problem. A first, and perhaps hardly surprising, result is that a constant level of benefit payments is optimal if the UI system's control function is so effective that the unemployed person himself cannot affect the probability of obtaining employment. But the more the claimant can influence this probability, and the more sensitive this probability is to the benefit level, the more sharply declining the benefit profile should be (or, alternatively, the larger the proportion of benefits should be paid as a severance payment). However, it should be emphasized that the costs of maintaining a control system are not taken into account in the models.

So far in the discussion, most of the arguments have been against a benefit payment profile which increases over time. If, on the other hand, we introduce the possibility that unemployed workers use private savings or loans to adapt to the fall in income resulting from unemployment, the solution may, in fact, be different. Shavell and Weiss (1979) show that the optimal solution may be an introductory period with a rising benefit level, whereupon the level should fall.

The literature written so far in this area has without doubt contributed to the understanding of choice problems within the U I system, but a variety of objections can be raised against the models which have been used. A primary objection has already been made: they ignore the possibility that the benefit level and the time profile of benefits can affect the probability of becoming unemployed. Generous severance benefits can also increase the incentive to search for firms where there is a high risk of unemployment. Therefore, certain limits on entitlement to severance benefits would probably need to be set, especially for persons who become unemployed after short periods of employment. Such rules also apply for Swedish severance payments.

A second objection is that certain factors which support a rising time profile of benefits have not been considered in the literature. Above all, it is reasonable to suppose that the psychological cost of unemployment increases with the length of the spell. Similarly, various losses of human capital rise as the period becomes longer; professional and trade skills can be forgotten, and new skills are not obtained. In order to compensate for this, benefit levels should rise over time. There are also other kinds of capital losses which are relevant for the design of the unemployment compensation system. In certain cases, those who lose their jobs incur a once and for all loss due to the fact that the market value of their skills suddenly falls. In order to compensate for this, some kind of severance benefit would be appropriate.

In the same vein, one may raise the objection that the models do not consider different advantageous aspects in a satisfactory manner. The models maximize expected utility for a person who becomes unemployed. In addition, all unemployed persons are assumed to be alike. But expected utility is of course not realized by all unemployed persons. There is an element of randomness in job search; some people may have luck and obtain a job very quickly, while others may be unlucky and be forced to search for a long time. With a system of severance payments, everyone would get the same amount of benefits from the insurance system. This leads to significant inequality among those encountering unemployment. One can therefore ask how one should consider the distributional aspect in the analysis, and how the result would be changed in this case. A relatively radical way would be to apply a Rawlsian framework, i.e. maximize the outcome for the 'worst unlucky case' (Rawls 1971). This would certainly suggest, ceteris paribus, a rising time profile of benefit payments, since a large part of the resources at the system's disposal would go to those with long durations of unemployment. But since this has adverse incentive effects, it is not certain that the optimal solution implies a rising benefit profile.

It is also possible that the optimal solution would be different if one dropped the assumption that all unemployed persons are identical. The duration of unemployment is not merely random, but depends on the individual's education, experience, etc. A time profile of rising benefits can thus be a way to give more resources to those who have a weak position in the labour market. The risk, however, might be that most of the resources are given to those who are most adversely affected by bad incentives.

In conclusion, much work still remains, theoretical as well as empirical, in order to determine the best way to distribute a given amount of resources between lump sum and periodic benefits, as well as to determine the time profile of the periodic payments. Efficiency considerations probably suggest a declining time profile of benefits, possibly with a severance payment for those who have been employed for a long time with the same firm. Furthermore, the more adverse the effects of unemployment benefits on work incentives are, the larger are the efficiency gains of a declining profile. On the other hand, if one puts more emphasis on distributional considerations and wishes to improve the outcome for those who encounter long periods of unemployment, a rising time profile might be preferable.

14.4. Labour Market Policy as Unemployment Insurance

Unemployment compensation and labour market policy programmes in Sweden are closely related. Job search by unemployed workers is facilitated by free services from employment offices; mobility grants and training programmes are available; temporary jobs and wage subsidies have been targeted to unemployed persons. Unemployment criteria are used for eligibility to these programmes, so the latter can be regarded as integral parts of the Swedish UI system.

Labour market policy instruments such as providing information on vacancies, mobility grants, and retraining presumably increase a worker's probability of getting a job offer. It is likely that many people are very willing to pay for unemployment insurance which covers substantial costs for such instruments. However, the Swedish approach is to provide these opportunities in kind rather than offering a very high benefit level which covers the costs for retraining, etc. Is this reasonable? It may well be, because provision of labour market services in kind is likely to reduce the moral hazard problems that would be associated with very high benefits.

Hui and Trivedi (1986) have presented one innovative analysis of the rationale for labour market policies as a complement to pure unemployment benefits. They consider whether unemployed individuals, after some period of fruitless job search, should be offered training or (possibly) a job which provides experience. If such programmes can effectively increase the skills of the participants, thereby raising either subsequent earnings or the job offer probability, the policy problem involves the following trade-offs. On the cost side we first have the direct training costs (salaries for teachers, etc.) and the loss of output for those who otherwise would have obtained a job during the period of training. There is also a second, indirect, cost involved. If unemployed persons know that they will be offered an attractive training programme after some period of job search—denoted T_1—standard search theory predicts that the optimal strategy is to be more choosy in job search until T_1.

Hence, the probability of re-employment will decrease until T_1 and this represents a cost in terms of additional outlays for unemployment benefits. The benefit of such a programme, on the other hand, would be that individuals have a stronger position after completion of training. If training takes place from T_1 to T_2, the benefits will consist of both higher output and lower outlays for unemployment from T_2 onwards. The benefits will be higher if unemployment *per se* has a deleterious effect on the individuals whereas participation in training has not. Hui and Trivedi consider the so-called duration dependence of unemployment, meaning that the probability of re-employment decreases with the duration of unemployment, due to the stigma of long-term unemployment or the depreciation of job skills. If there is no stigma attached to or depreciation during the labour market programme, its benefits will obviously be higher.

The formal problem addressed is to find the policy which minimizes the difference between the costs of a 'benefits and training' and a 'benefits only' system. The costs consist of output forgone and outlays for unemployment benefits. The policy parameters are T_1 and T_2. Note that the difference $(T_2 - T_1)$ defines the length of the programme. ($T_2 = T_1$ implies no programme in operation.)

The precise solution to this policy problem requires detailed information about the size of disincentive effects of the existence of programmes for unemployed, the strength of duration dependence mechanisms, and the effect of labour market programmes on re-employment probabilities. Unfortunately, the available empirical estimates of the required parameters are very uncertain, for Sweden and other countries.

Hui and Trivedi performed some numerical explorations of their model, based on 'guesstimates' of the crucial parameters. They showed that a 'benefits and training' system was superior to a 'benefits only' system and that the disincentive effect, the duration dependence effect, and the training effect all play crucial roles. Even though some mechanisms are specified *ad hoc* in their study, the approach seems to present a theoretical justification for the Swedish training and job programmes for the unemployed.

15

Summary and Conclusions

Our presentation of the Swedish unemployment compensation system has shown that it has certain notable features which make it different from those in many other countries. This concluding and summarizing chapter will discuss these features in light of the literature we have surveyed.

One notable feature is the organization of the main system for compensation, namely unemployment insurance. In contrast to many other systems, it is not compulsory but relies on voluntary membership in UI funds. These funds are organized by the unions but subsidized by the government, and the rate of subsidization has increased over time. During the 1980s it has been above 90 per cent, and from 1 January 1989 the membership fees are in practice fixed amounts bearing no relationship to unemployment risks in the industry or occupation covered by the fund.

What are the pros and cons of this system as revealed by the economic literature? The promotion of a voluntary system by subsidies can be motivated by considerations concerning market failure, adverse selection, and positively correlated unemployment risks. The subsidies make it possible to obtain premiums even from low-risk individuals, and the UI funds are protected against severe recessions and structural shocks. However, the literature provides only some general and qualitative arguments in favour of public support for unemployment compensation systems and cannot help us determine the magnitude of the subsidy rate. Our own judgement is that a stable UI system for the majority of Swedish workers can be guaranteed with a lower subsidy rate than the present one.

Distributional arguments in favour of public intervention can also be made. Our analysis showed that unemployment benefits financed by payroll taxes, which are shifted over on lower wages, have favourable distributional consequences. Whether a highly subsidized UI system is an effective means to reach distributional goals is another issue which goes beyond the aims of this study.

An obvious disadvantage with the high subsidy rate is that

unemployment-prone industries are subsidized at the expense of industries which offer stable employment. The implicit industry subsidies which we have documented cause both an inefficient industrial structure and inefficient job contracts. The magnitude of these efficiency losses, however, are hard to ascertain.

The increasing subsidies of the UI system have also changed the incentives facing the UI funds in making the final decisions about the right to receive benefits. At the time when membership fees paid a significant part of the total as well as the marginal costs for benefits, the fund faced a trade-off between two groups of members, namely the unemployed and the employed. 'Hard' conditions for the receipt of benefits would permit lower membership fees and would thus be favourable for the employed. The opposite approach would be favourable for the unemployed but more costly for the employed. With the new system in effect from 1 January 1989, the fund always has an incentive to treat the unemployed benefit claimant as generously as possible because all costs are paid by a third party.

One policy reform which has been suggested in Sweden is to make membership in UI funds compulsory for all workers. This would guarantee a stable UI system without subsidies. Adverse selection would not make low-risk individuals drop out of the system, and UI funds would not run the risk of bankruptcy during deep recessions because they can raise the membership fees without losing members.

One obvious advantage with a compulsory system with lower subsidies would be that the implicit subsidies to industries with high unemployment risks could be avoided. Furthermore, the unions' choice between real wages and employment would probably be influenced in the direction of more employment. There are, however, problems involved. First, the distributional consequences might be negative, since the membership fees probably would be raised most for low income earners. Second, workers with very low unemployment risks and/or low risk aversion would be forced to contribute more to the system than they want. Hence, a type of efficiency loss is created.[1] Finally, there is a problem related to the distinction between anticipated and realized unemployment. Ideally, two UI funds with equal anticipated unemployment (equal

---

[1] See Barr (1988) for a discussion of the merits of a compulsory system.

risks) should have the same membership fees. If, however, realized unemployment will differ between the two funds because of unexpected structural events in the economy, the fees paid to the unaffected UI fund should be transferred to the affected one. Such pooling of inter-industry risks would require some kind of co-operation between the UI funds which so far has not existed. The high subsidy rate has perhaps made co-operation less important. Compulsion in combination with lower subsidies and higher fees would probably require an institutionalized pooling of risks between the funds which does not exist today.

Another notable feature of the Swedish system is that ambitious labour market policies are closely related to unemployment compensation. First, many services are offered to the unemployed in addition to cash benefits—information, counselling, training, temporary jobs, and mobility grants. Under certain circumstances, such services in kind can be a part of an effective unemployment compensation package (see Sec. 14.4). Second, the claimant seeking unemployment benefit is obliged to seek work at the employment office, which allows personnel of the office to implement the 'work test'. Even though this is not done rigorously, the fact that the system exists requires the existence of a network of employment offices which by international standards is very ambitious; this in turn increases the likelihood that claimants receive job offers. Third, the unemployed can qualify for future benefits by accepting a temporary job or by participating in a training course. These possibilities exist both for those who have never received unemployment compensation and for those who approach the end of their benefit periods (in general, after 60 weeks). These options make it socially acceptable to have a benefit system which has a maximum duration rather than the open-ended type of system used in many other countries.

We believe that the labour market policies are the most likely explanation for Sweden's successful unemployment record. In spite of a very marked extension of unemployment benefits in terms of coverage, duration periods, and replacement ratios, the relationship between unemployment and vacancies has been remarkably stable during a period when the relationship has deteriorated in many other OECD countries. This interpretation is supported by data from the labour force surveys on the job search activities of the unemployed. These show that the fraction of the unemployed who search via the employment offices has increased at the same time as the coverage of the two benefit systems has risen, and that search intensity has increased. Thus, it appears that the active labour market policies might have helped to counteract the disincentive effects of unemployment benefits *per se*.

Appendix: Calculations of Replacement Ratios for Average Unemployed Workers

Replacement ratios in Fig. 15.1 are calculated using the formula

$$R = \frac{B \cdot 5(1 - t')}{W \cdot H(1 - t')} \qquad \begin{array}{l} t' = t'(B, W, H, E, D) \\ t = t(W, H) \end{array}$$

where:

B = the average benefit level for an unemployed worker

W = expected hourly earnings for an unemployed worker, including basic wages on time—work and piece work, overtime supplements, extra shift pay, public holiday pay and other wage supplements

H = desired weekly hours of work among the unemployed

t = average income tax rate for a person with hourly earnings W and desired hours H

t' = average income tax rate for a person with hourly earnings W, desired hours H, benefit level B, E weeks in employment, and D weeks in unemployment. (Benefits were not taxable before 1974; hence, for 1965–73 $t' = 0$.) We assume that for 1965–77, $D + E = 46$, and for 1978–85, $D + E = 45$.

The tax rates are based on average municipality tax rates for an unmarried worker without children. D refers to the average duration of an unemployment spell and is obtained from $D = U/IU$, where U is the average number of unemployed and IU is the weekly flow into the unemployment pool.

The average benefit level is obtained from

$$B = \alpha_1 B_{\mathrm{UI}} + \alpha_2 B_{\mathrm{KAS}}$$

where:

B_{UI} = average UI benefit paid out per day (*utbetald dagpenning*),

B_{KAS} = average KAS benefit paid out per day (*genomsnittligt stödbelopp*),

α_1 = fraction of unemployment days covered by UI benefits

α_2 = fraction of unemployment days covered by KAS benefits.

(Note that $\alpha_1 + \alpha_2 < 1$ since not all unemployment is covered by benefits.)

The total number of unemployment days per year, UDAYS, is calculated as $U \cdot 52 \cdot 5$, where U is the average number of unemployed during each year.

Expected hourly earnings for an unemployed worker is given by

$$W = \beta_1 WM + \beta_2 WF + \beta_3 WY, (\beta_1 + \beta_2 + \beta_3 = 1)$$

where:

WM = hourly earnings for a male blue-collar worker in mining and manufacturing

WF = hourly earnings for a female blue-collar worker in mining and manufacturing

WY = hourly earnings for a teenage worker (*minderårig*)

β_i = the share of unemployment for males, females, and teenagers, respectively ($i = 1, 2, 3$).

Sources

WM, *WF*, *WY*	Statistics Sweden: SOS Wages.
U, IU, β_i	AKU (labour force surveys)
B_{UI}, B_{KAS}, number of compensated unemployment days	AMS (Swedish Labour Market Board)
Tax tables	*Riksskatteverket* (Swedish tax board)

16

Comment

Gary Burtless

If an economist from elsewhere in the galaxy arrived on this planet to investigate the state of economics, he or she would be impressed by the interest in and apparent uncertainty about the economics of unemployment insurance. Interest in this subject runs especially high in the United Kingdom and the United States. In those two countries, countless studies have been conducted to discover the rationale and impact of a social insurance programme that is ubiquitous in advanced capitalist economies and is now being introduced in some socialist states.

The English-language literature on this subject is so vast that an extra-terrestrial visitor could spend days merely investigating surveys of the literature; the number of articles grows so fast that a visitor would spend additional weeks bringing the most recent survey up to date.

A plausible hypothesis to explain this phenomenon is that English-speaking earthlings are particularly susceptible to some horrible side effects of unemployment insurance. A sensible visitor might also conclude that existing theories and findings about unemployment insurance must be highly uncertain as well as terribly important. How else can one explain the unequal distribution of research resources across economic subjects? Surely Anglo-Saxon economists must be rational; they believe other earthlings to be so. It therefore follows that these economists expect some positive benefit from their continued investment of time and effort into studying unemployment insurance programmes.

What benefits can be derived from the present paper? I see several important ones, which I shall explain in a minute. But I should first declare my bias before beginning the discussion. Over the past couple of years, I have written about unemployment insurance myself. Two of my papers have dealt specifically and at length with the Swedish system. Without a forerunner of this paper, I would not have had much to say. Anders Björklund and Bertil Holmlund have provided an indispensable introduction to the subject. If their work is seriously in error, I have compounded the error by repeating it.

The first great merit of the present paper is that it explains clearly and briefly the notable features of the Swedish insurance system. This is a useful and commendable achievement. For non-Swedes like myself, the paper gives an excellent overview of jobless pay in this country. What is more, it does so in the context of a good and reasonably complete survey of the economic theory of unemployment insurance. For Swedish and non-Swedish readers alike, this kind of discussion makes it clear why particular features of the Swedish programme are important.

The second merit of the paper is its succinct survey of the relevant economic literature. Economists and interested non-economists should learn enough from reading this paper to grasp the main lines of argument about unemployment insurance, and understand the major attacks that have been mounted against the programme, particularly in Great Britain and the United States. A related merit is that the paper has generated a first-rate bibliography with at least a brief discussion of most of the themes mentioned. Even economists who are specialists in unemployment insurance will find this aspect of the paper to be valuable.

The paper gives proper emphasis to the pure insurance aspects of jobless pay. The programme is first and foremost a source of insurance against fluctuations in earnings arising from unemployment. Some economists, especially in the United States, are so caught up in the second-order effects of the programme that they sometimes forget its underlying goal. Björklund and Holmlund do not make that mistake. The programme can raise the well-being of risk-averse workers by reducing the uncertainty of income derived from wage and salary employment. This is the main reason for the existence of unemployment insurance, and it is the correct starting point for analysing its effects.

The authors then review the problems in devising an efficient insurance program. The most celebrated problem is of course moral hazard. This problem arises when the state of nature insured—in this case, unemployment—is affected by the actions of the agent who is covered by insurance. The worker's own actions affect the probability of unemployment because they affect the chance of being fired when employed and the chance of being hired when out of work. While moral hazard cannot be eliminated from unemployment insurance programmes, there are ways the problem can be reduced, and the authors describe several of them.

Björklund and Holmlund consider reasons for government intervention in the unemployment insurance market. If the welfare gain to workers is large, why don't private companies provide insurance? One reason, although a minor one, is the moral hazard problem just mentioned. The government is in a stronger position than private companies to enforce the requirement that insured unemployed workers use their best efforts to become re-employed. Another reason for government intervention is adverse selection. Workers with a high probability of unemployment have the strongest reason to buy insurance, and premiums in a private market must be set accordingly. If premiums were high enough, workers with a low probability of unemployment might be priced out of the insurance market. Government intervention might be needed to make insurance available at a reasonable price to all workers subject to unemployment risk.

The most important reason for the present extent of government intervention, however, is the correlation of unemployment risk across workers. Workers tend to lose their jobs simultaneously. If cyclical unemployment is high, all unemployed workers experience longer spells out of work. While the government has enough resources to insure workers against such contingencies, private insurance companies do not. A private company rash enough to offer unemployment insurance to American workers in the 1920s would presumably have gone bankrupt early in the Great Depression of the 1930s. A private company's offer to insure the risk of unemployment in severe recessions and depressions is thus not credible. Yet a high proportion of all unemployment occurs in precisely these periods.

The authors next give us a summary of the main provisions of the Swedish system of unemployment insurance. As an outsider, I see three distinctive features of that system. First, the basic system is not compulsory. Basic coverage is provided by unemployment insurance societies, many of them associated with labour unions. Membership in these societies is in principle voluntary, implying that workers can refrain from becoming insured if they do not wish to pay the premium necessary to join a society. In 1985, 22 per cent of workers chose this option; only 78 per cent were covered by insurance. It should be noted, however, that membership in these societies is heavily subsidized by the central government. More than 90 per cent of the cost of basic insurance benefits are paid out of central government contributions to the societies. Workers who refrain from joining the societies in spite of the subsidies must believe they face a very low probability of becoming unemployed.

To the best of my knowledge, Sweden is nearly unique in providing basic insurance under a voluntary system. The other systems with which I am familiar provide for compulsory coverage of most wage and salary workers. Employers usually pay part or all of the premium for jobless pay as part of the basic social insurance tax.

In fact, however, the difference between the Swedish system and a compulsory programme is less important than appears on the surface. The main purpose of a compulsory system is to obtain premium payments from workers or firms who do not materially benefit from an unemployment insurance system—notably, those workers or employers for whom unemployment is a very rare event. Because more than 90 per cent of the cost of Swedish insurance is paid for out of central government revenues, those workers who do not face a high probability of unemployment are already making a compulsory 'contribution' to unemployment insurance through their regular or social insurance tax payments. In addition, there is a back-up system of insurance—KAS—that provides less generous insurance to workers not insured under the voluntary funds.

Economically, the distinction between 'compulsory' and 'voluntary' systems is less important than the difference between 'experience-rated' and unrated premium schedules. In most countries, all firms face the same premium schedule for unemployment insurance, irrespective of their contribution to the liabilities of the unemployment insurance system. In the United States, firms must pay higher payroll tax rates if their lay-off policies place above-average burdens on the system. Firms that only rarely discharge workers pay a low tax rate. Even though these firms are compelled to pay on unemployment insurance payroll tax, their tax contribution does not subsidize the unemployment of high-unemployment firms to the same extent as it would in Sweden or Germany, where the tax schedule is the same for each firm irrespective of its experience of unemployment.

The Swedish insurance programme for temporary lay-offs is quite different from that for permanent lay-offs. In some respects Swedish insurance for temporary lay-offs is more similar to that provided under the US system than it is to that provided under other unemployment insurance systems in Europe. Björklund and Holmlund show that temporary lay-offs are far less generously subsidized under the Swedish system than are permanent lay-offs. Firms are required to pay for a substantial share of the benefit costs of short-term lay-offs. However, the phenomenon of temporary lay-offs is far less important than it is in North America, so this aspect of the Swedish system does not appear to have major economic significance.

A second distinctive feature of the Swedish system is its benefit schedule. Although the fact is not emphasized by Björklund and Holmlund, the daily benefit appears to be largely unrelated to the unemployed worker's previous earnings. According to a report of the French Centre d'Étude des Revenus et des Coûts (CERC), 95 per cent of all payments in 1980 were between SEK 180 and 195 per day (CERC 1982: 23).[1] While this amount was about three-quarters of the wage paid to an average wage worker, it was a much higher percentage of the wage of a poorly paid worker. Thus, the Swedish unemployment benefit schedule, like that in Great Britain, would be expected to have disproportionately large incentive effects on low-wage workers. By contrast, benefit schedules in most countries, including France, Germany, and the United States, provide weekly benefits that represent a fixed proportion of previous weekly earnings.

The French, German, and US benefit schedules correspond more closely to my understanding of an insurance formula. They replace a fixed percentage of earnings lost through unemployment, up to some maximum loss per week. By contrast, the Swedish and British formulas seem to provide much poorer insurance of earnings loss. They insure workers against the loss of a job, and they insure long spells better than short ones, but the amount of the insurance payment does not vary with the amount of daily earnings lost. It seems a bit like a fire insurance policy that gives policy-holders a fixed payment per minute that their home is on fire, but fails to adjust the payment for the amount of damage done during each minute. My guess is that a private company offering an insurance

[1] CERC (1982). *L'Indemnisation du chômage en France et à l'étranger*, Paris.

policy of this type would find few home-owners eager to buy if there were other forms of insurance available.

·The last and probably most important feature of the Swedish system has nothing to do with unemployment insurance *per se*. Instead, it involves the active labour market policies for which Sweden is famous. Although I am not closely familiar with how Sweden's active and passive labour market policies interact in practice, I have a pretty good idea of how they might interact in theory. Since the facts seem to correspond with this theory, I shall briefly describe it. In recent years Sweden has spent several times as much on active labour market policies—such as worker retraining and job programmes—as it has on passive policies, like unemployment insurance and public assistance for able-bodied adults. In addition, Sweden has a law requiring employers to register all job vacancies with the state employment service, and this service is apparently quite effective in matching jobless workers with job openings.

The efficiency of the employment service combined with the enormous resources devoted to active labour market programmes provide the unemployment insurance programme with an effective check on moral hazard. Workers who might be tempted to malinger on the unemployment rolls can be referred to job openings in the private sector or to work and training opportunities in the public sector. If an unemployed worker declines these opportunities, he or she can be denied unemployment benefits.

The situation in Sweden contrasts strongly with that in the United States. A much lower percentage of unemployed workers receives benefits in the United States (about one-third); workers typically receive lower weekly benefits as a percentage of past earnings; and they are eligible to receive benefits for only half as long (Burtless 1987: 140). But the US government spends only trifling sums on active labour market policies—less than a fifth the amount it spends on unemployment insurance. In addition, the United States has a much less efficient employment service than the one in Sweden.

Even though unemployment benefits are far less generous in the United States, the potential moral hazard problem is probably more severe than it is in Sweden. Officials of the unemployment insurance service cannot refer jobless workers to very many suitable job vacancies, because employers are reluctant to list vacancies with the job service. Nor can they refer many workers to suitable public job or training opportunities because few such opportunities exist. This means that US authorities cannot effectively monitor job search among insured unemployed workers.

The United States, Great Britain, and several other countries have chosen to limit the extent of moral hazard in unemployment insurance by limiting the amount or duration of benefits. Sweden has implicitly chosen a different approach. It provides enough work and training opportunities so that the job search of unemployed workers can be effectively monitored. Although the Swedish approach is obviously far more costly than the one used in most countries, it may also be quite a bit more effective. The aggregate evidence suggests it is reasonably effective. Even though Swedish unemployment insurance has been dramatically liberalized and extended over the past two decades, by international standards Sweden continues to enjoy unusually low unemployment.

As shown in the paper, the low unemployment rate may disguise the true significance of unemployment insurance policies in Sweden. Some forms of insurance or aid, such as payments for early retirement and mandatory severance pay, can induce workers to leave the labour force rather than enter or remain in unemployment. None the less, the authors seem to me correct in their conclusion that the generous insurance system in Sweden has not imposed intolerable burdens on the Swedish labour market.

17

Comment

Eskil Wadensjö

Anders Björklund and Bertil Holmlund's study covers the structure
and effects of the Swedish unemployment insurance system in a very
readable way while providing the detail which is necessary to understand its effects. As such, it will surely constitute the starting point of
future studies of the Swedish unemployment insurance system. I
shall select two issues for comment: (a) that the unemployment
insurance system is a part of a more extensive employment insurance
system, and (b) that the growth of the unemployment insurance
system is slightly more complicated than is possible to ascertain from
Björklund's and Holmlund's study.

17.1. Unemployment Insurance as a Part of the Employment Policy

In most countries, the cost of unemployment insurance is the main
element in the cost of the labour market policy. Sweden is an exception here. The active labour market policy is greater than the passive
one, both regarding costs and number of persons. What is more
important, however, is that the two lines of labour market
policies—cash support and active labour market programmes—are
highly integrated. The integrating organization is the Labour
Market Board and, at the local level, the employment offices. The
employment offices have several functions. They are labour
exchanges, they place mainly unemployed persons in labour market
programmes, and they supervise the unemployed who receive
unemployment insurance benefits or cash benefits (KAS). It is
important to note here that unemployment insurance in Sweden is
not a compensation for those who cannot get a job in a specific
occupation. The unemployed are obliged to accept jobs in occupations other than their own, with or without retraining. What is also

important to note is that the unemployment insurance system is supplemented by a collective insurance scheme which leads to income compensation that in many cases exceeds 100 per cent.

This integration with labour market policy means that the Swedish unemployment insurance system differs from that of most other countries. I shall here choose a few examples of the interrelations between the two systems.

1. In most economic studies, the duration of unemployment is determined by the unemployed person's search for work. The person compares the wage rate for jobs with his own reservation wage, which is strongly influenced by the level of compensation in the unemployment insurance system. In the Swedish system, both the unemployed person and the employment office search for work for that person. If the employment office finds a job and the unemployed person refrains from applying for it, the person then loses his right to unemployment compensation. This is not simply a formality; it is actually practised for all but older workers (Christensen 1980). The low rate of denials of benefits is explained by the fact that most unemployed accept the jobs offered by the employment office. In some cases, the employment office uses public relief work or labour market training courses as tests of the unemployed's 'willingness to work'. This policy may explain why long-term unemployment is relatively less frequent in Sweden than in other European countries, despite the high level of unemployment compensation (OECD 1988: ch. 2).

2. However high income compensation is perceived to be in the Swedish unemployment insurance system, in practice it is still higher. Most workers 40 years of age or older are, as Björklund and Holmlund emphasize, also covered by a severance pay insurance according to an agreement between LO and SAF. The severance pay insurance consists of two parts, one lump-sum paid out after the lay-off and one unemployment-related compensation paid out after every three months of unemployment (for a maximum of 39 months). The unemployment-related compensation is also paid out for 39 months with disability pension if the latter is granted because of labour market reasons. The compensation is such that quite a few people receive compensation which more than covers the income loss. This is the case, for example, for those who are 58 years and 3 months or older at the time of the lay-off and who get a disability

pension after exhausting their unemployment benefit period. The employment offices generally do not apply the work test with this group of older workers.

3. Björklund and Holmlund refer to the discussion of lump-sum payments as an alternative to unemployment insurance. In a way, this is already an important part of the Swedish social insurance system. Firstly, there is an element of lump-sum payment in the severance pay insurance. Secondly, the active labour market programme may be seen as lump-sum payments in kind (and not in cash; see Wadensjö 1978). If we reckon as lump-sum payments the labour market programmes to the disabled (to get a training place, to get subsidized new employment, etc.), the main part of 'unemployment insurance' is already lump-sum payments. The present development is in the same direction. One example: in 1989 a youth job guarantee was introduced covering all youths up to the age of 20. This means that the youths get a lump-sum payment in kind instead of cash support.

4. Björklund and Holmlund present much interesting information on the development of unemployment. Some of the peculiarities according to the statistics can be explained by changes in public systems other than the unemployment insurance societies. I shall mention only two examples.

The number of youth unemployed, and especially the number receiving cash assistance, has decreased rapidly in the 1980s. The main explanation is the introduction of two labour market programmes—Youth Jobs, administered through the high school system since 1982 for those aged 16–17, and Youth Teams administered by the labour market administration since 1984 for those aged 18–19. Youths who refuse jobs under these programmes are not entitled to cash assistance.[1]

The great majority of older (55 +) workers registered as unemployed are members of unemployment insurance societies. There are two specific explanations for this. Firstly, unemployment insurance compensation is part of an early retirement system comprising several elements: unemployment insurance benefits, disability pension, and severance pay for those aged 58 years and 3 months and

---

[1] The Youth Jobs are low-paid jobs in the private sector subsidised by the government for 16–17-year-olds. Youth Teams are part-time jobs for 18–19-year-olds in the public sector.

older. Workers who lose their jobs at this age or also if they have left the labour force are classified not as retired but as unemployed.

Secondly, many who have retired from the health sector have been registered as unemployed. The explanation is the following: Up to a few years ago nurses and nurses' aids had a retirement age of 63. When they retired they registered as unemployed at the employment offices. In most cases, they were not looking for work and they were not entitled to unemployment benefits (receiving pensions made them ineligible). The reason for registering as unemployed was that they could therefore receive sickness cash benefits on becoming ill instead of their pension. Sickness cash benefits give a higher income compensation than old age pension. Hence, the unemployment figure was inflated for women aged 63 and 64.

To summarize: unemployment insurance is only a part of a greater employment and social security scheme. This explains, for example, the low incidence of long-term unemployment in spite of the high compensation level. It also explains many of the irregularities in the unemployment pattern not explained by the unemployment insurance scheme and standard economic variables.

17.2. The Long-Run Development of the Swedish Unemployment Compensation System

The casual reader will learn from Björklund's and Holmlund's study that state support for unemployment insurance societies was introduced in 1935 and cash benefits (KAS) in 1974, and that these, together with the extended coverage in the unemployment insurance in the last decades, are the main changes in the system. This is an oversimplification.

Many trade unions had unemployment insurance societies before 1935. To be able to get state support when it was introduced in 1935, more stringent rules had to be followed than most funds had applied before. As a result, most of the societies chose to stay outside the state-supported system in the 1930s (see Edebalk 1988).

In addition to the unemployment insurance societies, unemployment support was paid by the local communities. That support was partly financed by the state. This system was founded already before the start of the state support for the unemployment insurance, and existed alongside the unemployment insurance system even in the post-war period. In 1968 a complementary compensation system for unemployed older workers (55 years or older) was introduced (*omställningsbidrag*). When cash assistance (KAS) started in 1974, it replaced the two earlier existing systems, i.e. the state-supported unemployed compensation administered by the local communities and the special unemployment compensation system for older workers. In fiscal year 1972/3, the two earlier systems paid out SEK 70 million to the unemployed (39 and 31 million, respectively). In fiscal year 1974, SEK 64 million was paid out as cash benefits (KAS). The introduction of cash benefits mainly meant a restructuring of the programmes, with lower compensation for some groups, especially older workers, and higher compensation for others.

A corresponding analysis could be done for the disability pensions. Formally, disability pensioning for labour market reasons (in practice for those exhausting their unemployment benefits) was introduced in 1972, in practice, labour market conditions could be weighed together with medical ones (and many older workers have some medical problems) as much as two years earlier, in 1970. Before that, labour market conditions in practice were something which influenced the decision of the doctors and the social insurance societies.

To summarize: the cash support to unemployed workers has expanded during the last decades, but part of the registered expansion is quite likely a change of label.

References to Part II*

Akerlof, G. (1978). 'The Market for Lemons: Qualitative Uncertainty and the Market Mechanism', in Diamond and Rothschild (1978).

Albrecht, J. W., and Axell. B. (1984). 'An Equilibrium Model of Search Unemployment', *Journal of Political Economy*, 92: 824-40.

Albrecht, J. W., Holmlund, B., and Lang, H. (1986). 'Job Search and the Transition to Employment: Theory' FIEF Working Paper No. 26, Stockholm.

Arbetsmarknadsdepartementet (1981). 'Förslag till ändrat bidragssystem m m inom den frivilliga arbetslöshetsförsäkringen'. DS A 1981: 17. (Swedish Ministry of Labour: Proposals for changes in the system of subsidies to unemployment insurance.)

Atkinson, A. B., and Micklewright, J. (1985). 'Unemployment Benefits and Unemployment Duration', ST/ICERD Occasional Paper 6, London School of Economics.

Atkinson, A. B., Gromulka, J., Micklewright, J., and Rau, N. (1984). 'Unemployment Benefit, Duration and Incentives in Britain: How Robust is the Evidence?', *Journal of Public Economics*, 23: 3-26.

Baily, M. N. (1977). 'Unemployment Insurance as Insurance for Workers', *Industrial and Labour Relations Review*, 30: 485-504.

—— (1978). 'Some Aspects of Optimal Unemployment Insurance', *Journal of Public Economics*, 10: 379-402.

Barr, N. (1988). 'The Mirage of Private Unemployment Insurance', Discussion Paper WSP/34, Centre for Economics and Related Disciplines, London School of Economics.

Barron, J. M., McAfee R. P., and Speaker, P. J. (1986). 'Unemployment Insurance and the Entitlement Effect: A Tax Incidence Approach', *International Economic Review*, 27: 175-85.

Beenstock, M., and Brasse, V. (1986). *Insurance for Unemployment*. London: Allen & Unwin.

Björklund, A. (1978). 'On the Duration of Unemployment in Sweden, 1965-1976', *Scandinavian Journal of Economics*, 80: 421-39.

—— (1981). *Studies in the Dynamics of Unemployment*. Stockholm: EFI.

—— (1986), 'Arbetslöshet, arbetslöshetsersättning och inkomstfördelning

* Source material from SCB's Labour Force Surveys, AFA, Riksförsäkringsverket unemployment funds, the AMS insurance unit, and Trygghetsrådet SAF-PTK has also been consulted.

i Sverige' (Unemployment, unemployment compensation and income distribution in Sweden), Nordisk statistisk sekretariat, Tekniske rapporter 40.

Björklund, A., and Holmlund, B. (1989). 'Effects of Extended Unemployment Compensation in Sweden', in B. Gustafsson and A. Klevmarken (eds.), *The Political Economy of Social Security*. Amsterdam: North-Holland.

Boadway, R. W., and Oswald, A. J. (1983). 'Unemployment Insurance and Redistributive Taxation', *Journal of Public Economics*, 20: 193–210.

Burdett, K. (1979). 'Unemployment Insurance Payments as a Search Subsidy: A Theoretical Analysis', *Economic Inquiry*, 17: 333–43.

Burdett, K., and Hool, B. (1983). 'Layoffs, Wages and Unemployment Insurance', *Journal of Public Economics*, 21: 325–57.

Burdett, K., and Mortensen, D. T. (1978). 'Labor Supply under Uncertainty', in R. G. Ehrenberg (ed.), *Research in Labor Economics*, ii: 109–58. Greenwich, Conn.: J A I Press.

Burdett, K., and Wright, R. (1987). 'Optimal Firm Size, Taxes, and Unemployment'. Manuscript, Cornell University, Dec.

Burgess, P. L., and Kingston, J. L. (1976). 'The Impact of Unemployment Insurance Benefits on Reemployment Success', *Industrial and Labor Relations Review*, 30: 25–31.

Burtless, G. (1987),'Jobless Pay and High European Unemployment', in R. Lawrence and C. Schultze, (eds.), *Barriers to European Growth*. Washington, DC: The Brookings Institution.

Calmfors, L., and Forslund, A. (1989). 'Wage Setting in Sweden', in L. Calmfors (ed.), *Wage Formation and Macroeconomic Policy in the Nordic Countries*. Oxford: Oxford University Press.

Christensen, Anna (1980). *Avstängning från arbetslöshetsersättning*, (Suspension from unemployment benefits). Stockholm: Norstedts.

Clark, K. B., and Summers, L. H. (1982). 'Unemployment Insurance and Labor Market Transitions', in M. N. Baily (ed.), *Workers, Jobs, and Inflation*. Washington DC: Brookings Institution.

Classen, K. P. (1977). 'The Effect of Unemployment Insurance on the Duration of Unemployment and Subsequent Earnings', *Industrial and Labor Relations Review*, 30: 438–44.

—— (1979). 'Unemployment Insurance and Job Search', in S. A. Lippman and J. J. McCall (eds.), *Studies in the Economics of Search*. Amsterdam: North-Holland.

Danziger, S., Haveman, R., and Plotnick, R. (1981). 'How Income Transfers Affect Work, Savings and the Income Distribution', *Journal of Economic Literature*, 19: 975–1029.

Diamond, P. A. (1981). 'Mobility Costs, Frictional Unemployment, and Efficiency', *Journal of Political Economy*, 89: 798–812.

Diamond, P.A., and Rothschild, M., eds. (1978). *Uncertainty in Economics*. New York: Academic Press.

Edebalk, P.G. (1975): *Arbetslöshetsförsäkringsdebatten: En studie i svensk socialpolitik 1892-1934* (The debate on unemployment insurance: A study in Swedish social policy 1892-1934) Department of Economic History, Lund University.

Edebalk, Per Gunnar. 'Från motstånd till genombrott: Den svenska arbetslöshetsförsäkringen 1935-54' (From resistance to breakthrough: Swedish Unemployment Insurance 1935-54), *Meddelande från socialhögskolan i Lund*, 3 (1988).

Edebalk, P.G., and Wadensjö, E. (1978). 'Unemployment Insurance and Seasonal Unemployment', *Economy and History*, 21: 1.

—— (1986), 'Temporary Layoff Compensation and Unemployment: The Case of Sweden', Institute for Social Research, Stockholm. Mimeo.

—— (1987), 'Severance Pay Insurance in Sweden', Institute for Social Research, Stockholm. Mimeo.

Ehrenberg, R.G., and Oaxaca, R.L. (1976). 'Unemployment Insurance, Duration of Unemployment, and Subsequent Wage Gain', *American Economic Review*, 66: 754-66.

Enegren, B. (1988). 'Vägar in i arbetslöshet' (Transitions into unemployment). Institute for Social Research, Stockholm. Mimeo.

Erikson, R., and Åberg, R. eds. (1987). *Welfare in Transition: Living Conditions in Sweden 1968-1981*. Oxford: Clarendon Press.

Feldstein, M. (1976). 'Temporary Layoffs in the Theory of Unemployment', *Journal of Political Economy*, 84: 937-57.

—— (1978). 'The Effect of Unemployment Insurance on Temporary Layoff Unemployment', *American Economic Review*, 68: 834-46.

Feldstein, M., and Poterba, J. (1984). 'Unemployment Insurance and Reservation Wages', *Journal of Public Economics*, 23: 141-67.

Flemming, J.S. (1978). 'Aspects of Optimal Unemployment Insurance: Search, Leisure, Savings and Capital Market Imperfections', *Journal of Public Economics*, 10: 403-25.

Grassman, S., Lundberg, E., Stahl, I., and Ysander, B.C. (1978). 'Blandekonomi i kris?' (The mixed economy in crisis). Konjunkturrådets rapport 1978-9, SNS, Stockholm.

Gujarati, D. (1972). 'Behaviour of Unemployment and Unfilled Vacancies', *Economic Journal*, 82: 195-204.

Gustman, A.L., (1982). 'Analyzing the Relation of Unemployment Insurance to Unemployment', in R.G. Ehrenberg (ed.), *Research in Labor Economics*, V. Greenwich, Conn: JAI Press.

Hamermesh, D.S., (1977). 'A Note on Income and Substitution Effects in Search Unemployment', *Economic Journal*, 87: 312-14.

—— (1979). 'Entitlement Effects, Unemployment Insurance and Employment Decisions', *Economic Inquiry*, 17: 317-22.

Hamermesh, D.S. (1980). 'Unemployment Insurance and Labor Supply', *International Economic Review*, 21: 517–27.

Heikensten, L. (1984). *Studies in Structural Change and Labour Market Adjustment*. Stockholm: EFI.

Hellberg, I., and Wrethem, M. (1978). 'Företagskris och trygghetslagarna', (Firm behaviour and employment protection). LAS-projektet, Arbetsrapport nr 2. Department of Sociology, University of Gothenburg.

Hirschleifer, J., and Riley, J.G. (1979). 'The Analytics of Uncertainty and Information: An Expository Survey', *Journal of Economic Literature*, 17: 1375–421.

Holen, A. (1977). 'Effects of Unemployment Insurance Entitlement on Duration and Job Search Outcome', *Industrial and Labor Relations Review*, 30: 445–50.

Holmlund, B. (1981). 'Determinants and Characteristics of Unemployment in Sweden: The Role of Labor Market Policy', in G. Eliasson, B. Holmlund, and F.P. Stafford (eds.), *Studies in Labor Market Behavior: Sweden and the United States*. Conference Report, vol. ii. Stockholm: IUI.

—— (1986). 'Vägar ut ur arbetslöshet: Stockholmsungdomars erfarenheter 1981–1982', (Transitions from unemployment: The Experiences of Youth in Stockholm 1981–1982), *FIEF forskningsrapport*, 4.

—— (1989). 'Wages and Employment in Unionized Economies: Theory and Evidence', in B. Holmlund, K.-G. Löfgren, and L. Engström, *Trade Unions, Employment, and Unemployment Duration*, FIEF Studies in Labour Markets and Economic Policy. Oxford: Clarendon Press.

Holmlund, B., and Lundborg, P. (1988). 'Unemployment Insurance and Union Wage Setting', *Scandinavian Journal of Economics*, 90: 161–72.

—— (1989). 'Unemployment Insurance Schemes for Reducing the Natural Rate of Unemployment', *Journal of Public Economics*, 38: 1–15.

Hui, W.T., and Trivedi, P.K. (1986). 'Duration Dependence, Targeted Employment Subsidies and Unemployment Benefits', *Journal of Public Economics*, 31: 105–129.

Johnson, G.E., and Layard, P.R.G. (1986). 'The Natural Rate of Unemployment: Explanation and Policy', in O. Ashenfelter and P.R.G. Layard (eds.), *Handbook of Labor Economics*. Amsterdam: North-Holland.

Jones, S.R.G. (1986). 'Unemployment Insurance and Involuntary Unemployment: The Case of Adverse Selection', *Journal of Public Economics*, 30: 317–28.

Junankar, P.N. (1981). 'An Econometric Analysis of Unemployment in Great Britain', *Oxford Economic Papers*, 33: 387–400.

Lancaster, T. (1979). 'Econometric Methods for the Duration of Unemployment', *Econometrica*, 47: 939–56.

Lang, H. (1985). 'On Measuring the Impact of Unemployment Benefits on the Duration of Unemployment Spell', *Economics Letters*, 18: 227–81.

Layard, R., and Nickell, S. (1985). 'The Causes of British Unemployment', *National Institute Economic Review*, 85/1: 62–85.

—— (1986). 'Unemployment in Britain', *Economica*, 53 (Supplement): 121–69.

Löfgren, K. G., and Engström, L. (1989). 'The Duration of Unemployment: Theory and Empirical Evidence', in B. Holmlund, K.-G. Löfgren, and L. Engström, *Trade Unions, Employment, and Unemployment Duration*, FIEF Studies in Labour Markets and Economic Policy. Oxford: Clarendon Press.

McLure, C. E. (1977). 'The Incidence of the Financing of Unemployment Insurance', *Industrial and Labor Relations Review*, 30: 469–79.

Maki, D. R., and Spindler, Z. A., (1975). 'The Effect of Unemployment Compensation on the Rate of Unemployment in Great Britain', *Oxford Economic Papers*, 29: 128–40.

Minford, P. (1983). 'Labor Market Equilibrium in an Open Economy', *Oxford Economic Papers*, 35: 207–44.

Mortensen, D. T., (1977). 'Unemployment Insurance and Job Search Decisions', *Industrial and Labor Relations Review*, 30: 505–17.

—— (1983). 'A Welfare Analysis of Unemployment Insurance: Variations on Second-Best Themes', *Carnegie-Rochester Conference Series on Public Policy*, 19: 67–97.

Narendranathan, W., Nickell, S., and Stern, J. (1985). 'Unemployment Benefits Revisited', *Economic Journal*, 95: 307–29.

Nickell, S. (1979a). 'The Effect of Unemployment and Related Benefits on the Duration of Unemployment', *Economic Journal*, 89: 34–49.

Nickell, S. (1979b). 'Estimating the Probability of Leaving Unemployment', *Econometrica*, 47: 1249–66.

Nickell, S. J., and Andrews, M. (1983). 'Unions, Real Wages and Employment in Britain, 1951–1979', *Oxford Economic Papers*, 35 (Supplement): 183–206.

Nilsson, C., and Stenkula, P. (1978). 'Förundersöhning av förtidspension-ering utanför det offentligrättsliga systemet', (A preliminary investigation on early retirement). Rapport till Sysselsättningsutredningen och Arbetsmarknadsdepartementet, November.

OECD (1988). *Employment Outlook*, Sept.

Oswald, A. J. (1982). 'Trade Unions, Wages and Unemployment: What can Simple Models Tell Us?', *Oxford Economic Papers*, 34: 526–45.

—— (1985). 'The Economic Theory of Trade Unions: An Introductory Survey', *Scandinavian Journal of Economics*, 87: 160–93.

Pauly, M. V. (1974). 'Overinsurance and Public Provision of Insurance: The Roles of Moral Hazard and Adverse Selection', *Quarterly Journal of Economics*, 84: 488–500.

Pissarides, C. A. (1983). 'Efficiency Aspects of the Financing of Unemployment Insurance and Other Government Expenditure', *Review of Economic Studies*, 50: 57–69.

—— (1984a). 'Search Intensity, Job Advertising, and Efficiency', *Journal of Labor Economics*, 50: 128–43.

—— (1984b). 'Efficient Job Rejection', *Economic Journal*, 94 (Conference Papers): 97–108.

Rawls, J. (1971). *A Theory of Justice*. Cambridge, Mass.: Harvard University Press.

Rosen, S. (1985). 'Implicit Contracts: A Survey', *Journal of Economic Literature*, 23: 1144–75.

Sampson, A. (1978). 'Optimal Redundancy Compensation', *Review of Economic Studies*, 45: 447–52.

Sawyer, M. C. (1979). 'The Effects of Unemployment Compensation on the Rate of Unemployment in Great Britain: A Comment', *Oxford Economic Papers*, 31: 135–46.

Shavell, S. (1979). 'On Moral Hazard and Insurance', *Quarterly Journal of Economics*, 93: 541–62.

Shavell, S., and Weiss, L. (1979). 'The Optimal Payment of Unemployment Insurance Benefits over Time', *Journal of Political Economy*, 87: 1347–62.

Stafford, F. P. (1977). 'More on Unemployment as Insurance', *Industrial and Labor Relations Review*, 30: 521–6.

SOU [Statens Oftentliga Utredningar] (1971). *Bilagor till KSA: Utredningens betänkande.* (Appendix to the KSA Report.) Stockholm: Government of Sweden.

—— (1978). *Allmän arbetslöshetsförsäkring* (General unemployment insurance). Stockholm: Government of Sweden.

—— (1984). *Arbetsmarknadspolitik under omprövning* (Labour Market Policy in transition). Stockholm: Government of Sweden.

Ståhl, I. (1978). 'Unemployment Insurance: The Swedish Case', in *Unemployment Insurance: Global Evidence of Its Effects on Unemployment. Proceedings of a Conference in Vancouver, British Columbia, Canada.* Vancouver: Fraser Institute.

Topel, R. (1983). 'On Layoffs and Unemployment Insurance', *American Economic Review*, 73: 541–59.

Wadensjö, Eskil (1978). 'Planeringsmodeller för arbetsmarknadspolitik' (Models in planning labour market policy), in *Arbetsmarknadspolitik i förändring* (Labour market policy in transition).

—— (1984). 'Disability Policy in Sweden', in R. V. Haveman (ed.), *Public Policy Toward Disabled Workers*. Ithaca, New York: Cornell University Press.

Yaniv, G. (1982). 'Unemployment Insurance Benefits and the Supply of Labor of an Employed Worker', *Journal of Public Economics*, 17: 71–87.

Index

Aberg, R. 160
ABM programme 38, 61 n.
access 65
Adams, C. 39
adults 41–52
adverse selection 107, 109, 174, 181
AGB benefit system 119, 120
agents 79
Aid to Families with Dependent
    Children 44, 50
Akerlof, G. 107, 108
AKU (Swedish labour force
    surveys) 154
Albrecht, J. W. 140, 142, 166, 167
allocation of resources 48, 145–6
AMS, see National Labour Market
    Board
Andrews, M. 147
apprenticeships 62, 63
ARIMA (autoregressive integrated
    moving average) 85
Ashenfelter, O. 25 n., 26 n., 30, 35,
    42, 43
asymmetric information 11
Atkinson, A. B. 135, 148
ATP (supplementary pensions) 118
attitudes, see behaviour
attrition 15, 27
Axell, B. 142, 166, 167
Axelsson, R. 88–90, 89
Azariadis, C. 11

Baily, M. N. 10, 20 n., 105, 168
balance of payments 21
Balkenhol 11 n., 60 n.
Baltimore 56
bargaining 138, 139, 142, 143, 154, 165
    collective 20, 65
    Rehn–Meidner plan and 10
Barnow, B. 43
Barr, N. 174 n.
Barro, R. J. 68
Barron, J. M. 142
Bassi, L. 25 n., 30, 35, 43

Beenstock, M. 146
behaviour 27, 33, 79, 138, 141, 155
    firms' 144, 149
    optimal 139
    trade union 142
Bell, C. 68, 76 n.
Bendick, M. 49
benefit–cost analysis 23, 28–32, 45, 46,
    50, 57
benefits 30, 32, 40, 41, 78, 81
    financing 164–72
    social 9, 23, 29, 36, 54, 60
    welfare 50, 51, 52
    see also KAS; unemployment
    insurance
Bergström, Villy 66 n., 103 n.
Betsey, C. 19 n., 23 n., 27, 28, 43, 53
Bhagwati, J. N. 67 n.
Bishop, J. 19, 36
Björklund, Anders 66 n., 86 n., 88,
    91 n., 151–2, 154, 159 n., 160,
    179–81, 183, 186, 187, 188–9
Blitzer, C. 68, 76 n.
Bloch–Michel, C. 41
Bloom, H. 25 n., 43
Boadway, R. W. 67 n., 109, 167
booms 144
borrowing 71, 83
Bosworth, B. 10 n., 12
Brasse, V. 146
Britain, see United Kingdom
Brown, R. 27
Bruche, G. 37, 41
budgets 71, 72, 72–3, 103
Buffalo 49 n.
Bulow, J. L. 11, 14
Burdett, K. 11 n., 19 n., 140, 141,
    144–5, 149
Burgess, P. L. 149
Burtless, G. 37, 43, 103 n., 104, 184
business cycle 17, 18, 19, 34, 145

Cain, G. 14 n., 23 n., 25
Calmfors, L. 154

capital 18, 21, 69
capitalization 41
Casey, B. 37, 41
cash benefits, *see* KAS
Centre d'Étude des Revenus et des
    Coûts (CERC) 183
CETA, *see* Comprehensive
    Employment and Training Act
    (1973)
Chen, Paul 66 n., 103 n.
choice 65, 140, 168, 169
Christensen, Anna 187
Clark, K. 19 n., 150
Classen, K. P. 149
Cleveland 56
CLMS, *see* Continuous Longitudinal
    Manpower Survey
coefficients 87, 88, 154
collective bargaining 20, 65
Community Programme 38, 61 n.
Community Work Experience Program
    (CWEP) 50
comparison groups 24–7, 34, 40, 43,
    47–8, 53
compensation 71, 77, 105, 106,
    110–22, 141
    collective bargaining and 64–5
    programmes 34, 35
competition 16, 22
Comprehensive Employment and
    Training Act (1973) 42, 43, 44,
    47, 48
constraints 21, 69–70, 77, 79, 80, 83
    budget 71, 72–3
Continuous Longitudinal Manpower
    Survey (CLMS) 42, 47, 48
Contract Emploi-Formation 62 n.
contracts 138, 144, 167
control function 168
control groups 24–7, 42, 44–5, 47–8,
    50–1, 90–1
control–treatment comparisons 32
Cook, R. 39
Corson, W. 49
cost–benefit rules 13, 66–85
cost–effectiveness 52, 55
costs 29, 40, 48, 159, 186
    administrative 164
    benefit 162, 182, 183
    employers' 11, 12, 126
    information 159
    marginal 142, 165, 174
    opportunity 30

reduced inflation 20
    social 9, 17, 18, 36, 82
    training 71, 81–2, 171
    welfare 51
counter-factuals 23, 24, 39, 41
coverage 106, 175, 176, 181
Crane, J. 31
criminals 44, 45, 46, 53
    see also ex-offenders
cross-subsidization 166
Cuddington, J. T. 68, 76 n.
Current Population Survey (CPS) 42,
    43, 47, 48

Dabos, M. 91
Danziger, S. 148
Dasgupta, P. 67 n., 68, 76 n.
decay 33
demand 20, 68, 72, 81, 144, 157
    aggregate 60, 67, 76, 78, 83
    constrained 82, 91 n.
    elasticity of 13, 146
    supply and 12, 74, 80
    unemployment insurance 105, 108
    wage 10, 18, 145, 165
    see also labour
demand function 73
demographic information 42, 43
Denmark 22, 38, 52, 61 n., 62 n.,
    150
Denver–Phoenix programmes 56
depreciation 172
depressions 42, 181
Detroit 49 n.
devaluation 21
Devarajan, S. 68, 76 n.
Devine, J. 49
Diamond, P. A. 107, 166
Dickens, W. T. 14 n.
Dickinson, K. 43
Diewert, W. E. 67 n., 76 n.
differentials 13, 14, 142–3
direct job creation
    cost-benefit rules for job training
        66–85
    counter-cyclical measures 18, 19, 40;
        programmes 34–5
    employment and training policy
        9–22
    evaluation of 23–33
    labour market training 86–91
disability pensions 118, 188, 189, 190

disadvantaged groups 10–11, 20, 53, 59
  programmes targeted on 36–7,
    39–40, 42
disaggregations 152
discrimination 65, 88
disequilibrium 14, 68, 76–7, 83–4
disincentive effect 172, 176
dislocated workers 49–50
dismissal 125
displacements 27, 29–32, 35–6, 38, 83
distortions 12, 166
distribution 84, 159–63
disutility 66
domestic currency prices 70
Drèze, J. H. 21 n., 68, 76 n.
Drèze, J. P. 68, 76 n.
drop-out rates 55
drug addicts 44, 45, 46, 47
duration dependence effect 172

early retirement 110–11, 118, 121, 124,
    185, 189
earnings 88, 130, 171, 178, 180, 183
  direct job creation and 26, 43, 47,
    48, 87; ex-offender group 45–6;
    increased 30, 45; long-term gains
    40; YIEPP study 54, 55, 56, 57
  women's 129, 132–3
Eckstein, O. 67 n.
Economic Development
    Administration 35
Edebalk, Per Gunnar 112, 119 n., 126,
    128, 157, 189
Edin, P.-A. 87–8, 88
efficiency 17, 71, 168, 170, 184
  equity and 108–9, 151
  gains 18, 159
  losses 174
  unemployment benefits and 166–7,
    168, 170
efficiency wage 11, 12, 14, 143, 144
Ehrenberg, R. G. 149
elasticities 12, 13, 21, 147–8, 165
  wage 146, 154
Ellwood, D. 31, 51
employment and training 7, 8, 34, 35,
    38, 60
  policy 9–22
  programmes 40, 41–58, 59
employment offices 186, 187
Employment Promotion Act (1985)
    64 n.
Employment Tax Credit 61 n.

endogenous variables 68, 140, 145
England, *see* United Kingdom
Engström, L. 148
enterprise 8, 40–1, 63
equilibrium 69, 77, 138, 144, 166
  exchange rate 22
  general 11–12, 35, 38, 68, 147, 158;
    cost-benefit rules 13, 74–6, 79, 83
  partial 66, 67, 78, 84, 157
  search 142
  Walrasian 67
  see also disequilibrium
equity 71, 108, 109, 166
Eriksson, R. 160
error variances 85
Europe 7, 34, 42, 59, 86, 183
  high rates of unemployment in 8 n.,
    13
  see also Denmark; Finland; France;
    Germany; Ireland; Sweden;
    United Kingdom
evaluations 23–33, 59, 60, 151
exchange rate 16, 20–2
ex-offenders 44, 45, 46, 47
exogenous variables 69, 73, 74, 138,
    145, 147
  and expectations 68, 70
expansion 18, 20, 21
expectations 68, 73, 79
expenditures:
  benefits 103, 110–11, 113, 117, 136,
    164
  public 18
  training 19 n., 20, 35
experience rating 128–9, 166, 167
  and layoffs 144, 145, 146, 150, 182

factors 76, 168, 169
  of production 60
Farkas, G. 32
Feldstein, M. 144, 149
Finland 150
first-difference models 89
fiscal measures 19, 21, 38, 39, 40, 60
Flemming, J. S. 168
fluctuations 145, 156, 157, 180
foreign citizens 89–90
foreign trade 21
Forslund, A. 154
Fourgeaud, C. 68, 76 n.
Fraker, T. 47
France 38, 52, 62 n., 64 n., 183
Freeman, R. B. 13, 19 n., 74 n., 78 n.

Friedman, B. 62 n.
funds 48, 62, 182
  unemployment insurance 110–12,
    154, 155; growing membership
    in 132, 134; risks and 174–5
    subsidies and 110, 166, 173; white-
    collar workers' 160

gains 18, 28, 30, 40, 45, 158
General Equivalence Degree (GED) 58
Germany 35, 38, 61 n., 183
GNP (gross national product) 110, 111
goods 68, 82, 83, 84
  government purchase of 79
  prices 72, 73, 76
  social value 28, 29
  traded 70, 71; and non-traded 69,
    71
Gould, W. 31
governments 79, 81, 82, 84, 108, 168
  and employment and training 7, 30,
    34, 39, 64, 71; enterprise creation
    40–1; labour market intervention
    9–14; subsidies 35, 38, 39
  and production 60–1
  and UI funds 108, 110, 111, 112,
    113, 116–17, 118; intervention
    109, 159, 167, 181; layoffs 126,
    128, 149; subsidies 160, 164, 173,
    182
grants 35, 135, 136, 164, 171, 175
Grassman, S. 168
Great Britain, *see* United Kingdom
Great Depression 42
Grossman, J. 51, 68
growth 19, 20, 41
Gueron, J. 26 n., 50 n., 51
Gujarati, D. 147
Gustman, A. L. 148

Hamermesh, D. 19 n., 141, 150, 168
Hamilton, J. 66 n.
Harberger, A. C. 67 n.
Haveman, Robert 10 n., 11 n., 19,
    28 n., 29 n., 36, 84, 86, 90, 91
Heckman, J. J. 91
Heikensten, L. 154
Hellberg, I. 118
Helliwell, J. F. 13
Hirschleifer, J. 108
Hispanics 56
Holen, A. 149

Hollister, R. 19 n., 23 n., 24 n., 27,
    28, 33 n., 43, 44, 46 n., 53, 76 n.,
    84, 86, 90, 91, 103 n.
Holmlund, Bertil 66 n., 143, 151–2,
    153–4, 160, 165, 179–81, 183, 186,
    187–9
Hool, Bryce 11 n., 19 n.
Hotz, V. J. 91
hours of work 26, 43, 45, 64
households 71–3, 77
Houston 49 n.
Hui, W. T. 171, 172
human capital 18, 20, 30, 40, 76, 169
  formation 15

impacts 40, 89, 147, 148, 150
  evaluation of 34–6 *passim*, 43–8
    passim, 50 n., 57
  measuring 24–6
  substitution 27
imports 21, 22
incentives 84, 106, 130, 166, 168, 169
  and incentive effects 138–58, 170,
    183
income 72, 78, 85, 113, 125, 133
  distribution of 71, 84, 159–63
  exogenous 73, 74
  marginal utility of 81
  supplement to 156
  uncertainty of 105, 180
  see also taxation
individual optimization 67
Industrial Institute for Economic and
    Social Research (IUI) 103 n.
Industrial Relations 8 n., 23 n.
inefficiency 12
'infant industry' argument 21
inflation 11, 20
inputs 17, 71, 75, 78, 82
insurance, *see* unemployment insurance
interest rate 69, 71
interventions 36, 38, 107
  government 9–14, 109, 159, 167, 181
  see also Job Corps; Supported Work
investment 18, 21, 70, 76, 81, 82
  exogenous private 68
  loss of 11, 15
Ireland 52

Job Corps 27 n., 53, 53–7, 54
job creation, *see* direct job creation
Job Creation Law 52
Job Offer Scheme 38, 61 n.

job search 139–42, 153, 170, 185
  theory 138, 149, 152, 171
job security 64
Job Training Partnership Act (1981)
  42, 48–9, 54
Johansson, M. 66 n.
Johansson, Per-Olov 10 n., 13, 68,
  69 n., 75 n., 76 n., 79 n., 82 n., 85
Johnson, G. E. 11–12, 14, 15, 30, 39,
  43, 78 n., 144
Jones, S. R. G. 108
Junankar, P. N. 147

KAS (cash benefit assistance) 121, 137,
  141, 155, 186, 190
  denials of 116
  financing of 112
  income distribution and 160–2
  introduction of 110, 117–18, 150,
    152, 153, 189
  percentage receiving 122–4
  replacement ratios and 132–4
Keifer, N. 25
Kemper, P. 24 n., 27, 28 n., 29, 30,
  33 n., 44, 46 n.
Kesselman, J. 10 n.
Keynesian macro-economics 66, 67, 68
Killingsworth, M. 19 n.
Kingston, J. L. 149
Krueger, A. 13
Krutilla, J. 10 n., 67 n.
Kulik, J. 49 n.
Kydland, F. E. 79 n.

labour 71, 72, 83, 84
  demand for 11, 16–17, 21, 77, 142,
    145–8 *passim*; deficient 68; as
    function of prices and wages 78;
    increase in 67; seasonal
    fluctuations in 156
  supply of 66, 75, 138, 139–42, 149
labour exchanges 186
Labour Force Survey 124
labour unions, *see* trade unions
LaLonde, R. 47
Lancaster, T. 148
Lang, K. 14 n., 142
LAS (law on employment protection)
  121
Lawrence, R. 13
lay-offs 121–2, 183, 187
  temporary 125–9, 138, 144–5, 146,
    182; and labour supply 149–50

Layard, P. R. G. 11–12, 14, 19 n.,
  78 n., 144, 147–8
Lenclud, B. 68, 76 n.
lending 71
Lerman, R. 62 n.
Lesourne, J. 67 n.
Level of Living Survey 160
liquidity constraints 15
Little, I. M. D. 67 n.
LO (Swedish trade union
  confederation) 119
loans 21, 35, 169
local governments 38 n., 39, 118
Löfgren, Karl-Gustaf 66 n., 68, 69 n.,
  76 n., 79 n., 82 n., 103 n., 148
Long, D. 27, 28 n., 29
losses 75, 106, 163, 183,
Lucas, R. E. 11
Lundberg, E. 10 n
Lundborg, Per 66 n., 103 n., 143, 165

McKean, R. N. 67 n
McLaughlin, M. 25 n., 43
McLure, C. E. 142
macro-economics 9–14, 16–22, 31
Maki, D. R. 147
Malinvaud, E. 77 n.
Mallar, C. 25, 27, 28
management 24
Maneschi, A. 68
Manpower Demonstration Research
  Corporation (MDRC) 86
Manpower Development and Training
  Act (1962) 42
Marchand, M. 68, 76 n.
marginal change 74
Marglin, S. 67 n.
Margolis, J. 28 n., 29 n.
marketing 29, 35
markets 12–20 *passim*, 31–2, 68–9,
  74–82 *passim*, 107–8, 181
  clearing 20, 74, 75, 76, 78
  failure 9, 30
  imbalances 66
  switching 14, 18, 22
Mathematica Policy Research 51, 86
Maurice, A. 39
Maxfield, M. 51
Maynard, R. 27 n., 33 n., 44, 46 n.,
  47, 49 n., 51
membership fees 112, 173, 174, 175
Meyer, R. 58
Micklewright, J. 135

Minford, P. 147, 148
Ministry of Labour 167
minorities 7; *see also* disadvantaged
    groups
Minority Enterprise Small Business
    Investment Company 63 n.
Mintz, J. 68, 76 n.
Mirrlees, J. A. 67 n.
mixed work 8, 62–3
mobility 30
Modigliani, F. 21 n.
monopoly 12, 106, 143
monopsony 12
moral hazard 106, 171, 180, 181, 184,
    185
morale 11
Mortensen, D. T. 140, 141, 166, 167
multiplier effects 18, 66
Musgrave, P. B. 66
Musgrave, R. 66, 67 n.

NAIRU (non-accelerating-inflation rate
    of employment) 10–11, 19–20
Narendranathan, W. 148
Nathan, R. 31, 39
National Academy of Sciences 53, 57
National Labour Market Board 113,
    114–15, 123 n., 137, 155 n.,
    156 n., 186
National Supported Work
    Demonstration 40, 44, 90, 91
Neary, J. P. 69, 70 n., 80
New Jobs Tax Credit 36
Nichols, Donald 11 n., 20 n.
Nicholson, W. 49
Nickell, S. J. 11 n., 19 n., 147, 148
Nilsson, C. 118
non-traded goods 79, 80, 81, 82 n.

Oaxaca, R. L. 149
Occupational skills training 57
OECD (Organization for Economic
    Co-operation and Development)
    60, 63 n., 64 n., 175, 187
Ohlsson, H. 66 n., 76 n.
Oswald, A. J. 109, 143, 167
outcome 91, 105, 108, 143, 165
output 18–19, 28, 29, 40, 69–70, 79
    increased 9
    loss of 171
    public infrastructure 17

Palmer, J. 11 n., 19 n.
Papageorgiou, M. 19 n., 23 n., 27, 28,
    43, 53
Pareto-efficient 159
Pauly, M. V. 106, 108
payments 120, 183, 189, 190
payroll taxes 112, 142, 160, 162, 182
pensions 118
performance 17, 26, 27, 41, 48, 158
Perloff, Jeffrey 11 n.
persistence 33
Pestieau, P. 68, 76 n.
Phan-Thuy, P. N. 11 n.
Phillips curve 11, 19
Picard, P. 76 n., 68
Pissarides, C. A. 166
placement 58, 59
Poterba, J. 149
premiums 105–7, 109, 164–5, 181–2
Prescott, E. C. 79 n.
prices 17, 21, 78, 79
    exogenous expectations of 73
    foreign currency 69
    goods 72, 73, 76, 84
    market 80, 81; and market-
        clearing 74, 75, 76
Private Industry Councils (PIC) 48
probability 167, 168, 169, 171, 172,
    182
products 9, 19, 75
production 14, 36, 78, 81, 82, 157
    capital-intensive 22
    government 8
    in-programme 29
    sectors of 69–70
    shared public-private 61
    subsidization of 35
productivity 14–15, 18, 35, 70, 79
    future 75, 76
    participant 30
profitability, social 66, 68–9, 75, 78,
    82, 83
profits 71–2, 73, 80, 165
    maximizing 69–70, 167
Public Employment Program (USA)
    38, 39

quantity-unconstrained supply 80
quotas 83

random assignment 48, 50, 54
rationing 76, 91
Rawls, J. 170

Reagan administration 42, 48, 54
recession 7, 18, 108, 115, 181
recovery 35
redistribution 40, 160, 162
regional development 8
regulations 8, 64
Rehn, G. 10
reliability 26, 45, 48
relief work 38, 61 n., 88
relocation 49
replacement 30, 31
replacement ratios 129–35, 141, 152, 177–8
resources 18, 23, 60, 114, 135, 184
    allocation of 48, 145–6
    benefit-cost analysis and 28, 29
    counter-cyclical programmes and 40
    incentives and 168, 170
    movements of 22
    research 179
    targeting of 49
    underutilized 10
    welfare 51
revenues 36, 38
rigidity 13, 14
Riley, J. G. 108
risks 144–6, 159, 167, 170, 173
    adverse selection and 107, 109
    equal 174–5
    government intervention and 181
    and risk aversion 105, 108, 168, 174, 180
Rivera-Casale, C. 62 n.
Rivlin, A. 10 n.
Roberts, K. 51, 68, 80
Rosen, Sherwin 167
Rothschild, M. 107

SAF (Swedish employers' federation) 119, 120
sample attrition 27
Sampson, A. 168
saturation 54, 55
savings 169
Sawyer, M. C. 147
Schmid, Gunther 35, 103 n.
Schultze, C. 13
Schwanse, P. 23 n., 34
search theory 138, 149, 152, 171
selection 88, 91
    bias 27, 47, 53, 54
sensitivity analysis 32–3

services 28, 29, 48, 175
severance pay 119–21, 134, 167–71, 185, 187–9
shadow-pricing 76
Shavell, S. 106, 168, 169
shortage 30, 31
sites 54, 55, 56
Skedinger, P. 66 n.
Skidmore, F. 28
skills 28, 38 n., 41, 53, 59, 171
    see also human capital
slumps 103, 144
Smith, D. A. 49 n.
social profitability 66, 68–9, 75, 78, 82, 83
Social Security 25 n.
Social Security Administration (SSA) 42, 43, 47, 48
societies 181, 182, 188, 189
Söderström, Hans Tson 103 n.
Spindler, Z. A. 147
Srinivasan, T. N. 67 n.
stagflation 10
Stahl, I. 151, 152
standard of living 163
Starr, G. 64
Stenkula, P. 118
Stern, J. 76 n.
Stiglitz, J. 11, 13, 68, 69, 70 n., 76 n.
Stockholm 103 n., 154
Stromsdorfer, E. 49 n.
subsidies 39, 61–2, 111, 160, 164–5, 173–5
    experience-rating and 144, 149–50, 166
    marginal employment 12, 59
    seasonable industry 157
    society membership 182
    wage 10, 22, 35–8, 61, 136, 171; industry-specific 145
substitution 21, 27, 29, 38, 39, 40
Summers, L. H. 11, 13, 14, 150
supplementary pensions 11
supply 70, 75, 77, 91 n., 147
    and demand 12, 74, 80
support 41, 63
Supported Work 27 n., 33 n., 44–8, 53, 58
surplus 30, 31, 32
Sweden 35, 46 n., 62 n.
    training programmes 7, 38, 52, 61 n., 86–91
    unemployment insurance 101–90

target groups 44, 45
Targeted Jobs Tax Credit (TJTC) 61 n.
tariffs 83
taxation 12, 39, 84, 143, 168
  and budget constraint 71, 72
  income 106, 109, 129, 130, 131
  lump-sum 72, 77
  marginal tax rate 130
  payroll tax 112, 142, 160, 162, 182
  tax credits 36, 37, 62
  unemployment insurance 144, 165, 166
Taylor series expansions 84
technology 69, 70
temporary jobs 58
Thornton, C. 28 n.
time inconsistency 79
time-series 147, 151–4
Tobin, J. 10, 20 n.
Tomola, J. 39
Topel, R. 149, 150
tradables 69, 77
trade balance 83
trade unions 12–13, 130, 138, 173, 174
  behaviour of 139, 142–3
  close association between UI and 110–11, 150, 164–5, 181, 189
  severance pay and 134
trade-offs 166, 171
training, *see* employment and training
transfers 27, 29, 46 n., 77, 89, 160
Travaux d'Utilité Collective 38, 52
treatment groups 24, 25
Trivedi, P. K. 171, 172
Trygghetsrådet SAF-PTK 120

unemployment:
  classical 76, 77–9, 83
  involuntary 11, 12, 13, 14, 108
  Keynesian 77, 79–83
  part-time 116, 117
  seasonal 155–7
  structural 42
unemployment insurance (UI):
  financing 164–72
  incentive effects 138–58
  income distribution and 159–63
  optimal 164–71
  problems in insurance markets 105–9
  Swedish system 103–4, 110–37

United Kingdom 52, 147–50, 179, 180, 183, 185
  training programmes 38, 61 n., 62 n.
United States 8 n., 13, 86, 146–8, 179, 180–5 *passim*
  Congress 50, 54
  Council of Economic Advisers 10 n.
  Department of Commerce 63 n.
  Department of Health and Human Services 51
  Department of Labor 42, 48
  Employment Service 37
  General Accounting Office 19 n., 35
  growth of jobs 41
  income support 46 n.
  layoffs 138, 144, 149–50
  segmented markets 14
  training programmes 34–5, 38, 59, 61 n., 62 n.; disadvantaged groups 10–11, 20, 36–7, 39–40, 42; evaluation 23 n., 59; 'workfare' 50–2
  see also Continuous Longitudinal Manpower Survey; Job Training Partnership Act; NAIRU; Youth Conservative Corps; Youth Employment and Demonstration Projects Act; Youth Incentive Entitlement Pilot Projects
upturns 115
utility 72, 139, 142, 168, 170
  marginal 74, 81, 167
utility function 71, 73, 77, 81, 84

valuation 29, 45, 46 n.
value 28, 69, 70
Varian, H. R. 70 n.
Vaughan, R. 19 n.
Vernez, G. 19 n.
Vredin, Anders 103 n.
Vredin, V. 66 n.

Wachter, M. 14 n.
Wadensjö, Eskil 104, 188
wages 18–22 *passim*, 65, 70–9 *passim*, 88, 112 n., 114
  determination/setting 142–4, 147
  efficiency 11, 12, 14, 143, 144, 157
  real 68, 104, 174
  reservation 108, 139–40, 142, 148–50, 168, 187
  rigidity 13
  see also earnings; subsidies

Walker, G. 48
War on Poverty 42
Ward, M. 31
Weiss, L. 168, 169
Welch, F. 31
welfare 37, 51, 67–8, 73–4, 108, 158
  women on 44, 45, 47, 48, 50, 52
West, R. 43
Whitely, J. D. 11 n., 19 n.
Wilensky, H. 34
'willingness to work' 187
Wilson, R. A. 11 n., 19 n.
'windfalls' 30, 35–6, 38
Wise, D. 58
women 43, 46, 52, 59, 90, 188 n.
  on welfare 44, 45, 47, 48, 50, 52
Wooldridge, J. 24 n.
work experience 46, 52, 53, 54, 109

'workfare' 50–2
Wright, R. 145

Yaniv, G. 141
youth 44, 46–8 *passim*, 52–8, 59, 160,
    188
  black 7, 55
Youth Conservative Corps 61 n.
Youth Employment and Demonstration
    Projects Act (YEDPA) (1978) 7,
    19 n., 52–4
Youth Incentive Entitlement Pilot
    Projects (YIEPP) 53, 54–7, 58
Youth Teams 52, 61 n.
Youth Training Scheme 52, 62 n.

Zimmerman, D. 31

Index compiled by Frank Pert

DUE DATE

	~~APR 0 5 200~~		
			Printed in USA